Dispelling Fantasies

NEW SUNS:

RACE, GENDER, AND SEXUALITY

IN THE SPECULATIVE

Susana M. Morris and Kinitra D. Brooks, Series Editors

Dispelling Fantasies
Authors of Color Reimagine a Genre

Joy Sanchez-Taylor

THE OHIO STATE UNIVERSITY PRESS
COLUMBUS

Copyright © 2025 by Joy Sanchez-Taylor.
All rights reserved.
Published by The Ohio State University Press.

Library of Congress Cataloging-in-Publication Data
Names: Sanchez-Taylor, Joy, author
Title: Dispelling fantasies : authors of color reimagine a genre / Joy Sanchez-Taylor.
Description: Columbus : The Ohio State University Press, 2025. | Series: New suns: race, gender, and sexuality in the speculative | Includes bibliographical references and index. | Summary: "Examines how authors of color—including Tomi Adeyemi, R. F. Kuang, and Marlon James—write against white-dominated, Eurocentric fantasy narratives to counteract Christian and colonial tropes and offer alternate versions of morality, race, gender, and sexuality"—Provided by publisher.
Identifiers: LCCN 2025009238 | ISBN 9780814215906 hardback | ISBN 9780814284193 ebook
Subjects: LCSH: Fantasy fiction, American—History and criticism | American fiction—Minority authors—History and criticism | Jamaican fiction—History and criticism | Jamaican fiction—Authorship | White in literature | American fiction—Authorship | Literature and race—United States | Race awareness in literature | LCGFT: Literary criticism
Classification: LCC PS374.F27 T39 2025 | DDC 813/.0876609—dc23/eng/20250326
LC record available at https://lccn.loc.gov/2025009238

Other identifiers: ISBN 9780814259498 (paperback)

Cover image by Black Kirby
Cover design by Laurence J. Nozik
Text composition by Stuart Rodriguez
Type set in Palatino Linotype

To every person who made encouraging remarks about my first book, Diverse Futures: *you all gave me the confidence to write again.*

And to my daughter, Alessia, who inspires me to imagine better worlds.

CONTENTS

Introduction	Dispelling Fantasies	1
Chapter 1	Virtue: Revising the Moral Order of Epic Fantasy	26
Chapter 2	Envy: Blood Magic Is Not Always Black Magic	52
Chapter 3	Patriarchy: Reimagining Gender Roles in Fantasy	80
Chapter 4	Salvation: Rescuing the Dark Other from the White Savior	115
Conclusion	Decolonizing the Imagination	136

Acknowledgments   149
Works Cited   151
Index   169

INTRODUCTION

Dispelling Fantasies

When I set out to write this project, I had a vague idea that I would read fantasy by authors of color, identify common tropes or themes, and write a book discussing the ways that these authors' works are challenging current perceptions of the genre. I could not have imagined the scope of the project I was taking on. Fantasy literature is an extremely complex and varied genre, harboring epic adventures, magical systems, monster stories, and mashups with other speculative genres such as horror and science fiction. This variety of storytelling may be why it has taken fantasy scholars so many attempts to define what makes a work fantasy at all. Edward James and Farah Mendlesohn describe these varied attempts in their introduction to *The Cambridge Companion to Fantasy Literature*:

> Fantasy literature has proven tremendously difficult to pin down. The major theorists in the field—Tzvetan Todorov, Rosemary Jackson, Kathryn Hume, W. R. Irwin, and Colin Manlove—all agree that fantasy is about the construction of the impossible whereas science fiction may be about the unlikely, but is grounded in the scientifically possible. But from there these critics quickly depart, each to generate definitions of fantasy which include the texts that they value and exclude most of what general readers think of as fantasy. (1)

Beyond fantasy theory, James and Mendlesohn point to J. R. R. Tolkien's "On Fairy Stories" (1947), Brian Attebery's *Strategies of Fantasy* (1992), John Clute's definition of "full fantasy" in *The Encyclopedia of Fantasy* (1997), and Mendlesohn's own *Rhetorics of Fantasy* (2008) as significant influences on discussions of twentieth-century and contemporary fantasy literature.

What these theories and definitions as a whole demonstrate about the fantasy genre is that it is generally defined as works that address the impossible, but that do so using specific and recognizable structures, tropes, and modes of writing. C. Palmer-Patel explains that "although fantasy fiction is generally defined by its impossibility, fantasy fiction is not an illogical form. It is in fact governed by a sense of rules and structure, one that reflects our current understanding of the world and cosmology" (1). This explanation points to one interesting aspect of fantasy works: they are expected to provide a logical representation of a fantasy world. Whether it is Clute's structure of Wrongness to Healing or Campbell's structure of the Hero's Journey, fantasy is generally expected to include a hero in a magical realm who experiences hardships but ultimately restores order. Readers expect a fully formed, coherent world of magic that operates under specific rules created by the author. And like most genre-fiction categories, fans and readers of fantasy have great influence over which texts get defined as fantasy and which texts publishers recognize as fantasy. In fact, Attebery's theory of the "fuzzy set," or the idea that fantasy is grounded by a set of core texts that share common tropes of the impossible and that have been largely influenced by the enduring popularity of Tolkien's Lord of the Rings series (1954–55),[1] highlights the ways that fans and scholars of fantasy literature have influenced which texts are considered fantasy. In fact, Attebery has always acknowledged that the poll he conducted to attain the center of the fuzzy set had "no scientific validity" (14), a fact that Mendlesohn acknowledges in a talk titled "Peake and the Fuzzy Set of Fantasy" where she explains that the fuzzy set is, indeed, a self-fulfilling construct:

---

1. Attebery's theory of the fuzzy set is borrowed from two logicians, Lakoff and Johnson, who proposed that a more flexible means of categorizing objects and ideas is to begin with a central example (e.g., "robin" for the category "bird") and, from there, to radiate out to examples that technically or fuzzily fit the category (e.g., "penguin" or "bat") (12). Attebery then decides to poll other scholars of fantasy to figure out what texts would be at the center of a fantasy fuzzy set. Not surprisingly, J. R. R. Tolkien's Lord of the Rings is found to be the center of the fantasy set. While Attebery notes that his poll was informal and not comprehensive, its results mainly demonstrate that fantasy scholarship is still being heavily influenced by the Oxford school of authors, which includes Tolkien, Lewis, and their protégés.

> It is perfectly reasonable to argue that *The Lord of the Rings* proved a lodestone around which fantasy post-1975 was to form, one Terry Brooks figured out how to digest, and Stephen Donaldson worked out how to subvert. . . . *The Lord of the Rings* becomes the core of the modern fuzzy set because it becomes an inspiration, if not to the majority of the form, then to the most visible and successful subset of fantasy.
>
> But this means only that Tolkien is what fantasy *became*. At least one element of my contention here is that Tolkien was *not* what fantasy *was* (and within this contention, that Peake, not Tolkien, was far closer to the centre of the fuzzy set in 1950). (65)

The fuzzy set of fantasy demonstrates how assumptions about what fantasy is (The Lord of the Rings) have caused fantasy critics to deify a mostly white, Western, heterosexual subset of the vast amount of literature that has the potential to be read as fantasy. This deification and the Oxford school's[2] influence on the fantasy genre come at the expense of many fantasy authors who do not fit the Tolkienesque model and reinforce the perception that fantasy worlds are texts set in a predominantly white medieval Europe.

Maria Sachiko Cecire explains that the history behind the popularity of white, European medieval–set fantasy is rooted in a desire to maintain white supremacist systems of power:

> It is no coincidence that Oxford School–style fantasy—shaped by two men born in colonial settings (Tolkien in South Africa, Lewis in Ireland) who chose to live in England as adults—took root just as the British empire was coming to an end and Britain confronted a newly reduced role on the global stage. Such works unfold in a magical Middle Ages of youthful English power, bursting with globe-conquering potential. This earlier, fantastical setting allows most fantasy to avoid mentioning histories associated with settler colonisation and transatlantic slavery.

Sachiko Cecire's explanation highlights a major blind spot in the fantasy genre. While science fiction is known for its history of depictions of "postrace" settings,[3] fantasy has long been dominated by a "prerace" depiction; the false perception that there were no peoples of color present in medieval

---

2. The Oxford school of fantasy is typically described as including Tolkien, C. S. Lewis, and their writing group / social club the Inklings. I will discuss the influence of this group further throughout this text.

3. For a good overview of postrace depictions in science fiction, see Bould.

Europe[4] allows fantasy fans to accept "historically accurate" depictions of mostly white, patriarchal fantasy settings.[5]

Mendlesohn notes that an additional component of fantasy storytelling is linked to morality: "Fantasy, unlike science fiction, relies on a moral universe: it is less an argument with the universe than a sermon on the way things should be, a belief that the universe should yield to moral precepts" (*Rhetorics* 5). But if we consider the idea of the "fuzzy set" of fantasy being dominated by authors like Tolkien and C. S. Lewis for "high" fantasy and Robert E. Howard, author of the Conan the Barbarian series, for sword and sorcery, it is imperative that fantasy scholars and fans question how "habits of whiteness"[6] have affected what readers and authors view as the moral good of fantasy worlds. African speculative fiction author Mame Bougouma Diene observes in a keynote discussion on colonialism and fantasy that "magic has always othered other people's religions, never our own."[7] Diene's comment begs the question of whether the "moral universe" Mendlesohn invokes is based on Christian morality, and whether fantasy based on non-Christian ideals would insist on a universe that "yields to moral precepts." *Dispelling Fantasies* argues that fantasy's habits of whiteness are tied to a history of colonization and Christian missionary practices; depictions of Indigenous groups as primitive, deviant peoples in need of salvation, a portrayal based on the Western rational vs. magical binary and influenced by tenets of Christianity, contribute to depictions of "the dark fantastic"[8] or fantasy worlds where dark and othered characters are automatically viewed as evil and irredeemable. Fantasy and fantastic works by authors of color serve as critical counternarratives to the history of white-dominated, Eurocentric fantasy narratives, which often serve to reinforce Christian virtues and colonial, white supremacist structures.[9]

---

4. For examples of peoples of color in the medieval time period, see MedievalPOC.

5. Ebony Elizabeth Thomas gives a detailed explanation of the reception of the Black characters Rue in the *Hunger Games* film series and Gwen in the BBC's TV series *Merlin* in *The Dark Fantastic: Race and the Imagination from Harry Potter to the Hunger Games* (2019). Also, for an overview of the negative fan reception of the presence of peoples of color in the TV series *The Lord of the Rings: The Rings of Power*, see Blake.

6. I am referring to Helen Young's seminal critical text on fantasy, *Race and Popular Fantasy Literature: Habits of Whiteness* (2015).

7. Diene gave this keynote address at ICFA 45: Whimsy on Mar. 16, 2024, jointly with his wife and cowriter Woppa Diallo.

8. See my discussion of Thomas's *The Dark Fantastic* later in the introduction.

9. I am indebted to Taylor Driggers, who summarized my main arguments so well in a review of the manuscript for this project that I included, with permission, some of the language in this sentence.

It is well documented that Tolkien, Lewis, and the other members of their literary circle, the Inklings, were members of the Christian faith. In *The Fellowship: The Literary Lives of the Inklings: J. R. R. Tolkien, C. S. Lewis, Owen Barfield, Charles Williams* (2015), Philip Zaleski and Carol Zaleski link these authors' Christian belief to their fascination with medieval culture and legend and their disappointment in the modern world:

> A wit might say that the Inklings' aim was to turn the bird into a dragon and the baby into a king, for their sympathies were mythological, medieval, and monarchical, and their great hope was to restore Western culture to its religious roots, to unleash the powers of the imagination, to reenchant the world through Christian faith and pagan beauty. . . . The unavoidable harshness of life surprised none of them, for they were Christians one and all, believing that they inhabited a fallen world, albeit one filled with God's grace. (location 69, 98)

It is important to note that this description of one of the most influential groups of writers to the high-fantasy genre is one invested in the restoration of "Western" culture and "Christian faith" through the idea of the "pagan beauty" of a simpler, more magical world. While it may be impossible to know each of these authors' motives, the influence of the Inklings on the genre of fantasy and their known conversations and writings about Christian principles clearly draw a connection between these popular fantasy writers and Christianity. This connection is not surprising considering Oxford's historical ties to Christianity. Jan Morris notes in *Oxford* that "Oxford is a Christian city, built upon the Christian culture—as organically Christian as Bangkok is Buddhist. She has been Christian from the start. The oldest buildings in Oxford are churches" (164). Morris's assumptions about the "organic" nature of Oxford's Christianity and her decision to label Bangkok as Buddhist are some of the same assumptions that fantasy authors and readers might make about the normalization of a white, Western, Christian–dominated fantasy genre. Oxford has a history of intertwining the spheres of intellectualism and Christian faith, and its influence is so great that the Inklings are typically referred to as the Oxford school of fantasy literature and their writings are the central focus of the Oxford Centre for Fantasy.

While Robert E. Howard is best known for his authority-bucking figure Conan the Barbarian, his early writing shows a variety of influences and shifting views about civilization and race. Leon Nielsen notes that Howard was a voracious reader, and that he was especially interested in poetry and history pertaining to his Celtic roots. Poems such as G. K. Chesterton's "The

Ballad of the White Horse," an account of a king who united the Celtic and Anglo-Saxon tribes against the Danish, inspired Howard to write a poem titled "The Ballad of King Geraint" (23). Chesterton gives his explanation for the popularity of his heroic figure, King Alfred, in a preface to the poem: "Alfred has come down to us in the best way (that is, by national legends) solely for the same reason as Arthur and Roland and the other giants of that darkness, because he fought for the Christian civilization against the heathen nihilism" ("Ballad"). Just as the Inklings had been inspired by Christian principles and Arthurian legends, Howard absorbed influences from many epic sources that shaped his views about civilization. And it is significant that Howard's first major writing success came with the creation of the character Solomon Kane, "his first continued series, featuring the dour Puritan swordsman and his never-ending fight against evil, from the shores of Elizabethan England to the demon haunted jungles of Africa" (Nielsen 23). While Howard's own views of religion are not always clear, the idea of a civilized Puritan who fights the barbaric forces of evil, depicted as "savage" and "dark" forces often originating in Africa, offers a detailed picture of his views about civilization and race. Throughout his career, Howard wrote many stories concerned with varying degrees of barbarism and civilization and even exchanged letters with H. P. Lovecraft debating the merits of barbarism vs. civilization. While Howard often fluctuated in his views of barbarism, he ultimately concluded that even a debased civilization was superior to barbarism (Coffman 41). His choice to begin his career with European-set epic poetry and a virtuous Puritan character fighting Satan's dark forces demonstrates the influences of Western culture and Christian ethics on his writing. His later character, Conan, is a white barbarian who straddles the line between civilized and uncivilized man. Although Conan might be read as barbaric and unethical, Howard's stories frequently depict him as saving civilized white peoples from the hordes of dark barbarians who would defile them. Solomon Kane and Conan are two faces of Howard's fantastic tales, but both characters are heroic white figures who oppose evil, which is depicted as dark and linked to savagery.

One of the reasons it is important to discuss the history of white, male, Christian authors influencing the fantasy genre is because writers like the Inklings and Howard are still affecting depictions of contemporary fantasy. The Lord of the Rings movie series (2001–3) was highly successful and the new TV adaptation *The Lord of the Rings: The Rings of Power* (2022–present) continues to bring Tolkien's stories to new generations. Contemporary authors like George R. R. Martin have capitalized on writing epic, medieval-set fantasy stories while J. K. Rowling's Harry Potter series (1997–2007) comprises massively popular portal-fantasy novels featuring clear Dark Lord and Chosen One archetypes. And while Conan has been turned into multiple films and TV series throughout the 1980s and 1990s, it seems like the character of Solomon Kane might outlive Howard's other characters through the efforts of the modern gaming community. In 2018 the company Mythic Games ran a *Kickstarter* campaign for a Solomon Kane board game that raised over one million dollars. The game's website includes a description of Solomon Kane as a man fighting against an onslaught of evil: "Against this tide of corruption stands Solomon Kane. This mortal hero fights his lone crusade, aided by the silent might of the immortal Virtues. Together they fight against the relentless *Darkness*" ("Solomon"; emphasis in original). These stories, and through them, a reinforcement of Christian hierarchical values, are still present in contemporary fantasy literature and media.

Clute and Grant's definitions of "wrongness" and "thinning" in *The Encyclopedia of Fantasy* demonstrate that fantasy literature often works on very specific assumptions of what a real and fantasy world "should be" and utilizes a virtuous hero to restore a sense of moral rightness or order: "The sense of wrongness, in fantasy, is a recognition that the world is—or is about to become—no longer right, that the world has been subject to, or soon will be subject to, a process of Thinning." They note that Thinning often happens because of a "dark" character who seeks to harm the current order of the land due to "envy," which creates clear good–bad and light–dark binaries and makes envy, considered one of the seven deadly sins of Christianity, a key trait of fantasy villains. The influence of the Oxford school fostered the framework for the modern epic fantasy story and left little room for stories from cultures that hold alternate beliefs of kinship and connectivity. The texts discussed in *Dispelling Fantasies* each work to provide fantasy worlds that move away from a Western, Christian sense of morality and open dialogues about which peoples are "worthy" to be a hero. Because the influence of authors like the Inklings and Howard has permeated much of what fans define as fantasy, the body chapters of *Dispelling Fantasies* are organized around four Christian ideals that appear frequently in Western fantasy texts—virtue, envy, patriarchy, and salvation—to demonstrate how non-Eurocentric fantasy worlds can offer alternative versions of morality, race, gender, and sexuality that make space for authors to move away from the hierarchical and binary systems of mainstream Western fantasy.

Dispelling Fantasies is not a history of the fantasy genre or a historical overview of authors of color in the genre; this project is more concerned with how contemporary authors of color are working within the genre to dismantle the perception that all fantasy is white, European, Christian, and medieval. I decided to title this book *Dispelling Fantasies* using the plural "fantasies" to indicate that this text will go beyond a Western, Eurocentric depiction of fantasy literature; I am examining fantasy and fantastic literature written by authors of color, but this work is equally invested in exposing the fantasy that rationality, imagination, and magic belong only to white men, and the fantasy of a "pure" and morally "good" white medieval setting that allows readers to escape responsibility for the effects of colonization and xenophobia while subsequently creating worlds that depict dark-skinned peoples as an evil to be purged. As R. F. Kuang notes in her novel *Babel* (2022), "It's violent work that sustains the fantasy" (136). Fan backlash against the diversifying of fantasy TV series such as the new Lord of the Rings series *Rings of Power* and the new Game of Thrones series *House of the Dragon* is just the surface of the myriad ways that some authors and fans work to protect white dominance in the fantasy genre.[10] Fantasy by authors of color is a critical area of study because of its potential to broaden and complicate the types of stories that scholars and fans recognize as fantasy; these works create worlds that restore narrative agency and complexity to those historically deemed "other" while working to reclaim knowledge that has been suppressed by imperialism, colonialism, and white supremacy.[11]

If authors like Tolkien have been placed at the center of the established fantasy literature fuzzy set, then I intend to do a bit of genre origami in this project and fold the edges into the center. I do not intend to discuss race and fantasy from the Eurocentric "center" because such work has already been done admirably by scholars such as Elizabeth Leonard, Helen Young, and Ebony Elizabeth Thomas. Therefore, the only concern this work will have with the center of the fuzzy set of fantasy is to discuss it in terms of Helen Young's argument that the fantasy genre has formed "habits of whiteness" that have affected and continue to affect contemporary authors writing non-Eurocentric fantasy. Western, Eurocentric fantasy is still the majority of the fantasy media available on the market, and it is the fantasy that publishers[12] and fans expect to encounter. These influences may result in barriers for authors trying to write fantasy works with non-Eurocentric viewpoints; many of the authors discussed in this project have been told by fellow authors or publishers that their writing isn't strong because fantasy fans

---

10. For more information on the fan backlash against diverse fantasy characters, see Shanfeld; Barraclough.

11. I am indebted to Taylor Driggers for helping me with the language of the last two sentences of this paragraph.

12. It is important to note that publishing, in general, has been dominated by white, Western publishers, a point I discuss in more detail in the conclusion.

won't accept the setting or because the story doesn't follow an established Western narrative arc.[13] And there are also authors who don't necessarily identify as "fantasy" authors because of the genre's Eurocentric focus.[14] This project errs on the side of inclusivity while still recognizing the fact that fantastic writings, oral histories, and belief systems from non-Eurocentric cultures have historically been labeled "magical" or "fantastical" by colonizing cultures to portray these cultures as less civilized or inhuman. *Dispelling Fantasies* includes works from authors of color who are blending Western fantasy tropes with non-Eurocentric elements as well as some works that could be categorized as fantastic literature or magical realism. The works that I discuss as "fantasy" are writings that take some inspiration from established Western fantasy structures and tropes while also adding non-Eurocentric characters, settings, and worldbuilding elements that move the text away from canonical expectations and toward a more diverse representation of the fantasy genre. This choice is not intended to privilege Western fantasy; it is my attempt to avoid conflating oral histories, realist, or magical realist texts written by authors of color with the category of "fantasy."[15] I have also elected to include a few works that use references to non-Eurocentric magic, magical artifacts, or fantastic events; these works will be described as "fantastic" writing, Afrojujuism, or works of pantheology[16] to distinguish them from Western fantasy out of respect for the authors' intentions.

My decisions on which texts to include in this project focused on the structure and elements of the stories being considered and on the author's intent: Does the author engage in worldbuilding to create new or alternate worlds? Are there fantasy elements such as portals, magical artifacts, or world-orienting maps? Do the authors themselves label the fantastic abilities of their characters with the term "magic"? These are all questions I have asked myself to help decide which texts should be included in this project, which aims to identify and engage with non-Eurocentric fantasy

---

13. Authors such as Vida Cruz and E. G. Condé have made comments about beta readers and publishers rejecting their works because they did not have an expected Eurocentric setting or structure. For more information on this topic, see Cruz.

14. For examples of authors challenging the label of fantasy, see Nnedi Okorafor, Oghenechovwe Donald Ekpeki, and Joshua Uchenna Omenga's definitions and discussions of Africanjujuism and Afropantheology.

15. Authors like Nnedi Okorafor and Oghenechovwe Donald Ekpeki have noted in online posts and essays that their fantastic writings aren't connected to the often-expressed view of fantasy as "escapist" literature.

16. "Pantheology" is a term originally created by authors/scholars Oghenechovwe Donald Ekpeki and Joshua Uchenna Omenga to describe African writings "imbued with the African spiritual realities" (*Between* 1) but have since been applied by Ekpeki to other non-Eurocentric cultures in the Caribbean and Asia.

and fantastic literatures. The benefits of the fantasy genre's worldbuilding capabilities for authors of color should not be overlooked because of the perception that fantasy is a "white genre." Authors of color who write fantasy or fantastic literature often do so because of the inherent possibility within these forms of writing to build new or alternate worlds that have decolonial viewpoints.[17] And visions of decolonial worlds hold the potential to help readers of color overcome the "imagination gap" identified by Thomas[18] and, instead, immerse themselves in worlds full of cultural recovery and renewal. Overall, the texts discussed in *Dispelling Fantasies* prove that it is not only possible, it is critical, to write diverse fantasy worlds.

What is considered "fantasy" in texts written by authors of color can be a slippery definition because the terms "real" and "magic" are often defined by colonizing cultures. Scholars of Indigenous cultures such as Miriam C. Brown Spiers note that many Native figures and traditions such as the Medicine Man or Woman and skinwalkers are often depicted in Eurocentric cultures as mystical or magical to the detriment of Indigenous peoples; she points to J. K. Rowling's decision to include such figures in her story series *History of Magic in North America* as a prominent example of this trend (xvi). Author and scholar E. G. Condé notes that many Western fantasy tropes, like written scrolls or the term "black magic," stem from European colonizers' biases against Indigenous cultural traditions and oral communication practices.[19] Authors/scholars Nnedi Okorafor, Oghenechovwe Donald Ekpeki, and Joshua Uchenna Omenga each argue that African and African-descended authors have been harmed by the colonial label of "fantasy" being applied to their works without a deeper conversation about the African beliefs and mythologies that are centered in these works; Okorafor has remedied this oversight by labeling her fantastical writings as "Africanjujuism," or "a subcategory of fantasy that respectfully acknowledges the seamless blend of true existing African spiritualities and cosmologies with the imaginative" ("Africanfuturism");[20] while Ekpeki and Omenga identify their writings as "Afropantheology," defined as "the gamut of African works which, though having fantasy elements, are additionally imbued with the African spiritual realities" (*Between* 1).[21] Okorafor, Ekpeki, and Omenga all

---

17. For fantasy fiction with a decolonial viewpoint, see the works of Darcie Little Badger, E. G. Condé, Nalo Hopkinson, Nisi Shawl, and Andrea Hairston, among others.

18. See E. Thomas 5.

19. E. G. Condé made this comment in a writing workshop I attended on Oct. 29, 2023, sponsored by Palabras del Pueblo.

20. Okorafor tweeted this definition on Aug. 11, 2022.

21. See Okorafor's *Nnedi's Wahala Zone Blog* post "Africanfuturism defined" from 2019 and her subsequent tweets and the introduction to Oghenechovwe Donald Ekpeki and Joshua Uchenna Omenga's *Between Dystopias: The Road to Afropantheology* (2023).

admit that some of their writings do include elements of fantasy or fantastic literature, in addition to African mythology and cosmology, which is why I still include their works in *Dispelling Fantasies*, but these notes of caution and specific definitions are an important warning to fantasy readers and scholars to take care not to label cultural traditions or oral histories as fantasy. One solution I have employed is to avoid labeling fantastic figures such as gods or tricksters or practices such as Vodun, juju, or Santería as "fantasy" or "magic." While there can be fantastic characters or magical systems based on these cultural elements, the elements themselves are not "fantasy."

What is "magical" or "impossible" also depends heavily on the culture and viewpoint of the person answering this question. Early records of Indigenous cultures written by European colonizers were fraught with miscategorization and mislabeling of Indigenous beliefs as nonrational, especially views centering on the divide between life and death and spiritual healing practices.[22] Many cultures make room for fantastic happenings in their belief systems; Alejo Carpentier argues that magical realism is recognized by this normalization of fantastic events or happenings: "The marvelous real that I defend and that is our own marvelous real is encountered in its raw state, latent and omnipresent, in all that is Latin American. Here the strange is commonplace and always was commonplace" (qtd. in Zamora 104). Carpentier's definition can help readers and scholars to avoid labeling all texts with fantastic elements as fantasy; one way to differentiate between genres like magical realism and fantasy is to consider what the author or the culture the author is depicting would consider to be part of their cultural identity compared to what that culture might consider impossible. For this reason, I choose to not include magical realist stories in *Dispelling Fantasies* that use a fantastic element that would not be considered "magic" by the culture the author is writing from, with the exception of a few fantastic stories that blur the line between magical realism and fantastic writing by including narrators who are unsure whether the fantastic events or magical happenings they encounter are real or imagined. So a story like Carlos Hernandez's "More than Pigs and Rosaries Can Give," a magical realist tale of ghostly possession, is not included because possession would not necessarily be categorized as "magical" in Cuban culture. But Rebecca Roanhorse's Between Earth and Sky trilogy would be considered fantasy because it combines its pre-Columbian-inspired culture with epic worldbuilding and nongodly magic wielders. And Nnedi Okorafor's Akata Witch series is Afrojujuism because of Okorafor's choice to combine elements of African

---

22. For examples of how European colonizers viewed Indigenous belief systems, see Pané; Thornton.

cultural practice with a clearly defined magic system and magical portals. Overall, there is seldom one right answer to the question "Is this fantasy?," but it's important to consider the author and culture that the text is coming from when making decisions about how to categorize non-Eurocentric writing with fantasy or fantastic elements. As Condé notes, magic does not have to be limited to dragons and other Western fantasy tropes; there is magic in the everyday as well.[23] But if the "magical" element is part of an established cultural tradition, fantasy scholars need to take great care with how they are categorizing such works.

While the genre of mainstream fantasy is still dominated by white authors and is often problematic in its depictions of characters of color, or their monstrous counterparts, authors of color still turn to fantasy and other speculative genres because of these genres' potential. Fantasy affords the opportunity to build fictional worlds where peoples of color can be the heroes of their own adventures. But this work is not easy; as Matthew Sangster notes in his discussion of Junot Díaz's references to Tolkien and The Lord of the Rings in his novel *The Brief Wondrous Life of Oscar Wao* (2007), specifically to Oscar's desire to be the "Dominican Tolkien": "[Oscar's] sense that a Dominican *Lord of the Rings* would need to be substantively different highlights the fact that Tolkien's fantasies imaginatively accommodate some readers more easily than others" (21). I would add that Oscar being shunned by his white-fan social group and not living to become the fantasy author he desires to be demonstrate the social and structural difficulties authors and fans of color face when attempting to insert themselves into a genre that has been, whether correctly or incorrectly, labeled as predominantly white. It is also worth noting that Díaz's references to The Lord of the Rings serve as recognizable markers that help non-Dominican readers understand the epic and evil scope of the Trujillo regime. In the end, *Oscar Wao* is not fantasy; it is a work of magical realism with fantasy references created to highlight how Dominicans have survived atrocities Western readers might think of as impossible. As *Oscar Wao* demonstrates, reimagining fantasy literature in a nonwhite, non-Western context is more difficult than simply reworking the Tolkien model. Authors of color who grew up as fans of Western fantasy eventually realize that stories like The Lord of the Rings were not written for them and that they must find a way to reconcile this fact within their fantasy writing.

But if authors of color can overcome the significant barriers of Eurocentric dominance and Christian idealization, fantasy holds the potential to imagine decolonial spaces. In "The Magic Is in the Roots: Cultural Reconnection

---

23. Condé made this comment in the writing workshop mentioned in n. 19.

through Magical Realism," Lysz Flo notes that the act of reclaiming cultural knowledge and actively resisting cultural erasure is a form of magic:

> Slavery and colonization were apocalypses for Black and brown people, and through systemic oppression, continues [sic] to affect Black and Indigenous folks to this day. To exist and maintain ancient traditions, rituals, and recipes that are historically traceable is to defy the daily odds of erasure. This is where our cultural myths and traditions, our magic, create a thread between all of our existences despite being separated by genocide, cultural erasure, and assimilation. Despite having to hide all the ways we are tied historically and culturally to our origins we find ways to keep sustaining and nurturing our roots; magic is the thread. (129)

While it can be difficult work to break free of the fantasy genre's colonialist tendencies, it is also necessary work. Reclaiming the everyday magics of non-Eurocentric cultures is often a decolonial practice invested in reinforcing the validity of non-Christian religious and non-Eurocentric cultural practices. Fantasy authors who depict such magics or who utilize magic as a means to combat cultural erasure can potentially decenter Western models of fantasy. Ken Liu describes such work in an interview about his Dandelion Dynasty series as "re-interpreting modernity through a non-Western lens (or more accurately, a decolonized perspective that melds Western and non-Western ideas)" (*Arley Sorg* blog). In *Dispelling Fantasies*, I am specifically choosing texts that work within a fantasy or fantastic framework, but that also use these frameworks as a tool of radical resistance.

"The Dark Fantastic" and Diverse Fantasy Literature

In *The Dark Fantastic: Race and the Imagination from Harry Potter to the Hunger Games* (2019), Ebony Elizabeth Thomas identifies a trend in mainstream fantasy literature that she labels "the dark fantastic"—a construct under which dark-skinned characters in mainstream fantasy literature are often made monstrous or othered, confined to liminal spaces, and subjected to violence and erasure to alleviate societal anxieties. As Thomas notes, most fantasy texts still privilege whiteness and depict darkness and dark-skinned beings as evil, which causes readers of color to internalize "the implicit message . . . that *we are the villains. We are the horde. We are the enemies. We are the monsters*" (23; emphasis in original).

Thomas is writing about popular fantasy literature and media created by white authors like J. K. Rowling's Harry Potter series and Suzanne Collins's

Hunger Games series, but I am more interested in how her theory of the dark fantastic connects to non-Eurocentric fantasy works. One might expect to see a reversal of the dark fantastic in a fantasy world with predominantly nonwhite characters. However, Thomas indirectly addresses this idea when she discusses fantasy texts and other media with all-white casts through her argument that "any impetus toward whitewashing the imagination, memory, dreams, and magic is futile, for any work of the fantastic which is all White signals (if not *screams*) that darkness is just beyond the turn of the page, the flicker of a frame, or the click of a thumb" (25; emphasis in original). I would argue that for non-Eurocentric fantasy works, the reverse is true; even in a world with no white characters, the specter of whiteness and its effects, specifically colorism and other internalized racisms stemming from colonization, are still present throughout the story.

One example of the dark fantastic in a nonwhite fantasy world is Tomi Adeyemi's *Children of Blood and Bone,* the widely popular first novel in the Legacy of Orïsha series, which is loosely set in a West African–based kingdom.[24] In this series, Adeyemi depicts a world where all the characters are Black and brown; this choice of characterization draws attention to the historical absence of Black-skinned heroic characters in fantasy literature. Adeyemi's choice to name the kingdom of her story Orïsha, an homage to West African deities, is a result of both her Nigerian heritage and her fellowship time studying West African culture in Brazil (Lodge). The Legacy of Orïsha series demonstrates how contemporary fantasy authors are combining non-European religious figures, myths, and legends with fantasy character archetypes and plot structures to produce diverse fantasy worlds. At the same time, Adeyemi does not shy away from issues of colorism and xenophobia in this series. She explains that "[*Children of Blood and Bone*] was real, or at least I tried to make it as real as possible from a personal struggle, which was, you know, black identity, marginalization and police brutality." The dark fantastic may look slightly different in Adeyemi's series, but it is not entirely absent.

Adeyemi and Thomas have both discussed the effects of colonization and white privilege on fantasy literature and the barriers for authors and fans of color who engage with this genre. Thomas narrates a pivotal moment of racial self-reflection she experienced in *The Dark Fantastic* where she participated in an online conversation about Salvador, Brazil (which is also, incidentally, the city where Adeyemi studied West African culture). In this

---

24. Adeyemi's series has received criticism from some African authors due to incorrect portrayals of cultural elements. For one example, see Chaosattractor.

online conversation, a Black American woman described the city of Salvador and the region of Bahia as Afrotopias. Thomas explains that a Brazilian anthropologist's response to this comment caused her to rethink her own racialized assumptions; the anthropologist stated, "*This is why myth-making is dangerous for subordinate peoples: your imagination is more controlled by the dominant social formation than you're probably willing to admit*" (16; emphasis in original). Thomas replies, "The idea that my imagination had been controlled in any way floored me" (17) and goes on to explore how young readers of color are affected by racial assumptions in the texts that they read. Adeyemi has discussed similar racial barriers through comments about the imaginative challenges of writing Black characters in fantasy literature; she explains in interviews that she predominantly wrote white characters in her stories when she was in her teens, a result of an internalized belief that Black people didn't belong in fantasy texts, and notes that during the writing of *Children of Blood and Bone*, she struggled to find the terminology to describe dark-skinned characters and their natural hair in positive or even neutral ways due to a lack of literary examples (Grady). Thomas and Adeyemi's lived experiences demonstrate the difficulties of overcoming the imagination gap for readers and authors of speculative genres who have only experienced darkness in these genres as linked to evil. These experiences also demonstrate that overcoming this gap will require speculative creators to think carefully about how they represent darkness and peoples of color in their narratives.

It is not strange that specters of whiteness would haunt fantasy authors of color even in worlds with no white characters because issues of internalized colorism, racism, and xenophobia continue to affect the treatment of people in communities of color; Adeyemi makes it clear in her writing that even in a world without white skin, colorism still fosters a race-based system of oppression. One of the first scenes in the novel is the main character, Zelie, being called "Maggot" by a lighter-skinned classmate. The term "Maggot" brings to mind N. K. Jemisin's derogatory slur "Rogga" in her Broken Earth trilogy; Adeyemi and Jemisin each create racial slurs for specific groups of people in their series that contain double consonants. This wording choice highlights the continued effects of racialized slurs on Black bodies. Anthony Russell Jerry notes in his ethnographic research on the N-word that this racial slur serves to position the Black body as Other, which serves to reinforce the white Self (37). Jeffrey Jerome Cohen expands on this idea of the othered Black body to explain the creation of monsters in Western culture and myth; he argues that "from the classical period into the twentieth century, race has been almost as powerful a catalyst to the creation of monsters as culture, gender, and sexuality. Africa early became the West's significant other, the sign of its ontological difference simply being skin color. . . . These differences were quickly moralized through a pervasive rhetoric of deviance" (10). The dark other as monstrous is present in many cultures, and the challenge for authors writing fantasy is to resist reinforcing depictions of evil as linked to dark skin.

Thomas notes in *The Dark Fantastic* that "what is most chilling is that *even when those who are endarkened and Othered dream in the fantastic, the Dark Other is still the obstacle to* overcome" (22–23; emphasis in original). I would argue, however, that "overcoming" the Dark Other in non-Eurocentric fantasy does not always imply the violent purging or banishment that has become the norm for this genre. Vida Cruz notes that a major difference between Western and non-Western storytelling is the potential for the hero to achieve their goals through understanding rather than violence. In a 2021 essay for *Fantasy Magazine* titled "We Are the Mountain: A Look at the Inactive Protagonist," Cruz explains that the ideal of the active protagonist in fantasy literature is harmful because it upholds the typical hero as a default young, healthy, white male. Cruz argues that the active nature of such a protagonist, one that is extremely typical in the fantasy genre, "is a mobility that is not afforded to anyone who isn't young, healthy and able, neurotypical, affluent/middle class, white, cis, straight, and/or male." She then argues that an inactive protagonist, who is more likely to be living in a world that was not made for them to succeed in, yet who survives anyway, often through community building or communal action, is an equally valid hero figure. Yet, she notes, such figures are often not accepted as valid by US publishers:

> What is perceived as "activeness" in a character manifests the American values of rugged individualism, of "pull yourself up by the bootstraps," of Manifest Destiny. "Activeness" in character, as promoted by the US publishing industry, ignores the contributions and influence of community and society on the personality and actions of the character.
>
> Much of classical and contemporary literature and comics from both East and West is full of protagonists who simply observe (*The Great Gatsby*), who simply survive bleak or volatile circumstances (*Beloved, The Unbearable Lightness of Being*), who have no choice but to navigate the political sea around them at great cost (*The Remarried Empress*). But there is a strange insistence from contemporary US publishing to make characters in SFF "do something that affects the plot." It demands that marginalized writers imagine characters with a mobility that they themselves do not have, resulting in characters that feel untrue to the writers but somehow fit a narrow vision of "marketability."

Cruz's comments demonstrate that the assumptions Western publishers make about the need for active protagonists is superimposed onto fantasy authors even as authors of more "literary" fiction are given the freedom to break such rules. As a subsection of literature, fantasy literature is often even more regulated because it does not often achieve the high sales and recognition of genres like romance and literary fiction.[25] Cruz's essay highlights some of the many barriers that keep authors of color from fully engaging with the fantasy genre, which I discuss further in the conclusion.

The Cost of Writing in Multiple Speculative Genres

While Cruz is speaking to barriers that authors from non-Eurocentric cultures face when trying to get their fantasy stories published, another barrier that authors of color experience is the pressure to stick to one genre of writing. Speculative authors such as Tananarive Due, Silvia Moreno-Garcia, and Nalo Hopkinson and scholars such as Kinitra Brooks have discussed the costs of writing across speculative genres for authors of color, especially female authors. Although Due and her husband Steven Barnes have recently received significant media attention for their literary contributions to the Marvel and Star Wars franchises as well as their horror-genre TV and film writing, both authors have been writing fantasy and science fiction for decades. Due explains that science fiction and fantasy literature was a more welcoming space in the 1990s than horror, stating, "Genre had an easier road for me than if I had tried to enter publishing as a horror writer, as a black woman" (qtd. in Swinson). For authors of color trying to make a living as authors, genre-hopping and writing across age groups can help them to grow their fan bases and make a living as creators. Many authors of color also note that single-genre writing feels limiting to them and choose to write in multiple genres.[26] The current reality of the publishing market is that fantasy authors of color make more money and receive more media attention writing for Marvel, Star Wars, or YA fantasy series like Rick Riordan Presents than they would writing only adult fantasy. This fact is one reason that

---

25. I am basing the first half of this comment on a 2022 *Publishers Weekly* article stating that romance book sales rose 52.4 percent compared to fantasy sales at 17.4 percent ("Romance"). The second half is based on the fact that out of the forty-two books that achieved no. 1 bestselling status on the *New York Times* fiction list in 2022, only four were fantasy (and one of those was written by Stephen King).

26. For examples of authors who write across genres, mediums, and age groups, see interviews of N. K. Jemisin, Tananarive Due, Nnedi Okorafor, Nghi Vo, Silvia Moreno-Garcia, Zoraida Córdova, Carlos Hernandez, David Bowles, and Daniel José Older.

I plan to include some texts that are considered YA (some correctly, some more suspect) in this project.

Moreno-Garcia notes the challenges she faced from editors and publishers as an upcoming author who knew she wanted to write in multiple genres and who also wrote fantasy novels set in countries like Mexico. She connects her desire for genre fluidity to her identity as a Mexican American living in a border zone:

> You also could chalk up this desire to straddle categories to two things at once. I spent my early childhood growing up in the Mexico-United States border zone in Baja California. My parents filled our home with eclectic books. They were hoarders in many ways, avid readers who didn't care what shelf something sat on. I learned to read in Spanish and in English because they had books in both languages, and I was as likely to bump into award-winning Mexican writers, French poets or early 20th century American pulp fiction in the chaotic piles of books that mushroomed in every corner of our messy home. ("Silvia")

Fantasy authors are often encouraged to write trilogies or to write more books in whatever world they have created that is appealing to readers, but as Moreno-Garcia notes, this approach may not necessarily work for authors of color, who often write from a range of experiences and identities. To date, Moreno-Garcia has written historical fantasies, dark fantasies, romantic fantasies, noir, and science fiction. While she has managed to overcome barriers of genre-hopping, her experience begs the question of how many other authors are pressured to "stay in their lane" and keep writing in the genre they started in.

N. K. Jemisin also argues that the science fiction and fantasy genres are intertwined, and that attempts to categorize her work into one genre are not productive:

> I have no interest in genre definitions beyond "fantastical" and "realist." . . . With the Broken Earth series, for example, I basically had fun playing with the idea of "any sufficiently advanced science/sufficiently complex magic," and I'm honestly a little surprised to see how many readers throw themselves into conniptions trying to classify it. A lot of the "science fiction" our culture embraces is magic, or spiritual beliefs with the serial numbers stripped off; a lot of the "fantasy" we embrace is actually alternate history, which is typically considered a science fictional subgenre, or something else skiffy. So what does it matter what it's called? (qtd. in Sorg)

Jemisin's comments echo many other authors of color, who frequently state that the story they are trying to express is more important than what genre of literature they are writing. Nnedi Okorafor is one such author, and she has expressed frustration with fans and scholars who mislabel her work: "I really wish people would stop calling me a 'fantasy author.' Sigh. It's a constant battle. I sometimes write 'fantasy' yes, but I'm not a 'fantasy author.' Is that hard to understand?!? I just feel like there's this dismissal of the science fiction that I write. This reluctance to accept that I ALSO (even MAINLY) write science fiction. I sense what's behind that reluctance and it infuriates me. I am coming to despise the term 'fantasy.'"[27] Okorafor's comment speaks to her concern that Western audiences are trying to label her as a fantasy author to dismiss the non-Western sciences in her writing as fantasy. Her concern about being labeled as a fantasy author echoes many authors of color in the last few decades who were hesitant to be classified as science fiction authors because of stereotypes about genre fiction not being "serious" literature and because of this genre's ties to colonialism.[28] One of the major difficulties I have come across as a US scholar of science fiction and fantasy who is supposed to care about genre distinctions is making sure to avoid the pitfall of labeling any "nonrational" technology or cultural practice as "magic." And yet, it is authors who challenge or break down the barriers between science fiction and fantasy that are often doing some of the most exciting work in both genres, which is why I am including hybrid fantasy works in this project.

Double Estrangement in Fantasy Literature

In my previous book *Diverse Futures: Science Fiction and Authors of Color* (2021), I used the phrase "double estrangement" to describe science fiction texts that add a layer of racial self-consciousness to the estrangement of science fictional writings. This term juxtaposes the ideas of cognitive estrangement expressed by science fiction critic Darko Suvin with W. E. B. Du Bois's writings on racial double consciousness.[29] Although this term was specifically created to describe the experience of writing science fiction as an author of color, multiple levels of estrangement also exist within fantasy writings by authors of color.

---

27. Okorafor published this comment on Twitter on Feb. 25, 2023.
28. For one example of the conversations around science fiction and "respectability" for authors of color, see "Junot Díaz." Also, see Hopkinson.
29. See Suvin; Du Bois.

The term "double estrangement" has been used in fantasy studies to discuss immersive fantasy worlds that shield readers from the implication that the created fantasy world is not "real." Farah Mendlesohn explains this concept in *Rhetorics of Fantasy* (2008), noting that "if we imagine different levels of 'reality' as concentric shells around the world, then the reader of the immersive fantasy must be able to sit between the shell that surrounds the narrative and the shell that protects the world as it is built from any suggestion that it is not real—a position Gary Westfahl has termed double estrangement" (237).[30] This description of double estrangement is linked to the idea of reader expectations that an immersive fantasy world be a complete and contained space that abides by the worldbuilding rules set by the author and relies on the idea that its impossible worlds should follow some sort of logic; the world still needs to make "sense" to the reader and needs to abide by the rules its author sets. The double estrangement of Western fantasy is therefore often about creating and finding order even in impossible spaces.

It is important to note that this original use of the term "double estrangement" in fantasy is situated in a Eurocentric context; while many authors of color have been influenced by Western fantasy literature, fantasy produced in or depicting non-Western cultures may have a different interpretation of the relationship between the fantasy world and the world of the reader. Also, as previously noted, the idea of "reality" in general has been influenced by ideals of white supremacy. As African speculative author Oghenechovwe Donald Ekpeki notes in his essay "Too Dystopian for Whom?," one person's dystopia is another person's lived experience. I would argue that the same is true for fantasy: one person's idea of fantasy is often another person's lived experience. When readers of color encounter mainstream fantasy works where the marginalization of white characters in the fantasy world mimics the actual lived existence of marginalized peoples in the real worlds, the line between fantasy and reality becomes blurred. Ebony Elizabeth Thomas also notes that readers of color are more likely to see themselves reflected in the monstrous characters of mainstream fantasy, which is problematic because in many of these texts, the killing of the "Dark Other" is used as a cathartic restoration of white, conservative, heteronormative beliefs. Thomas explains that the dilemma of the Dark Other "is inescapable, for readers and for writers, and must be reconciled. It is most often resolved by enacting symbolic and/or actual violence against the Dark Other. This is what readers and

---

30. I have not been able to obtain a copy of Westfahl's original use of the term "double estrangement" in hard copy or eBook format, so I am forced to rely on Mendlesohn's reference to the term.

hearers of the fantastic expect, for it mirrors the spectacle of violence against the endarkened and the Othered in our own world" (24). Throughout this project, I identify some of the ways authors of color bypass the dilemma of the Dark Other in their works, such as exorcising what I call "the specter of whiteness," challenging Eurocentric ideals of "rationality," offering alternate protagonists and means of conflict resolution, and writing stories where main or narrative characters are acutely aware of their racialized and/or gendered otherness.

One fantasy novel that plays with the boundaries of double estrangement in fantasy is R. F. Kuang's *Babel*; in this work, the narrator uses well-known fantasy references and structures to critique the Eurocentrism of the genre: "Of all the marvels of Oxford, Babel seemed the most impossible—a tower out of time, a vision from a dream . . . it all seemed to have been pulled straight from the painting in Professor Lovell's dining room and dropped whole onto this drab grey street. An illumination in a medieval manuscript; a door to fairy land" (72). Kuang uses her narrator's disbelief and the well-known fantasy tropes of a young protagonist being taught by a seasoned mentor in a magical school setting to critique the horrors of colonialism from within a recognizable frame. Her references to "medieval manuscripts" and "fairy land" take the most expected aspects of Western fantasy worldbuilding and use them to express the alienation of her Chinese protagonist, Robin, who is given an English first name from a children's rhyme book by his English tutor and is later forced by Professor Lovell to take an English surname; he chooses "Swift" after the character in *Gulliver's Travels*, "a stranger in a strange land" (12).

Within Kuang's English fantasy setting, Robin and other characters of color are constantly questioning their choice to participate in the colonial machine. The fact that non-European languages are the key to the continuing dominance of England's magic reminds readers of England's history of colonial exploitation and also critiques Western fantasy's use of minor characters of color to "diversify" contemporary fantasy worlds such as J. K. Rowling's Harry Potter series and Suzanne Collins's Hunger Games series, which often results in the sacrifice of these characters to move the hero forward. If double estrangement in fantasy is the act of shielding the reader from any speculation that an immersive fantasy world is not real, then a work like *Babel* offers an important example of how non-Eurocentric fantasy can use a self-conscious awareness of racial or gendered estrangement within the borders of the fantasy world to break out of the prerace or "diverse" depictions of popular Western fantasy by creating additional levels of estrangement.

Description of Chapters

While the chapters of *Dispelling Fantasies* are designed to work together to provide a broad overview of the current state of contemporary fantasy literature written by authors of color, each chapter is also a self-contained discussion of a specific Eurocentric Christian value found in fantasy literature. I wrote this project with teachers, scholars, and fans in mind; a reader can choose to read the entire text or pick and choose the topics that interest them. This project is not, however, designed to be a comprehensive history of fantasy writing by authors of color; I am happy to say that authors of color have been contributing to the fantasy genre for decades (and potentially longer depending on how one defines fantasy literature) and there are simply too many authors for me to include them all, although I offer additional-reading lists at the end of each chapter. I am also choosing to focus on fantasy and fantastic literature although there is much potential for media studies scholars and visual arts scholars to do great work within these topics.[31] Many of the authors discussed in *Dispelling Fantasies* are US-based members of a diasporic group, but I have also included some authors from outside of the US, including authors from the Caribbean, the UK, Australia, Africa, and Canada. I have also had to limit my choices to Anglophone fantasy literatures due to my inability to translate global fantasy works, but I hope that other scholars who have translation abilities will further this important research. My ultimate goal for this book is to provide a snapshot of some of the current practices I have noticed in my research on fantasy literature by authors of color; I am aware that there are many more ideas and authors within this topic than I can address in one book, and I encourage other scholars to build on this effort so that fantasy fans and scholars can gain a better understanding of the contributions authors of color have made and continue to make to the fantasy genre.

Chapter 1, "Virtue," discusses epic fantasy texts that include characters of color and elements of non-Eurocentric cultures, providing an alternate view of who gets to be the "hero" in epic tales. This chapter will address texts utilizing the structures and tropes of "high fantasy" as well as African and African-diasporic revisions of the sword and sorcery genre.

Chapter 2, "Envy," addresses the idea of darkness and "black magic" in non-Eurocentric fantasy. European colonizers created racialized fantasies about dark skin and Indigenous practices as evil to justify slavery,

---

31. For further reading on fantasy, race, and media studies, see E. Thomas; Carr and Carstarphen.

assimilation, and extinction practices. From the US "one-drop rule" that depicted Black and brown blood as a contaminant to the use of blood in African-based religious practices, blood plays a significant role in many non-Eurocentric cultures and in the fantasy genre itself through depictions of "blood magic." This chapter discusses texts that revise depictions of blood and magic to depict worlds where dark skin and blood practices are not inherently evil.

Chapter 3, "Patriarchy," examines depictions of sex and gender in non-Eurocentric fantasy literature. Whether through rewritings of the hero's journey, revisions of figures like the bruja/witch, or by combining multiple speculative genres, authors of color are offering exciting and complex depictions of sex and gender in contemporary fantasy.

Chapter 4, "Salvation," discusses the ways that colonial views of Indigenous peoples fostered a fantastic narrative about the need for white peoples to "save" darker-skinned peoples through exploitation and slavery. This chapter analyzes fantasy texts that use magic and fantasy worlds to depict the colonial erasure of nonwhite cultures. Each of these texts revises the hierarchical and binary structures of Christian-influenced Eurocentric fantasy texts and, instead, uses Indigenous practices of connection and ethical responsibility for all beings to produce fantasy texts that do not restore a Eurocentric order to their fantasy worlds.

Is it Possible to Write Decolonial Fantasy?

In a reading of The Lord of Rings, Brian Attebery points out that even the most "good" or "pure" characters can be corrupted by power, symbolized by the effects of the one ring. As a result, good and evil become the effects of specific actions rather than an inherent quality (33). And yet this characterization is not equally applied to dark-skinned characters; dark characters in Tolkien's writing are inherently evil, and they remain inherently evil at the end of the text. So how can fantasy authors challenge the idea that light/white is good and darkness/black is evil?

One important way that fantasy authors can challenge current perceptions of good and evil in fantasy texts is to show empathy for the monstrous, either by taking the perspective of the monstrous or by depicting humans working with the monstrous rather than eliminating it altogether. It is worth pointing out that monsters are often defined as an othered being that exists outside of binaries or hierarchies; Jeffrey Jerome Cohen defines the monster as "a mixed category [that] resists any classification built on hierarchy or a merely binary opposition, demanding instead a 'system' allowing polyphony, mixed response (difference in sameness, repulsion in attraction), and resistance to integration" (7). This aspect of the monstrous makes it useful for authors who want to disrupt the ordered, hierarchical structures of Western fantasy literature. For example, Eliza Chan's "The Tails That Make You" (2022) employs fox spirits and the nine-tailed fox of Chinese mythology, dualistic creatures said to embody both good and bad omens, to comment on the double bind of gendered expectations of women in Chinese and Western cultures. Xiaofei Kang notes:

> For the Chinese, the fox has long been "betwixt and between": it roams in the wild and remains untamable for domestic uses, yet it preys on domestic fowl, builds dens in human settlements, and demonstrates quasi-human intelligence. No clear line divides natural and supernatural foxes in popular imagination. . . . The marginality of the fox has generated manifold interpretations over the course of history. For example, *"huli jing"* (fox essence), a colloquial expression, connotes a dualism recognized by all: the enchantment of a female beauty and her power of lustful destruction. (2)

Chan gives her narrator tails that appear at moments of sexual significance or gendered violence; the narrator feels othered because of the tails, which are both a source of pleasure and shame. The fact that the story is told from the point of view of the other allows readers to empathize with the narrator, who feels trapped by the gendered expectations of her family and society. The use of a "monstrous" quality enables a more nuanced depiction of gender than the virtuous-female-helper or temptress characterizations found in many fantasy texts.

Another important way that fantasy worlds can resist the trope of the one good hero overcoming envious evil is to create fantasy texts with elements of communal action or kinship. Texts like Shelley Parker-Chan's Radiant Emperor series (2021–23), Nghi Vo's Singing Hills Cycle (2020–24), Zoraida Córdova's Brooklyn Brujas series (2016–19), and Aiden Thomas's *Sunbearer Trials* (2022) each depict main characters with the ability to both recognize the potential of socially othered groups—women and/or nonbinary people, people of lower classes, magical creatures, or animals—and bring these othered beings together to achieve the main character's goals. The main characters of these series refuse to conform to the hierarchical expectations of their societies and, instead, inspire kinship between disparate groups of peoples that allows for a structural shift in the social hierarchies of the worlds they inhabit. Often, the magic in these worlds is also based on connectivity and communication between peoples, their environments, and other species or ghosts. In many non-Eurocentric fantasy texts, the lone heterosexual male hero is replaced by a character of color and/or a gender-nonconforming character, and these characters, despite their powerful abilities, cannot enact change without kinship and community.

The works referenced in this introduction are only some of the many examples of contemporary fantasy authors of color who are utilizing combinations of Eurocentric fantasy figures with elements of non-Eurocentric cultures, folklore, and mythology to disrupt the light-as-good/dark-as-evil binary. The worlds that these authors create are diverse depictions where characters of color are the focus and racial and gender hierarchies are disrupted. While such depictions of fantasy are not limited to authors of color, these authors are well-positioned to recognize the Eurocentrism of Western fantasy and are therefore more likely to address it in their writing. When people of color read Eurocentric fantasy and find themselves depicted as, at best, outsiders or, at worst, monstrous, such experiences can result in an internalization of the idea that people of color can't be the heroes of fantasy worlds.[32] The authors discussed in *Dispelling Fantasies* are working to make sure that this belief is eradicated for generations to come.

---

32. For examples of authors who have been affected by reading Eurocentric literature at young ages, see Adichie; Grady.

CHAPTER 1

Virtue

Revising the Moral Order of Epic Fantasy

Someone who is virtuous is typically thought to be a person who is morally good in thought and action ("Virtuous"). The way that Christianity defines goodness is through the example of Jesus Christ, who loved his neighbor, helped the needy, forgave sinners, and engaged in self-sacrifice to save the souls of mankind.[1] Christianity is also a monotheistic religion, with a clear hierarchy from God to mankind. The Gospel of John contains clear descriptions of Jesus referencing his descent from on high in Heaven to the mortal world:

> If I have told you about earthly things and you do not believe, how can you believe if I tell you about heavenly things? No one has ascended into heaven except the one who descended from heaven, the Son of Man. And just as Moses lifted up the serpent in the wilderness, so must the Son of Man be lifted up, that whoever believes in him may have eternal life. (Coogan, John 3:12–15)

---

1. For more information on the major beliefs and practices of Christianity, see S. Brown.

Jesus "descended" from heaven, indicating that he traveled downward to literally and metaphorically "lower" himself to live among mankind. If man must be "lifted up," then mankind is clearly both lower than God and in need of salvation. The gospel's reference to Moses is an example from the Old Testament (Numbers 21:9) where Moses saves people from fiery serpents after they criticize God. However, Jesus is depicted as greater than Moses because he will lift up all mankind. Jesus becomes both a virtuous example for mankind to follow and a self-sacrificing savior who will allow mankind to overcome its wickedness through salvation and achieve a place in Heaven.[2]

One of the hallmarks of heroic or epic fantasy tales is the trope of the hero as a "messianic figure" (Palmer-Patel 84). The idea of a male figure engaging in sacrificial heroic acts for the good of others, echoing the story of Jesus, occurs frequently throughout the fantasy genre. *The Encyclopedia of Fantasy* identifies epic fantasy stories in particular as those that include a hero "whose acts have a significance transcending their own individual happiness or woe." Some fantasy heroes literally reenact the death and resurrection of Jesus, such as Aslan from C. S. Lewis's Chronicles of Narnia series or Harry Potter from J. K. Rowling's Harry Potter series. Some fantasy texts force a humble hero into action through tragic loss, such as Paul Atreides from Frank Herbert's Dune series or Luke Skywalker from George Lucas's Star Wars franchise. Some fantasy texts depict unlikely heroes who turn out to be morally superior, such as Frodo from Tolkien's Lord of the Rings series or Howard's Conan the Barbarian. What brings together these vastly different fantasy depictions is a male heroic character who is willing to sacrifice in times of danger to uphold or restore the moral order of his fantasy world. The example is so common that Joseph Cambell added it to his definition of the hero in an interview with Bill Moyers: "A hero properly is someone who has given his life to something bigger than himself or other than himself" ("Ep. 1"). Such characterization becomes problematic, however, in stories where main characters are not white, male, heterosexual, and able-bodied, or stories set in a culture that does not believe in the ideals of sacrifice or salvation. Sarah E. Bond and Joel Christensen note that Campbell's insistence on the idea of a common heroic figure across Western and non-Western cultures led to the creation of a Western-influenced "Monomyth" that privileges

---

2. I am not saying that ideas of resurrection are only found in Christianity; many ancient and Indigenous creation stories have elements of resurrection. For examples, see Roos. But when resurrection is connected to the salvation of mankind, then I would argue that it is being influenced by Christian depictions of Jesus.

the individual male hero and leaves out peoples and examples that do not conform to Campbell's formula:

> Campbell's hero is ruggedly individual; it uses weaker people as instruments; and it has no room for collective action, for families, or for bodies that fail to conform: the aged, the disabled, the sick. . . . The Monomyth sets up unrealistic expectations. It harms people who don't see themselves represented and it traps people in roles based on the bodies they inhabit, on skin color, race, sex, gender, and ability.

Bond and Christensen's points demonstrate that heroism in fantasy is filtered through a Western, Christian lens of ability and morality, and it is largely defined through individual virtuous acts of self-control and self-sacrifice. The monomyth creates the idea that most fantasy narratives follow this "logical" sequence, which leaves out alternative narrative arcs of kinship and community. Through a discussion of non-Eurocentric epic fantasy, specifically high fantasy and variations of the sword and sorcery subgenre, this chapter will explore how fantasy authors of color are utilizing non-Eurocentric cultural practices and beliefs to revise the Western, Eurocentric notion of the virtuous, self-sacrificing hero.

Non-Eurocentric Morality

Is it necessary to sacrifice oneself for the greater good to be considered a hero? If the moral universe of the fantasy genre has been predominantly Christian, then it stands to reason that non-Christian-based fantasy might have differing views of what a "moral universe" entails. One important difference between Christian views of morality and those of many non-Christian cultures is the idea of hierarchy vs. connectivity. Rather than following a Christian hierarchy, many non-Eurocentric cultures teach that all beings are equal and interconnected. Vincent Shen notes that one difference between Christianity and religions like Confucianism, Daoism, and Buddhism is that the non-Christian religions move away from a hierarchical line from God to man and toward a more balanced concern with serving life, self, and Heaven:

> In Christianity, the spiritual aim is mystic union with God, and thus spirituality is integrated into mysticism. While Chinese spirituality also contains a mystic dimension, it is more concerned with the nurturing of life

(yangsheng 養生), the cultivation of the mind/heart (xiuxin 修心), the formation/achievement of virtues (chengde 成德), and finally, serving Heaven (shitian 事天). This is to say that the mystic dimension of the Three Teachings (Confucianism, Daoism, and Buddhism) is usually integrated into their spirituality. (34)

In a belief system that does not follow a strict hierarchy or a need for man to sacrifice himself to serve God's plan, mortals have more space to serve Heaven while also addressing their individual needs and those of their communities.

Another important component of some non-Christian religions is the shift from individual responsibility to a more communal responsibility. Whether it is the Yoruba concept of "àse/ache/ashe," the "'vital force' in all living and non-living things" (Abiodun 310) that has traveled to diasporic cultures in Brazil, the Caribbean, and the United States, or the idea of "qi," the balanced force that makes up all living and nonliving beings found in many Asian cultures (Lee 42), many non-Christian belief systems teach the concept of one vital energy that is found in all things, even alternate planes of existence. And because these cultures teach that all beings share the same force/power/energy, it makes sense that these beings are connected by this force and thus affect each other to some degree. The idea of connection and its effects leads to concepts of reciprocity and the ethical responsibilities necessary to maintain such relationships. Leonard Tumaini Chuwa explains in *African Indigenous Ethics in Global Bioethics: Interpreting Ubuntu* that a key moral concept found in African cultures is that of Ubuntu, or "the often unrecognized role of relatedness and dependence of human individuality to other humans and the cosmos" (ix). Similar to the web-of-life concept found in many Indigenous teachings,[3] the idea of recognizing interdependence and community as key moral concepts shifts the idea of a moral universe from one where a solitary hero, or even one with a key mentor, can restore order, to one where entire communities of humans and other beings/planes of existence need to work together or at least coexist to maintain a moral universe.

Although many non-Eurocentric cultures include teachings of relatedness and connectivity, it is important to note that these beliefs often stem from Indigenous teachings and have been significantly impacted by European colonization and Christian missionary practices. One major influence

---

3. For more information on Indigenous cultures and web-of-life kinship, see Salmón, "Kincentric Ecology."

of European colonization and trade was an adoption of gender binaries that encouraged the subordination of women and the erasure of nonbinary gender designations. Rosemary A. Joyce notes in "Gender in the Ancient Americas" that "colonial documents record a process through which indigenous societies made themselves intelligible to Europeans, at times at the cost of leaving out what did not fit European understanding" (269). She notes that gender roles were not always strictly defined or maintained in precolonial cultures and explains that "multiple scholars have proposed that societies in Mexico and Central America, the Andes, and the Amazon conceived of more fluid possibilities of gender than a male/female dichotomy, including gender-neutral and dual-gender beings" (274). Jana Tschurenev notes that a similar colonial influence affected gender relations in India: "The reform and regulation of gender relations, sexuality, and reproduction were central concerns of British colonial governance in India. From the 1820s onwards, interventionist social policies were formulated in the name of an imperial civilizing mission" (241). Current research in the fields of gender and empire highlight that even within cultures that stress duty to one's family and community over individualism, there can still exist a strict hierarchy of gender roles and a refusal to acknowledge gender fluidity.

Revising the Eurocentric Virtuous Hero

Many authors of color are redefining the qualities that make someone heroic; whether it is through racial and gender representation or through characters who would not be considered virtuous by Christian standards, these authors utilize non-Eurocentric settings, characters, and practices to reimagine the epic fantasy hero.[4] The texts discussed in this chapter have clear epic fantasy worldbuilding elements: sweeping landscapes, magical artifacts or creatures, and worldbuilding maps are present. But beyond a nonmedieval setting, the authors discussed also employ elements of non-Eurocentric cultures such as a refusal to provide a eucatastrophic payoff, communal action or inactive protagonists, and nonhierarchical systems of thought to create epic fantasy that revises the individualistic, self-sacrificing heroics of Western fantasy literature.

---

4. I am not implying that all fantasy works include a male, self-sacrificing hero. There are contemporary fantasy works that feature nontraditional or questionable heroic characters. My point is that that the virtuous male hero is a common, central trope of the fantasy genre.

In high fantasy, the hero is often a young man fated to save the world from the powers of evil. W. A. Senior notes that a common trope for a quest fantasy is to have a hero from an ordinary background who is forced to leave a place of security to save the fantasy world from a Dark Lord figure (190–94). These characteristics highlight how often Western fantasy heroes are defined by their humble origins, their ability to not be corrupted by power or glory, and their choice to sacrifice something to achieve their fated role. The Western fantasy hero is on a path that may have slight differences from author to author, but ultimately, he goes through trials, gains the skills or abilities he needs, finds companions willing to sacrifice for him, and defeats evil to restore the fantasy world to its former state. The hero thus becomes a representation of Jesus and Christian moral goodness in general. In fact, J. R. R. Tolkien makes this connection explicit in his essay "On Fairy Stories" through his invention of the term "eucatastrophe," defined as "a sudden and favorable resolution of events in a story; a happy ending" ("Eucatastrophe"). Tolkien notes that the birth and resurrection of Christ are eucatastrophes and that fantasy writing can be employed to defy "universal final defeat" and, in doing so, serve as a form of *"evangelium"* or evangelism (69; emphasis in original). According to Tolkien, fantasy literature should thus provide not only a brief respite from modernity, but also a eucatastrophic payoff that allows for hope that mankind can be redeemed.

While authors of color may choose to include elements of Western fantasy, many deliberately change elements of their fantasy narratives to draw attention to the idea that not all peoples are included in the active, mobile, self-sacrificing heroic narratives that Western fantasy stresses. One way that fantasy authors of color reimagine such heroic figures is by writing stories where the hero is part of a marginalized group, often one that has experienced war or genocide. Texts like N. K. Jemisin's Hundred Thousand Kingdoms series (2010–11), Tomi Adeyemi's Legacy of Orisha series (2018–24), Ken Liu's Dandelion Dynasty series (2016–22), R. F. Kuang's Poppy War series (2018–20), and Naseem Jamnia's *Bruising of Qilwa* (2022), among others, include main characters who are lesser or ousted nobility, survivors of genocide, or refugees. Often, these characters are not seeking to restore the fantasy world to its former glory; the dead and their cultural knowledge cannot be brought back, so many fantasy texts written by authors of color focus on revenge, societal restructuring, or recovery rather than restoration.

Two examples of non-Eurocentric epic fantasy texts that reimagine the heroic fantasy figure are Marlon James's *Black Leopard Red Wolf* (2019) and Tasha Suri's Burning Kingdoms series (2021–24). At their heart, James's novel is a quest narrative and the first two books of Suri's series are an epic battle between royal siblings; however, both authors deviate from the expected Western fantasy characteristics of self-sacrifice and restoration to create narratives that refuse to provide the eucatastrophic payoff that Western epic fantasy readers have come to expect from the genre.[5] In doing so, both authors highlight the fact that self-sacrifice is not endemic to all cultural belief systems and that many peoples of color never escape the effects of cultural erasure, oppression, and xenophobia.

Black Leopard Red Wolf begins with a very typical quest fantasy setup; the narrator, a man named Tracker who is known for an extraordinary sense of smell that helps him locate missing people, is invited by a friend to join a party of nine tasked with finding a lost child. What differentiates James's narrative from a typical quest narrative is that the story starts with Tracker saying, "The child is dead. There is nothing left to know" (3). *Black Leopard Red Wolf* begins by eradicating any sense of the reader's safety and stability; rather than starting in an idyllic setting, like a shire, or in a "simple," rural area, James's narrative begins in a city with Tracker killing his abusive father, who he later discovers is actually his grandfather. Tracker is told that his father/grandfather was a coward who failed to avenge the death of his uncle. He is also told that he will never be a man because his father/grandfather didn't have him circumcised to remove the "female" part of his genitalia. Tracker feels shame because of his family history, because he is not circumcised, and because he desires other men. James sets up his quest narrative with an emotionally damaged narrator who chooses not to care about others and a plot where the entire quest that Tracker is about to embark on is pointless because the child is already dead as the story begins.

James has noted that his refusal to provide resolution or restoration is deliberate, explaining, "The African folktale is not your refuge from skepticism. It is not here to make things easy for you, to give you faith so you don't have to think" (qtd. in Tolentino). Although James engaged in extensive research on African culture and language while writing *Black Leopard Red Wolf*, especially West and South African folklore and monster stories, his writing is equally influenced by the Jamaican culture he was born and raised in. James himself has struggled with feelings of shame because of his

---

5. I am aware that *Black Leopard Red Wolf* is the first book of James's Dark Star trilogy; I am not discussing the second book, *Moon Witch Spider King* (2023), because this novel has the same storyline as the first novel, told from a different character's perspective. At the time of writing, book 3 is not yet published, but since the first novel tells a self-contained story, my argument about the lack of eucatastrophe still holds. Also, I am not referencing the third novel in Suri's series here because I am basing my arguments in this chapter on the Malini–Chandra war storyline, which is one of the main storylines that runs through the first two novels of the series.

homosexuality; he was born in Jamaica, where antihomosexual laws have yet to be repealed and where members of the LGBTQIA+ community are often victims of violence and discrimination because of cultural views about homosexuality.[6] At one point, James requested an exorcism to eradicate the demons inside him causing him to feel desire toward men and hate toward his family (Tolentino). Upon being accepted to an MFA program at Wilkes University in Pennsylvania, he wrote on his blog, "I love my country but I've never missed it, perhaps because I have never forgotten the reasons I left" (qtd. in Tolentino). *Black Leopard Red Wolf* is full of characters marked as different or monstrous, from Tracker, who has his unusual sense of smell and, later in the novel, a wolf's eye, to a shape-shifting man/leopard, to the children they save marked as "mingi," or cursed. James creates characters who are shunned by society but makes these characters some of the most powerful in the novel. His writing does not hold back from the pain, anger, and sorrow that many peoples of color feel when they experience trauma at the hands of their own culture and other cultures. In *Black Leopard Red Wolf*, he asks readers to accept that documenting Tracker's journey is more important than a resolution for the reader.

Suri's Burning Kingdoms series is narrated by multiple characters, but the two main characters who drive the action of the series are Malini, a princess who desires to overthrow her brother and become empress, and Priya, a temple child turned servant after her nation, Ahiranya, is conquered by Malini's empire, Parijatdvipa. Malini is banished to Ahiranya after she is discovered to be plotting against her brother, the emperor Chandra, and refuses to willingly be burned at a stake to cleanse her of her sin. Malini befriends Priya, a servant assigned to wait on her during her imprisonment, out of desperation. She uses Priya to help her escape, and Priya allows herself to be used because she cares for Malini, but also because she wants Malini to help her free her people after she becomes empress. The end of the first book in the series finds Priya entering the deathless waters, a source of power for temple priests where chosen individuals hollow themselves out to make room for godlike powers (and for the gods themselves, as is revealed later). However, this choice marks Priya as monstrous and gives the gods, the yaksa, an opening to return and take over. Malini and Priya both make questionable choices and use each other, other people, and magic to achieve their goals.

Suri goes against the fantasy ideal of the heroic, self-sacrificing male figure from the beginning of her epic series by critiquing sacrifice, especially

---

6. For more information on the topic of homophobia in Jamaica, see Ghoshal.

sacrifices asked of women in patriarchal cultures. Suri is of Indian origin, so it is not surprising that she begins her series by critiquing the practice of sati, where widows were encouraged to commit suicide by throwing themselves on the funeral pyres of their husbands.[7] Malini refuses to be willingly burned at a stake and tells her brother Chandra, "I will never burn for you"; as a result, she is forced to watch her two handmaidens, her childhood friends, burn instead (*Oleander* 34). After Malini's banishment, Chandra begins burning women, willingly or unwillingly, to create a magical fire called mother's fire that he uses against Malini in battle. Mother's fire is linked to the religion of Parijatdvipa while Priya's magic is linked to the more ancient yaksa deities, nature deities connected to the religions of Hinduism, Jainism, and Buddhism (Dokras). In both cases, Suri links the price of magic to what she describes as "my complicated feelings on faith and religion and what they often demand from their [believers]" (qtd. in Roman). The character Malini, in particular, has to work hard to balance her desire for power with the patriarchal and religious beliefs of her male commanders, who want her to play the role of a virtuous feminine figure for them. Toward the middle of the second book in the series, Malini loses some of her commanders' faith when her soldiers see Chandra's forces using mother's fire, a magic that is supposed to indicate that a ruler has been blessed by the mothers of flame. She thinks to herself:

> Righteousness, rightfulness—oh, how she hated those words. Their sole purpose seemed to be to keep her in her place: a life with narrow walls and standards of purity that pressed her thin, erased her to nothing but her blood and her good bones and the worth of a pleasing face. A life where she would never contemplate ruling; a life where she would obediently bare her neck for a knife, or gladly embrace the pyre. (68)

Malini must appease and use men to overthrow Chandra, but she is not interested in being virtuous because she understands how this ideal is used to trap women into specific societal roles. The connection of "righteousness" and "rightfulness" could be seen as a critique of religious teachings or missionaries, who often link these ideas to justify their religion as the only true one. Malini has no intention to sacrifice herself for either man or religion; she is driven by a desire to rule and will do what is necessary, even pretending to be blessed and virtuous, to achieve her goals.

---

7. The practice of sati was not banned until the passing of the 1987 Commission of Sati Prevention Act. For more information, see Pallapothu.

Yaksa are typically portrayed in Indian folklore as deities of nature that humans often turn to for protection or boons (gifts or answers to prayer),[8] but Suri upends the typical restoration of a bygone-era trope in Western epic fantasy by portraying the return of the yaksa as negative; instead of protecting humanity, the yaksa in Suri's novel want to subordinate humankind by any means necessary. One of the temple children, named Ashok, is brought back from death and his body is made into a vessel for one of the yaksa; however, what is left of Ashok manages to maintain enough of his attachment to his friends to influence the yaksa inhabiting his form into giving his temple sister Bhumika knowledge that helps the humans fight back. After he delivers Bhumika's abandoned child to one of the children she previously helped survive, a move that mimics his childhood protecting Priya after the downfall of the temple, Ashok reflects on the meaning of all that has occurred:

> There was a vicious satisfaction in knowing that nothing ended, that all griefs in the world came back over and over again, spinning like a terrible wheel. He'd thought he would be able to forge a better world once. He'd thought he could bring back all the goodness and joy Ahiranya had lost.
>
> That he had only managed to bring back this—his own childhood made strange, as if seen through water—seemed . . . fitting. It seemed fitting. (465; ellipsis in original)

The restoration of an idyllic past is not possible in Suri's series. Instead, her eucatastrophe is the fact that humanity survives the yaksa at all. There is no return to safety and stability; there is only an endless cycle of pain and trauma as the surviving humans in Ahiranya try to rebuild their society once again without knowing if the yaksa will return. Priya's hollowing and blessing by one of the oldest yaksas, an act that allowed her to win a war but that also rendered her monstrous, resists resolution and leaves Priya wandering alone and met by a completely transformed Ashok. Like James, Suri's use of human main characters marked as different or monstrous allows her to subvert any real binary between good and evil precisely because "the monster resists any classification built on hierarchy or a merely binary opposition, demanding instead a 'system' allowing polyphony, mixed response (difference in sameness, repulsion in attraction), and resistance to integration" (Cohen 7). While the yaksa are portrayed as wanting to dominate humans, the fact that Priya and Ashok are the last two beings the reader encounters at

---

8. For more information on yaksas, see Dokras and Nguyen-Thi.

the end of *The Oleander Sword* seems to suggest that a posthuman existence, one more connected to nature, is possible. James and Suri look beyond the good–evil binary found in many epic fantasy texts and offer narratives full of multiple voices, both human and other, while exploring the lengths some characters will go to for survival.

A Different Fantasy Map

Another important element of Western fantasy worldbuilding is the landscape itself. In *Here Be Dragons: Exploring Fantasy Maps and Settings* (2013), Stefan Ekman notes that fantasy maps are central to the worldbuilding efforts of Western fantasy authors; although they are not "actual maps" (though they are often based on actual maps), maps help Western fantasy authors and readers orient themselves to the fantasy landscape and are thus an integral part of the Western fantasy narrative (20–21). It stands to reason that if maps are part of the Western fantasy narrative, then the representations of these maps can influence the ways that authors portray the characters and cultures located within a map and the fantasy reader's response to the world of the fantasy narrative. Eurocentric worldbuilding tends to utilize a single continent map that often evokes Europe with a clear distinction between Westerners and other peoples. The common justification for this type of mapmaking is that it occurs because fantasy stories are frequently set in a medieval European setting, making the continent of Europe the logical inspiration for fantasy maps. However, many Western fantasy texts, from Tolkien and beyond, also imported stereotypes about the peoples living within and outside of Europe: "The north is often a harsh tundra full of barbarian tribes, the east a mysterious land whence ride the Hordes from the East, and the south a hot land of jungles, tropical islands, and savages" ("Left-Justified"). Such stereotypes demonstrate that Eurocentric fantasy maps are about more than mapping the unfamiliar onto the familiar; they serve to reinforce the perspective that Western cultures are superior.

Two novels that make interesting deviations from the monocontinent and West–other binary found in many Eurocentric epics are Ken Liu's Dandelion Dynasty series and Moniquill Blackgoose's *To Shape a Dragon's Breath* (2023). Liu's and Blackgoose's works each include islands as main settings in their novels. Galen Strickland notes in a review of the first book of Liu's series, *The Grace of Kings*, that the scale of the islands is a significant part of the story: "If the scale is correct, Big Island is not that big, smaller than Spain or France, but it is home to six of the seven nation states, with several of them claiming adjacent islands." Strickland also notes that the state that eventually rises to conquer the other states, Xana, is one of the smallest nations in the series. Another interesting feature of the map is that it is oriented with West at the top of the map, meaning that Xana is a more Western island, while the biggest island is more South and East oriented. Liu has made frequent comments about his writing serving as a decolonial counterpoint to Western, Eurocentric epic fantasy texts,[9] and his map and geography for The Dandelion Dynasty series demonstrates this non-Eurocentric, decolonial viewpoint. He notes, "I decided to create a new fantasy world inspired by East Asia, and China in particular, but not directly analogous to it. Instead of a continental country, Dara, my fantasy world, is an archipelago and a place of magic as well as technology" ("Interview: Ken"). Liu utilizes islands in his worldbuilding to subvert the view that his fantasy world is either a Eurocentric copy or a reimagined ancient China.

The cultures of The Dandelion Dynasty were formerly defined by mutual respect between states in the Tiro system until a man from one of the islands decided to conquer the others and name himself emperor. Liu follows the traditional trope of desire to restore a past hierarchical order in his fantasy series, but complicates this restoration with descriptions of colonization:

> The origin of the old Tiro system was lost in the mists of time. Legend had it that the Islands of Dara were settled long ago by a people who called themselves the Ano, refugees of a sunken continent far over the seas to the west. Once they had defeated the barbarians who were the original inhabitants of the Islands, some of whom intermarried and became Ano, they promptly fell to fighting among themselves.
> ... Some scholars claimed the great ancient Ano lawgiver Aruano created the Tiro system in response to the chaotic wars among the states. The classical Ano word *tiro* literally meant "fellow," and the most important principle of the system was that each Tiro state was an equal of every other Tiro state; no state had any authority over another. (*Grace*, 510–11)

The Tiro people are former refugees who colonized an Indigenous population, went to war, and eventually devised a system of mutual coexistence. Liu has stated that one of his goals for the series was to explore the establishment of nations and the dynamics of revolution: "What history taught me is that societies are not static, and that the straight line of progressive

---

9. Liu discusses his choice to avoid writing a "Magical China" text to eschew Western stereotyping in "Interview: Ken Liu."

ideals—this thinking we have that a society will just magically become more egalitarian over time—is patently false. It helped me create more interesting and dynamic worlds" ("Historical Worldbuilding"). While Liu's main character, Phin, and his cousin Mata have a desire to avenge their clan after it is decimated by Emperor Mapidéré, the reality of the series is that cultures and nations are constantly shifting and changing, which challenges the more static cultural representations of many Eurocentric, medieval-set fantasy epics. Liu uses change to drive his characters and the narrative arc of the series.

Blackgoose's novel begins with a map titled "The Known World," which is a world map of Earth with different nations given European-influenced names. While the large scope of the world map is likely because the author is planning for later events in the next book of the promised Nampeshiweisit series, it is also interesting to note that the events of *To Shape a Dragon's Breath* take place in a relatively small geographic area for an epic story. The island of Nack is a reimagined Martha's Vinyard, an island off the coast of Massachusetts in the United States, which was originally settled by the Indigenous Wampanoag tribe that Blackgoose is a member of. The town that the main character, a young woman named Anequs, travels to is just south of Boston, Massachusetts. The two locations are less than one hundred miles from each other, and the novel is set in an alternate nineteenth-century backdrop with steam locomotives as the primary mode of transportation. This means that the journey to the dragon training school Anequs travels to takes less than a full day. In a genre where characters could be traveling on a quest by foot for months on end, Blackgoose chooses to make the setting of her epic dragon narrative relatively intimate. Fantasy stories with more intimate settings are currently being used for a variety of reasons by fantasy authors, including authors of "cozy fantasy" and urban fantasy texts. Blackgoose shows us through Anequs's internal dialogue that traveling to an "Anglish" city full of people with completely different customs, a people responsible for her tribe's colonization, can be just as dangerous and epic as traveling thousands of miles.

Blackgoose also chooses to reverse the directions of East and West in her novel. Although these directions are not written on the compass of the map, Anequs describes a world map during a session in her "Erelore" class, the study of "all things that have happened in foregone times and why they happened that way" (162). The description of the map includes many of the assumptions that Western cultures make about Eastern cultures: "There were no clear borders in the East, and the names of the nations were simply written across the land in large letters. Moving westward, Russland and Roveland in the North has clearer borders, and Indusland in the south." The fact that the Western countries are now located east on Blackgoose's map serves to both upend stereotypes about "civilized" peoples coming from the West and could even be poking fun at the Anglish knowledge; the Anglish mapmakers could very well have reversed the directions by accident. Either way, the Anglish become the "backward" peoples in Blackgoose's novel.

Blackgoose employs cultural conflicts between the colonizing Anglish cultures and the Masquisit culture of the main character to demonstrate the negatives of hierarchical societal structures. When Anequs first meets her new roommate, Marta, they both discover that they have differing opinions about dragons. Anequs explains that dragons are sacred in her culture and that the Masquisit word for "dragoneer" translates to "person who belongs to a dragon" (111). Marta replies by instructing Anequs on her lack of knowledge:

> Primitive superstition and folklore aside, dragons are beasts—as much as dogs and horses are. I very dearly love Magnus, and I'm sure that every dragoneer would say the same of their dragon, but I hold no particular illusions about him. He's an animal of a witskrafty nature. If he weren't bonded with me, or some other dragoneer of firm resolve, he would be vicious and dangerous. (111–12)

In Anglish culture, animals are below humans and are only tolerated if they are useful and not an immediate danger. Anequs responds to Marta's comment by noting how the Masquisit have a widely different view of their animal neighbors: "The dragons—and the wolves and great cats—were all here long before people were. My people have always endeavored to be good neighbors to them, and if your people find them menacing, then I can only presume that you haven't taken the same care" (112). Masquisit people embody a culture of kinship; Anequs and her people share common goods, engage in sustainable farming practices, and work to be good neighbors to dragons, all other animals, and the environment. Blackgoose is clearly using Marta's and Anequs's dialogue to critique Western cultures that believe in a hierarchical right to take and exploit land and animals as they see fit. Blackgoose includes many more scenes where Anequs is forced to deal with the backward opinions of Anglish peoples, which reverses the "civilized–savage" binary and stresses the superiority of Indigenous kinship practices.

The "Inactive" Protagonist

Another way authors of color are disrupting the Western fantasy narrative of the lone, self-sacrificing hero is by creating narratives with "inactive" protagonists. Nghi Vo's Singing Hills Cycle (2020–present) utilizes such a protagonist to produce an "anti–club story" where the protagonist's life is constantly endangered as they attempt to record a people's history of the world they live in. Vo's series challenges many ideas of Western epic fantasy, including that an epic story must be of epic length. Her novellas are all narrated from the point of view of a nonbinary cleric and their bird companion, which allows her to make room for alternate versions of heroes and heroism. In the world of Vo's Singing Hills Cycle, everyone has the right to have their story heard, and the protagonist is not an all-knowing entity.

A club story is a type of portal-quest fantasy where a group of travelers, typically predominantly male, listen to a closed narrative in a safe space. Mendlesohn explains:

> In the club story, the storyteller, whatever his designation, is possessed of two essential qualities: he is uninterruptible and incontestable; and the narrative as it is downloaded is essentially closed. Although not entirely relevant here, it is hard to avoid the acknowledgment that the club story has a gendered origin, and that there are consequences embedded in these foundations. The club narrative is diegetic, a denial of discourse, an assertion of a particular type of Victorian masculinity, a private place uninterrupted by the needs of domesticity or even self-care (there are always servants in the club), combined with a stature signaled by the single-voiced and impervious authority. (6)

This description of the club story depicts a closed, masculine space where mostly white men of means convene and celebrate their accomplishments. The narrator is depicted as a white male and an absolute authority; there is never a question of the validity of the storyteller or the story he tells. Mendlesohn notes that the club story has had a significant influence on portal-quest fantasy and argues that one of the main characteristics of this subgenre is the upholding of the "unquestionable purity of the tale" (7). These arguments highlight an important element of Western fantasy structures: the fantasy world, its characterizations, even the rhetoric used to tell the story, all these storytelling aspects serve the overall purpose of forwarding a received truth—the "rightness" and validity of the Western fantasy tale must be upheld for the hierarchy on which it is built to be maintained.

If a club story involves a group sequestered in a safe space, often a place of wealth or security, hearing a telling of an "incontestable" and "closed" oral narrative story set in the past and recounted by a male figure (6), then Nghi Vo's Singing Hills Cycle of novellas (*The Empress of Salt and Fortune,* 2020; *When the Tiger Came Down the Mountain,* 2020; *Into the Riverlands,* 2022; *Mammoths at the Gates,* 2023, *The Brides of High Hill,* 2024) gives readers an almost polar-opposite narrative. Rather than being in a safe, uninterrupted space, Cleric Chih's accounts, which are also oral histories, are only possible because they go out into the world. They hear multiple narratives from the individuals they encounter, typically from lower-class or othered groups such as servants, animals, workers, and mercenaries. The cleric's life is frequently in danger as they struggle to stay alive long enough to record and deliver the histories they have encountered. And rather than recounting a closed narrative, Vo makes sure that Cleric Chih hears multiple, even varying versions of some tales, and that they often don't get the entire tale in one sitting. The third book in the series, *Into the Riverlands,* goes even further by questioning whether Cleric Chih has the right to record certain stories. Throughout the Singing Hills Cycle, Vo undermines the idea of one incontestable narrator and narrative, a stand-in for one incontestable historical narrative, by utilizing a nonbinary main character and multiple points of view to challenge the typical white, male, heterosexual, authoritative narrator found in Western club story narratives.

The first novella of the series, *The Empress of Salt and Fortune,* introduces the character of Cleric Chih, a young, nonbinary cleric who has been tasked with going out into the world to collect the history of their people. Their companion is a neixin bird named Almost Brilliant who has absolute recall and who helps Chih record the stories they encounter. Upon meeting an older woman at Lake Scarlet, a location of exile for the former empress that has been recently declassified after her death, she asks the woman for her name and upon hearing it, says, "Welcome to your place in history, grandmother" (16). After the older woman, Rabbit, expresses happiness that "the true history of Lake Scarlet will be told," Chih thinks about the former Divine, their mentor, whom they describe as encouraging Chih to speak to as many people as possible to obtain an accurate historical account: "She sounded a little like the former Divine, who had always encouraged their acolytes to speak to the florists and bakers as much as to the warlords and magistrates. *Accuracy above all things. You will never remember the great if you do not remember the small*" (16–17; emphasis in original). And when Rabbit tells them that the female attendants of the empress called Lake Scarlet by the name "Thriving Fortune," Chih admits that they have never heard this nickname (17). Vo is thus working from the beginning of her first novella in the series to reverse reader expectations around the club story; rather than the reader receiving a tale told by an authority figure in a safe space, they are put in the place of a novice cleric out in the world who has been taught to listen to the stories of others, no matter their sex or station, to record the most accurate oral history possible.

Chih does not passively receive the story of Empress In-Yo's exile from Rabbit. Rather, they uncover the story in pieces through Rabbit's secondhand accounts and their attempts to categorize the empress's belongings. Rabbit was a servant girl and confidant of the empress, and she helps Chih by explaining the meanings of certain items and drawing attention to items they would have overlooked. A scroll filled with hair and a feather is considered trash, until Rabbit explains that it was a coded message the emperor sent In-Yo to mark her exile (43–44). A box of black salt signals the start of a war and star charts become coded messages of war (53–63). Empress In-Yo utilizes the people and resources at hand and builds a network of women and fortune tellers to help her pass messages of war to her family in the North. Rabbit reports that "In-Yo would say that the war was won by silenced and nameless women, and it would be hard to argue with her" (85). In-Yo uses her ability to forge connections with overlooked peoples to win the throne for the North.

Rather than recounting the oral histories they have learned from a safe and enclosed location, Chih is constantly thrown into dangerous situations and conflicts. They do not have fighting skills, so they are often forced to diffuse situations through mediation or find ways to travel in groups with people who are more skilled fighters. In *When the Tiger Came Down the Mountain*, Chih convinces a trio of tiger-people to tell them her story not only to record it, but also to keep herself and two mammoth corps officers alive until reinforcements arrive. *Into the Riverlands* finds Chih traveling with a famous martial artist and serving as a witness to a battle between the martial artist and bandits, which they describe as *"a battle between people who don't fight like people, who are what legends are made of"* (82; emphasis in original). Chih is frequently in danger, and they are never the authority of the story. Instead, they serve as a living record of the events they encounter.

One of the most important themes of the Singing Hills Cycle is the idea that there are multiple versions of stories and that not all stories are meant to be told. In *Into the Riverlands*, Chih travels with the martial artist Wei Jintai, a woman described as too wild for "the civilized world" (82). During their travels, Chih learns the story of the bandits Wild Pig Yi and

Gravewraith Chen, and how they rescued a noblewoman named Beautiful Nie, a tale that ends with all three characters pledging themselves to one another. When Chih realizes after the battle that the old couple they are traveling with are Wild Pig Yi and Gravewraith Chen, they try to ask Yi for her story. Yi replies: "What my story is, cleric, is *mine*. You have the rest, and you'll tell the rest. Be happy with that. My story's mine, and you don't get to have it" (95; emphasis in original). Chih is disappointed, but respects Yi's desire to keep her story to herself. Chih has been taught by their abbey mentors that "truth showed up in its own time, often late and sometimes entirely unlooked for" (98). Rather than embodying the all-knowing authority of the stories being told, Chih is a witness to greatness who must live with recording an incomplete account of the story of Wild Pig Yi and her companions. Yi also questions the validity of the stories that Chih and others will tell about Wei Jintai:

> "They'll tell stories about Wei Jintai if they've not already started," she continued. "You have one now. I imagine you even think it's the truth."
>
> There was something arch and catlike about her tone, and Chih considered before they answered.
>
> "I know what I have seen," Chih said finally. "There's what Almost Brilliant has seen. There's what the people who survive her have seen. Auntie, there's what you will say as well." (97)

Chih's answer makes everyone responsible for the oral history of Wei Jintai. Rather than Chih or their abbey being the sole authority for historical accounts, they are simply recorders of as much oral history as they can access. The responsibility of historical narrative in Vo's storytelling comes from community effort, and all play a role in providing a detailed account.

Vo creates a narrator who upends moral and gender expectations in epic fantasy stories. Chih is a cleric, a religious figure, and yet they consistently bend the rules of their abbey and ignore social and gender hierarchies to form bonds and record their stories. Rather than depicting a lone, virtuous, male authority figure, Vo portrays an asexual, nonbinary figure who receives stories from others. Vo's epic worlds include both sweeping landscapes and intimate spaces full of people and animals that are often overlooked by the society they exist in. Chih is "inactive" by Western fantasy standards because they observe action rather than initiating it. However, they sacrifice their safety and comfort to go into the world and record their people's histories.

Sword and Soul

The trope of the morally ambiguous hero is common in the epic subgenre of sword and sorcery, which often differentiates itself from high fantasy through depictions of morally ambiguous characters. The most famous of these characters is Conan the Barbarian. Jonas Prida notes that Conan is a cultural figure that has spanned almost eighty years, one that has had a large influence on the sword and sorcery subgenre (2). There has been a sustained popular interest in fantasy stories inspired by sword and sorcery; one good example is the popular role-playing game Dungeons & Dragons, which has been in the public consciousness for fifty years and has again returned to film in *Dungeons & Dragons: Honor Among Thieves* (2023). Conan and the sword-wielding action heroes he inspires are still present in Western fantasy literature and popular media today and have influenced a number of fantasy authors.

One of the earliest sword and sorcery–style series by an author of color is Samuel Delany's Tales of Nevèrÿon series (1979–87). Delany's sword and sorcery series reverses several tropes associated with the subgenre; the main character is a brown-skinned, subservient, homosexual man who does not fit the sword-wielding-warrior trope while the "barbarians" of the series are white. Delany also includes references to a matriarchal society and makes one of the main female characters, Raven, a warrior from this society. The Tales of Nevèrÿon series marks a groundbreaking shift from the predominantly white, Eurocentric, heterosexual norms of sword and sorcery. Delany deserves much critical acclaim for writing a sword and sorcery series that utilizes depictions of culture and technology to debunk the fantasy of the all-white, static Middle Ages. Jo Walton notes in a review of the series that "one of the subthemes of the book is how dynamic technology is, how fast everything changes, which isn't what we expect from fantasy, but why not? . . . It's interesting to wonder why we imagine the technology of fantasy worlds as static—as we (wrongly) imagine the Middle Ages as unchanging." Delany's series upends the static, Eurocentric orientations of sword and sorcery and offers many layers of cultural critique; the S&M scenes explore themes of sex and slavery while the addition of elements such as a "mock-academic Preface and Appendix written pseudonymously by Delany himself" (Burnett 257) make this series a metatextual exploration of academic authority. Much of Delany's early work seems to have been ahead of its time, but the Tales of Nevèrÿon series is a significant contribution to the diversification of the sword and sorcery genre and an early challenge to the normalization of all-white, heterosexual, patriarchal settings of medieval-set fantasy literature.

Another major influence of the Conan series on fantasy literature by authors of color is a subset of fantasy action stories featuring African-inspired characters or settings defined as "sword and soul." Author and publisher Milton J. Davis frequently discusses how he and Charles R. Saunders both read Robert Howard's Conan stories and found themselves frustrated with the stereotyped, negative depictions of African characters in them. This frustration led both men to become the first known authors of adventure fantasy featuring African settings and characters, albeit twenty years apart; they eventually teamed up to create and promote the subgenre of sword and soul, the name Saunders gave to their reimagined adventure stories. Saunders is best known for his Imaro series (1981–2005) while Davis is the founder of MV Media and has branched out into science fiction, "cyberfunk," historical fiction, comics, and graphic novel series. The term "sword and soul" was originated by Saunders and made visible by Davis, who met Saunders in the early 2000s and began to work with him to produce sword and soul anthologies such as *Griots: A Sword and Soul Anthology* (2011) and *Griots: Sisters of the Spear* (2013). In the introduction to the first Griots anthology, Saunders explains that while sword and soul is connected to real and fictional African settings and characters, it is also open to new iterations:

> The setting can be the historical Africa of the world we know, or the Africa of an alternate world, dimension, or universe. But that's not a restriction, because a sword-and-soul story can feature a black character in a non-black setting, or a non-black character in a black setting. . . . A sword-and-soul story may also be set in a future in which science and magic have become interchangeable, or one in which modern technology has long been lost. Regardless of the setting, magic and heroism form the underpinnings of sword-and-soul. (9)

Saunders's definition leaves open a world of possibilities for authors who wish to write within the subgenre. However, the main thread that Saunders's definition identifies is the Black character as heroic figure. This idea makes one of the main goals of sword and soul the reversal of Howard's depiction of Black barbarians as "savage."

Although Davis has written several blogs introducing fans to the genre of sword and soul and discussing the history and examples of this work, he has yet to explain why Saunders decided to use the term "soul" in this title. This may be because the concept of "soul" in African American culture has many connotations. Phillip L. Mason explains that the concept of "soul," specifically when referring to African American music and food, implies a physical and spiritual nourishment enjoyed communally. He goes on to link the music of jazz musician Pharoah Saunders to the idea of African spiritual practice:

> You have only to listen to Pharoah Saunders's rendition of "Let Us Go into the House of the Lord" on Summun Bukuman Umyum (Impulse AS 9199) to hear how he lifted the African-American spiritual . . . out of the context of the traditional diaspora and propelled it toward a Neo-African realization of universal consciousness. Saunders's approach to the music of the spiritual finds its analogy in the work of the African juju or conjure man who takes the raw elements of the earth, separates them from their context, endows them with certain symbolic meaning, and thereby works spiritual magic. (49)

While Mason's conflation of juju practices with "magic" is problematic, the idea of an artist reworking an existing creation and using it as inspiration for a communal, spiritual experience centered on African and African American cultural references is exactly the work that sword and soul undertakes. The word "soul" in this context differentiates sword and soul fantasy writing from the white, colonialist writings of Howard and reorients it toward a unique cultural terminology that embodies African American spiritual and cultural nourishment. Just as Afrofuturist musician Sun Ra infused jazz and science fictional thinking with his unique visions of African mythology, Saunders, Davis, and subsequent sword and soul authors are infusing fantasy with a blend of mythology, history, and spirituality found in African and African American cultures. African slaves in the Americas historically hid their African cultural practices from colonizers and made use of European cultural artifacts to continue their spiritual practices.[10] African American culture is a product of this practice; African Americans incorporated Christianity into their cultural beliefs, but added their own rhythms, social structures, and kinship practices to create the Black Church.[11] I would argue that sword and soul does the same: it takes the sword and sorcery genre and plays with it, riffs on it, to produce a subgenre of fantasy literature that has employed the story structures and heroic attributes of sword and sorcery to decolonize thinking about African "primitivism" through the introduction

---

10. The religious and cultural practice of Santería is one example of how African slaves were able to continue their West African practices by aligning them with Christian figures. For further information, see Ayorinde.

11. For more information, see the PBS series created by Henry Louis Gates Jr., *The Black Church: This Is Our Story, This Is Our Song* (2021).

of African settings and cultural practices. In sword and soul, Black culture is valued and Black characters are the heroes of their own stories.

Davis's *Changa's Safari* (2011) is one of the most prominent examples of the sword and soul genre and was adapted into a graphic novel in 2020 to reach more readers. The story is set in fifteenth-century Africa and follows a young prince named Changa Diop who becomes a slave after his father is murdered. Once he is freed from the fighting pits by a benevolent merchant, he vows revenge against the sorcerer Usenge and becomes a merchant with the goal of amassing enough wealth to return to Kongo and free his people. Nisi Shawl notes the importance of having escapist, adventure fantasy rooted in a historically accurate portrayal of African and African American cultures:

> Though this book and its sequel, *Changa's Safari Volume 2*, are undoubtedly fantasies, they're rooted in historical fact. The ruins of the Great Zimbabwe where the novel's initial conflict occurs persist to this day. The routes plied by Changa Diop's dhows are attested in contemporary texts, as is the floating embassy of Admiral Zheng He, inspiration for Milton Davis's character Zheng San. This non-Eurocentric medieval background is essential to many readers' enjoyment of the books' swashbuckling adventure foreground, because it's much easier to relax into pure and playful pleasure when you don't have to expend energy suppressing (possibly unintentional) imputation of your culture's inferiority. . . .
>
> And then there's the team spirit evinced by *Changa's Safari*'s ensemble cast of characters, which is so typical of the African American community and many other non-Western societies, and so atypical of the lone wolf hero of European-derived traditions. ("Modern")

Davis uses his interest in African history to create plausible settings that, as Shawl notes, deviate sharply from Eurocentric depictions of a backward, savage Africa. Davis and other sword and soul authors often use the adventure-fantasy format to refute stereotypes about early African cultures while also providing a cast of characters, similar to a found family, working together to achieve specific heroic goals.

Davis makes Changa a practical man; when he comes into possession of a mysterious magical object, a jade obelisk, at the beginning of the novel, he has an indifferent view of spirituality and magic: "He never had time for spiritual matters and didn't understand them. Every situation he ever faced could be solved by either a handshake or a sword" (*Changa's Safari* location 388). Davis follows the Conan formula in his depiction of Changa by making him a strong and straightforward man, but rather than a white barbarian figure, he makes Changa a fallen African prince who may, at times, act in his own self-interest, but is ultimately a virtuous hero on a quest to restore his people.

Although Changa does not want to deal with magic and its effects, he does believe in fate. His crew member and eventual lover, Panya, is a sorceress who explains the magic of the obelisk to Changa and recruits him to help save humanity by stopping the evil sorceress, Bahati, from taking over the mortal and immortal realms. After Prince Zakee tells Changa that they shouldn't be engaging in a ritual to summon the godlike warrior Kintu to save the mortal world from Bahati, Changa states: "I don't believe in many things, my life has been too harsh to allow much for faith. But I do believe in fate. We were all meant to be here at this moment for some purpose. So the choice was never yours" (*Changa's Safari* location 1049). It is no coincidence that Davis sets *Changa's Safari* in fifteenth-century Africa, a time when the Kongo people were first being introduced to Christianity by European missionaries. Thornton notes that the Kongo people integrated Christianity into their belief systems without fully eradicating their original belief system, which includes the use of spiritual objects, a "hidden power" that could be harnessed to achieve good or evil ends, and an "Other World" that did not require a God's salvation (74). Davis's choice to value "fate" over "faith" moves his story away from a Eurocentric, Christian perspective and toward an Afrocentric perspective that values the idea of all people having a greater purpose and being employed by the heavens to achieve this purpose.

Changa's defining features are his valor and strength. Like Conan, he is the strongest man in his world. Although Panya is a great sorceress, she needs Changa to kill Kintu when he is seduced by Bahati and unable to fulfill his duty to humanity. Later in the novel, he kills the sorcerer Chongli, whom Panya fears and describes as a demon. Changa is stronger than gods or magic, and he also fights several demons, magical creatures, and animal-monsters throughout the Changa series. As in Howard's Conan stories, the fight scenes are very visceral and Changa describes some of the creatures he encounters as "beasts." However, Davis challenges the dark savagery of Howard's Conan stories by omitting descriptions of dark or othered people as savage. Davis is not interested in describing Changa as a "civilized" man in opposition to "savages," but he does make Changa a prince, which automatically gives readers the impression that he is a noble person forced into a lower social station by fate. Although Davis does not make derogatory statements about commoners or creatures and even depicts strong female characters, he does still maintain some of the social and species hierarchy found in the Conan tales that he was inspired by.

Davis and other sword and soul authors are working to infuse adventure fantasy with "soul," or realistic depictions of African and African American cultures that spark a sense of joyful communion in readers. These stories are often set in a historical or imagined ancient Africa, and they have heroic characters and magical elements, such as sorcerers and magical creatures, that are recognizable to Western fantasy fans. Today, African fantasy writers, many of whom know of or have worked with Davis, are branching out in their depictions of African fantasy. Rather than following a Conan-style adventure story with various races and magical talismans, authors like Nnedi Okorafor, Marlon James, Eugen Bacon, Oghenechovwe Donald Ekpeki, and Joshua Uchenna Omenga, among others, are writing more intimate stories that speak to the ways in which the fantastic is woven into the fabric of life in Africa and the African diaspora, a concept defined as Afrojujuism or Afropantheology.[12] One example of this shift is Bacon's short story "The Water's Memory" (2020), which is based on Bacon's memories of her mother and grandmother. Bacon explains that her goals for this story were to preserve her family and cultural knowledge while also blending African storytelling with speculative elements: "I set about writing ["The Water's Memory"] with great urgency, seeking to demystify tradition, to claim it before it could further diminish. . . . Her story became my story. I created a brand new design, neatly packaged and speculative, from the original" (Bacon and Davis 55). Bacon combines her knowledge of African folklore with speculative elements to create writing that utilizes the speculative to recover the stories she has grown up with, stories that are not typically valued by Western cultures.

"The Water's Memory" centers on the costs of colonization for a small African village. The mother in the story sees a red leopard on the night of her wedding, a foretelling of the death of her yet-to-be-born daughter. As her daughter, Adaeze, which means "princess," grows up and becomes beautiful and educated, the mother begins to believe that the curse of the red leopard has been overcome. Bacon links Christian missionary efforts to ecological disaster to show the consequences of colonization on the village: "But, like the foreignness that came to the lake, suffocating the Nile perch, tilapia, kingfisher, and *daggaa,* Christianity came to native lands. It suffocated the gods of the thorn tree and the mountain" (Bacon and Davis 50). Adaeze dies young, fulfilling the fate prophesied by the red leopard, and the mother dies watching the decline of her people and their lake. Bacon's story does not have the maps, magical artifacts, or sorcerers of *Changa's Safari*; indeed, many African authors might argue that the story is not fantasy at all and, instead, draws on African cultural knowledge of fate and omens.[13]

---

12. See my discussion of these terms in the introduction.

13. For an example of such an argument, see my discussion of Afrojujuism and Afropantheology in the introduction.

But Bacon admits to making the story "speculative," so there is an element of the fantastic in it. Like James's story, the reader knows that the daughter is doomed from the start, but the death of Adaeze, who fulfills both the role of a princess of amazing beauty and accomplishment and a strong woman who goes against cultural norms, is treated as something fated to occur. Adaeze's death is supposed to be a warning for the village, but her mother never speaks of the omen she witnesses out of fear of making it come to pass. Her decision dooms her village, which, without the warning, gives in to colonization and ecological ruin. Based on history, however, one could say that the village was doomed either way; the sheer size and power of Christian missionary efforts caused the destruction of many villages. Bacon goes against the traditional resolution of the death of evil and triumph of the hero to demonstrate, like James and Suri, that eucatastrophe does not always occur in fantasy or fantastic narratives.

While sword and soul has not received much attention from fantasy scholars, it makes an important contribution to depictions of Blackness and Africa in fantasy literature. Davis's company, MV Media, has established a strong independent outlet for publishing Black speculative authors and has since broadened its scope to include graphic novels and animation. Sword and soul is also a popular genre that has produced strong online communities where fantasy authors and readers of color can join forces and connect directly to their fan base. The publication of texts such as Bacon and Davis's *Hadithi & the State of Black Speculative Fiction* (2020), Oghenechovwe Donald Ekpeki and Joshua Uchenna Omenga's *Between Dystopias: The Road to Afropantheology* (2023), and multiple editions of *The Year's Best African Speculative Fiction* demonstrates that African-based fantasy literature and its authors are expanding definitions of African-based fantasy and becoming strong voices in the conversation about what non-Eurocentric viewpoints can add to the creation and study of the fantasy genre. Rather than trying to address these varied depictions of African fantasy all in one chapter, I will be incorporating discussions of African fantasy texts throughout this project.

Conclusion

The goal of this chapter is to shed light on how fantasy authors of color are critiquing the Christian foundation of the self-sacrificing, virtuous male hero in Western epic fantasy and sword and sorcery narratives. Western fantasy often assumes that its Christian, hierarchical elements are "natural" or endemic to the fantasy genre. But not all heroes fit Campbell's description or follow a clear path from Wrongness to Healing. Sometimes, there is no eucatastrophic moment, no restoration of "a better world," which has never been "better" for everyone anyway. The heroes of the stories in this chapter are heroic because of the bonds they forge to survive; they are heroic because, despite overwhelming racism, sexism, homophobia, and xenophobia, they still exist. When people of color facing active attempts at social and cultural erasure still manage to tell their stories and choose to broaden the scope of fantasy literature at the same time, they become the real heroes of their stories.

Further Reading

Sofia Samatar, Olondria series (2013–16)
Kai Ashante Wilson, Sorcerer of the Wildeeps series (2015–16)
Nisi Shawl, Everfair series (2016–24)
Evan Winter, The Burning series (2017–present)
P. Djèlí Clark, *The Black Gods Drums* (2018), *A Dead Djinn in Cairo* (2021)
Amélie Wen Zhao, Blood Heir Trilogy (2019–22)
Zen Cho, *The Order of the Pure Moon Reflected in Water* (2020)
Andrea Hairston, *Master of Poisons* (2020)
Jordan Ifueko, Raybearer series (2020–21)
Zelda Knight and Oghenechovwe Donald Ekpeki, *Dominion: An Anthology of Speculative Fiction from Africa and the African Diaspora* (2020)
Chelsea Abdullah, The Sandsea Trilogy (2022–present)
Joyce Chng, *Twelve Paths to Glory: A Shapeshifter Clan Novel* (2022)
Saara El-Arifi, The Ending Fire Trilogy (2022–24)
Isabel Ibañez, *Together We Burn* (2022)
Naseem Jamnia, *The Bruising of Qilwa* (2022)
Tahereh Mafi, This Woven Kingdom series (2022–present)
R. R. Virdi, *The First Binding* (2022)
Eugen Bacon, *Languages of Water* (2023)
Hadeer Elsbai, The Alamaxa Duology (2023–24)
S. L. Huang, *The Water Outlaws* (2023)
Ehigbor Okosun, The Tainted Blood Duology (2023–24)
Aparna Verma, The Ravence Trilogy (2023–present)
K. S. Villoso, The Dageian Puppetmaster series (2023–present)
R. S. A. Garcia, *The Nightward: Book One of the Waters of Lethe* (2024)

CHAPTER 2

Envy

Blood Magic Is Not Always Black Magic

One of the most common villain tropes of Western fantasy, typically modeled on fantasy works like The Lord of the Rings, is the Dark Lord trope. Clute and Grant note that the Dark Lord is often described using Christian terminology: "Dark Lords are, or aspire to be, the Prince of this world, and as such are a malignant Parody of the Gods.... The Dark Lord may not be explicitly a Devil or an Antichrist, though names like Sauron, Ba'alzamon and Lord Foul indicate that he most usually is." The Dark Lord figure is thus filtered through a Christian lens and is portrayed as a symbol of envy and unredeemable evil. In the Old Testament, darkness and light were both associated with creation and Satan was depicted as God's partner, who tempts and punishes mankind with God's permission.[1] Later depictions of Satan in the books of Matthew, Luke, and Revelations depict him as God's adversary; in these accounts, Satan tempts Jesus, enters into Judas and causes him to betray Jesus, and goes to war with Heaven.[2] Satan thus shifts from a being made to test mankind's faithfulness to the embodiment of evil, and his alternate name, Beelzebub, or "Lord of Flies," implies that Satan is the highest

---

1. One example of the relationship between God and Satan is the story of Job, where Satan is given permission to test Job's faithfulness through a series of trials (Coogan, Job 1:1).

2. See Coogan, John 13:2 and Revelation 20:1.

form of evil. The fact that Satan tempts man to sin associates his persona with sin. And the title "Prince of Darkness," which originated from Milton's *Paradise Lost* (book 10, line 383), makes a clear connection between Satan, evil, and darkness in Western culture. Finally, the Wisdom of Solomon, an apocryphal text, explains that "through the devil's envy death entered the world, / and those who belong to his company experience it" (3:24). These various depictions highlight the ways that the New Testament and Western literature portray Satan as the highest form of unredeemable evil and associate him with darkness and envy.

Over time, depictions of darkness in Christianity were connected to descriptions of Africans and other dark-skinned peoples to justify slavery and colonization. Sheldon Cheek notes that in the medieval depiction of the Last Supper by the artist Liutoldus, the figure of Judas, the betrayer of Jesus, is depicted as standing in shadow. Cheek points out that although Judas is portrayed as a shadowy figure, with slightly different features to distinguish him from the other apostles, Judas is not depicted as Black or with African features. Cheek explains this distinction in terms of the racial thinking of the artist's time: "Though rather naturalistically rendered, the artist's conception of Judas does not yet reveal the awareness of the black body or the association with evil imposed upon it in subsequent periods of Western art." Once Europeans began engaging in colonization and slavery, connecting dark-skinned peoples, especially Africans, to evil became necessary to justify the enslavement of dark-skinned peoples and the theft of Indigenous resources. David M. Goldenberg explains in *Black and Slave: The Origins and History of the Curse of Ham* (2017) that the first known connection between Black peoples and Noah's curse of Canaan comes from multiple versions of the Syriac Christian work *Cave of Treasures* (believed to have been written at some point within the third to seventh centuries). He explains:

> In these versions of the *Cave of Treasures* the biblical story is retold, Canaan is cursed with slavery, and then, in an addition to the biblical account, we are informed that Canaan's descendants were various dark-skinned peoples and "all those whose skin color is black." Here, for the first time we see the explicit association of blackness with servitude in the context of the Noah story. (78)

If dark-skinned peoples are a result of God's curse and meant to be slaves, it is a small step from this depiction to one where dark-skinned peoples are inherently evil and unredeemable. White colonizers were also able to label dark-skinned peoples as evil through the association of Indigenous cultural practices with "black magic."[3] Western, Christian portrayals of darkness and evil and their connections to racial thinking are important to understand because they influence the tropes of good and evil that are found in much of the Western fantasy genre. Fantasy literature's worldbuilding and characterizations are not immune from associations of evil with darkness, dark-colored clothing, and dark skin. In The Lord of the Rings series, Tolkien's depictions of Orcs and Sauron's other forces as dark-skinned and his decision to make these people the enemy of white men and "pure" white elves have been criticized by scholars as racist.[4] For these reasons, fantasy authors and readers who have been influenced by the dominance of Tolkien-like fantasy may have a hard time seeing dark-skinned characters as anything other than evil.

Ebony Elizabeth Thomas notes the importance of shifting views of the dark fantastic toward a more inclusive perspective, one that does not make automatic judgments about the dark or "monstrous" characters she identifies as "the Dark Other," based on appearance: "Therefore, would-be storytellers must somehow liberate the Dark Other from her imprisonment and impending doom, not only in the text itself, but also in the imaginations of his or her readers" (36). Fantasy literature and other media are permeated with light-as-good, dark-as-evil tropes, stemming from Christian divisions of good and evil; but the fantasy genre also needs stories that complicate or consider the perspective of the Dark Other.[5] While the authors discussed in this chapter are not the only ones working to revise the dark-as-evil tropes in fantasy literature, their works utilize a racial self-consciousness and multiple levels of estrangement to provide a multifaceted depiction of dark characters and "black magic."

---

3. For a good overall introduction to Western and Christian beliefs about magic, see Middleton et al. It is also important to note that dark-skinned women were particularly vulnerable to being labeled as witches. For more information on this topic, see Schiff; Delgado.

4. See Rearick; Reid et al.

5. Some of this work has already begun in contemporary fantasy literature. Authors such as Jacqueline Carey, Adrian Tchaikovsky, Ari Marmell, and others have used the Dark Lord trope as a starting point for stories that question the premise that evil characters are always unredeemable. Authors like Gregory Maguire, Victoria Schwab, and John Gardner take the perspective of evil or monstrous characters. Such stories often tell "the other side" of a well-known tale or fairy tale or depict a dark character who is drawn back into their evil ways through trauma or for the greater good; or they may use dark characters to question the idea of the moral good in fantasy.

The Significance of Blood

The "black magic" and "blood magic" discussed in this chapter are significantly different from the definitions of these terms that have previously been used in Western fantasy literature. *The Encyclopedia of Fantasy* defines black magic as "magic worked with evil intent; the term is virtually synonymous with Sorcery" (Clute and Grant). This definition alludes to the fact that sorcerers, also called black magicians, became so common in Western fantasy literature that the term was included in the subgenre title of "sword and sorcery" to differentiate the heroic sword-wielder from his evil nemesis. Finally, Clute and Grant note that the difference between the terms "sorcerer" and "witch" in Western cultures is mostly gendered:

> Although anthropologists sometimes differentiate between Witchcraft and sorcery in respect of certain African tribes, the two terms are nearly synonymous in the Western tradition; the qualification is necessary because in literature as in legend male sorcerers employing Ritual magic tend to be much more imposing figures than female witches, who are often imagined as disreputable hagwives.

While male sorcerers might be considered more powerful than female witches, both terms come with the association of using ritualized magic for evil purposes, and both labels have historically endangered the lives of people in Western cultures who were labeled as black magic practitioners. For the purposes of Western fantasy reading and roleplay, there is a clear distinction between "good" and "evil" magic and magic users.

"Blood magic" is a specific term in fantasy literature and roleplay referring to magic that is either strengthened by blood or that allows a magic user to control their or another person's blood.[6] It is considered a powerful, albeit dark, form of magic because blood itself is frequently linked to life and death in Western and non-Western cultures. Blood is often connected to both a vital life force and death because the loss of too much blood results in death. Blood is also linked to birth because the absence of menstrual blood is linked to pregnancy (Verplaetse and Brown 33–34). Rituals involving blood are included in Christian, pagan, and many African and Afro-diasporic forms of religion. Rebeca L. Hey-Colón explains in *Channeling Knowledges: Water and Afro-Diasporic Spirits in Latinx and Caribbean Worlds* that blood and

---

6. For a full description of blood magic and its uses in fantasy, see Blankmarks.

water are often considered equally important in religious practices: "Like water, blood is a life-giving and life-sustaining element that circulates all around us. Because there is no blood without water, both liquids are central to the ontological and epistemological frameworks of Afro-diasporic religions" (10). But while water is often associated with cleansing religious practices, blood rituals are often labeled as water's opposite by Western cultures: a powerful substance often obtained through violence against innocents and used for evil purposes. At specific historical moments such rituals caused early Christians and pagans to be labeled through rumors as evil and sadistic (Verplaetse and Brown 27–29). Accusations of child murder, cannibalism, ingestion of menstrual blood, and animal sacrifice demonstrate that, while powerful, rituals involving the use of blood were also feared and often inflated to justify violence against and erasure of specific groups. Although Christians were formerly accused of cannibalism for "eating" the body of Christ, they also began to utilize descriptions of blood rituals and animal sacrifice as "pagan" or "savage" because pagan religions were in direct competition with Christianity's more symbolic rituals.[7] And darker-skinned peoples, such as Africans, began to be described in the early twentieth century as bloodthirsty: "It was claimed that African soldiers cut off body parts and were cannibals. *The Daily Herald* wrote that 'pitch-black' colonial soldiers bit through the arteries of their victims and sucked up their blood" (Verplaetse and Brown 42). Over time, shifts in descriptions of blood rituals from Christian to pagan ritual and their association with dark-skinned cultures formed the rhetoric that would be used to justify colonization practices.

Western fantasy literature frequently links blood magic to "evil" characters such as Dark Lords, sorcerers, mages, witches, necromancers, and vampires. The fact that these figures are often described as wearing black clothing or as "dark" figures perpetuates the myth that darkness is intrinsically linked to evil and must therefore be eradicated, a view described by Thomas as one of the central issues of the dark fantastic:

> The very presence of the Dark Other in a text of speculative fiction, across genre and mode, creates a profound ontological dilemma. This dilemma is inescapable, for readers and for writers, and must be reconciled. It is most often by enacting symbolic and/or actual violence against the Dark Other. This is what readers and hearers of the fantastic expect, for it mirrors the

---

7. Jan Verplaetse explains in *Blood Rush: The Dark History of a Vital Fluid* that "sacrificial blood acquired something horrific, especially among those—such as the early Christians—who wanted ritual sacrifice to disappear altogether, because this pagan practice was a formidable rival to their own ritual procedures" (67).

spectacle of violence against the endarkened and the Othered in our own world. It is a familiar template, an archetype that comforts, especially when the position of the Other in the real world is uncertain. (24)

Readers have become accustomed to the "habits of whiteness"[8] embedded within Western fantasy literature; one of the most significant habits is the good-is-light/evil-is-dark binary that allows fantasy texts to symbolically enact violence against dark, evil characters. Readers want the comfort of knowing that evil is punished and good wins in fantasy literature. However, when that comfort comes with the price of reinforcing racist stereotypes about dark-skinned peoples, then authors and readers need to begin to question why the Dark Other is always intrinsically evil and what peoples Western culture is actually trying to eradicate.

I would be remiss if I didn't also note a significant link between blood and racial classification in the history of the United States: the "one-drop rule" that posited one drop of Black blood as sufficient to label a person as Black, allowing for the stripping of rights or even potential enslavement,[9] fostered a social view of Black blood as a tragic contaminant, a view that Black authors used as a trope for tragic mulatto and racial passing narratives like Nella Larsen's *Passing* (1929) and early speculative fiction such as George S. Schuyler's *Black No More: Being an Account of the Strange and Wonderful Workings of Science in the Land of the Free, A.D. 1933–1940* (1931). Authors like Larsen and Schuyler challenged the view of Black blood as a contaminant by highlighting the ridiculousness of the US racial classification system and by making their Black protagonists regret their decision to pass for financial and social gain. The one-drop rule is significant because it highlights the ways that cultures link blood to family lineage; the idea that there could be a hidden "drop" of Black blood in one's ancestry became both a cause of anxiety for white people and a way for Black authors to challenge the racism that produced such an extreme societal rule. This history of Black blood as both lineage and contaminant becomes one tool that fantasy authors of color can utilize to reimagine depictions of hierarchical lineage and nonred blood in Western fantasy literature.

In addition to the use of blood magic by dark figures, fantasy also makes use of different types of blood or ancestral bloodlines in its worldbuilding. Like science fiction's depictions of nonred alien blood, fantasy literature frequently depicts nonhuman characters such as gods or monsters as having

---

8. See Young, *Race*.
9. For a full definition of the social and historical significance of the one-drop rule, see the definition of "(Racial/Ethnic) Classification" in Ansell.

unique-colored blood; in both cases, nonred blood is an easy way to mark certain races' or characters' difference, divinity, or monstrousness. The idea of "pure-bloodedness" or half-bloodedness has been utilized in popular Western fantasy series such as Andre Norton and Mercedes Lackey's The Halfblood Chronicles (1991–2002), Rick Riordan's Percy Jackson series (2006–23), and J. K. Rowling's Harry Potter series (1997–2007) to highlight social or class issues in various magical societies. Fantasy has also incorporated Western culture's fascination with blood and blood ritual to allow fans to vicariously indulge in the "wickedness" of blood through blood magic. Overall, nonred blood and mixed lineages are powerful markers of difference, but a difference that is often briefly discussed and that gets subsumed by the hero's need to eradicate the evil forces of their world. Many fantasy series, such as the Percy Jackson series and Mike Mignola's Hellboy series, also distinguish royalty or gods through the use of gold blood. This characterization serves to create a clear hierarchy of worthiness from nobility to commoners, or from gods to part-gods to humans. While I cannot claim that all fantasy authors of color take a different approach in their use of nonred blood, I will note that many authors of color have employed the trope of different-colored blood to avoid a top-down hierarchy and to center a self-conscious awareness of racial or gendered difference by creating main characters who are marked as monstrous because of their blood difference.

Authors of color have incorporated the idea of nonred blood by linking it to the idea of blood as an excuse for humans to subjugate specific groups. Several have also tapped into the Western fantasy trope of gold blood being linked to divinity to make the blood of darker-skinned characters divine.[10] Two series that utilize gold blood as a marker of difference for their main characters are Namina Forna's Gilded Ones series (2021–24) and N. E. Davenport's The Blood Gift Duology (2022–23). Forna and Davenport utilize the fantasy trope of gold blood, but they each avoid the typical noble/god to commoner/human hierarchy by using gold blood initially as marker of monstrosity. While the main characters of both series are eventually revealed to be linked to gods, the gods in both series are portrayed as suspect, so although this knowledge allows the characters to embrace their difference and the powers that come with it, the link to gods is not viewed as entirely

---

10. The idea of gods bleeding gold blood seems to be fairly new and is likely based on Greek myths about ichor, which was sometimes described as "a bright ethereal fluid" (Berens) or, in the case of the story of Talos and Medea, as "melted lead" (Apollonius). The Percy Jackson series employs the trope of Greek gods with golden ichor. This description makes sense considering the symbolic importance of gold in many religions; see Holland, Behr.

positive. These two series are less concerned with establishing a top-down hierarchy and more concerned with using the trope of gold blood to mark Black blood as powerful and valued.

In Forna's Gilded Ones series, the main character, Deka's, town priests preach that red blood is a sign of purity, while gold blood is a sign of impurity that marks certain women as monstrous demons. Once Deka is revealed to have gold blood, her best friend and father turn on her. After her father beheads her to release the demon inside of her and she comes back to life, Deka describes the hatred she feels toward her difference: "I look down at my veins, stomach lurching as they shimmer, the gold glittering inside them, demonic essence forever marking me impure. I want to rip them out, want to dig so deeply I empty them" (*Gilded Ones* 32). Forna specifically uses gold, typically considered valuable and used by religions to produce statues, images, sacred objects, and protective amulets, as the color that marks Deka as "impure." Although her fellow townspeople want her dead, she is also bled numerous times by greedy town leaders because her gold blood is valuable. Deka is treated as a slave and only saved because the current emperor has decided to use girls with gold blood as soldiers to fight the deathshriekers, creatures described as monsters who are threatening the empire. Forna uses the idea of nonred blood and monsters to demonstrate how easily humans can use the slightest differences as excuses to subjugate each other. Women in this series have been taught to subjugate themselves to men, and the ritual of purity and killing of gold-blooded women reinforce lessons of female impurity. But Forna also refuses to reinforce the idea of Blackness as ugly or evil; although Deka is an outcast in her Northern town because of her mixed lineage, dark skin, and curly hair, once she is brought to the South, she lives in a culture that views dark skin as beautiful. Forna is clearly interested in challenging current Western racial and gender hierarchies, and the fact that she uses organized religion as the foundation of the damaging hierarchies and binaries that cause Deka's racial and gendered self-consciousness points to the influence of Christian missionary practices on racial and gendered hierarchies.

Deka eventually discovers that she has been lied to by the priests; her gold blood is linked to divinity, not monstrousness, and she is descended from the gods of Otera. She embraces her difference and fights for the Gilded Ones, a group of four female goddesses who were trapped by men by being covered in gold blood. Deka eventually comes to realize that even the goddesses have lied to her; they believe that men are lesser and are trying to destroy their male god counterparts by denying them worship. The goddesses gift Deka with a necklace made of gold blood that turns out to be a method of control. Once Deka realizes she is being used as a pawn in the battle between the goddesses and gods, she uses a god's blood to access his memories and discovers that she is actually descended from a third species of god, one that refused to split their gender to appeal to mankind. At this point, Forna is more interested in highlighting the ways that binaries of gender and sexuality harm specific groups, but it is significant that Deka's powers all stem from her gold blood and her ability to perform blood magic. Once Deka escapes the control of the empire and its label of "demon," her friends and boyfriend are never repulsed by her difference or use of blood magic. Blood magic in *The Gilded Ones* links a Black character's gold blood to power, a challenge to Western fantasy literature's assumption that blood magic is inherently evil.

N. E. Davenport utilizes the idea of blood purity linked to race early in her duology to mark her main character, Ikenna, as the target of racism: "The Praetorian's grin spreads wider. 'Listen to your friend, Stay seated and stay in your place akulu.' He spits the slur at me. It's a word that benignly means the color black in the Khanaian tongue of Grandfather's paternal people. When Mareenians speak it, though, it oozes their disdain and prejudice against those with darker skin" (7). Davenport employs the Western fantasy trope of the Northern/white vs. Southern/Black racial binary, but she also links Ikenna's lineage to power through her gift of strong blood magic. Ikenna is part Accacian, another dark-skinned people that Mareenians hate because of their shared heritage with the Blood Emperor. The blood magic in Davenport's series works on two levels; the blood-gifted heal rapidly from wounds and, depending on ability and training, can manipulate blood to control others and create weapons. Ikenna initially keeps her gift secret because Mareenians view blood-gifts as linked to the evil gods and Blood Emperor who were the cause of a war that killed a third of the human population (81). Ikenna is also described as possessing a bloodlust that drives her to avenge her grandfather's murder. Davenport uses the trope of blood magic to present Ikenna as someone who is considered monstrous by Mareenian society and has to "pass" as a result.

Ikenna eventually learns that her blood-gift is linked to Amaka, the goddess of blood rights. She refuses to listen to her gift and grow it because of her fear. Eventually, Amaka intervenes when Ikenna is weakened by poison and explains that if Ikenna keeps refusing her gift, she will destroy herself. She explains their link: "You are my daughter. A blessed child of Amaka. One of my Chosen. I am threaded into your DNA and your blood. You will not continue to dishonor me by dampening my gift and blocking your access to me" (315). The references to DNA and blood help to stress the deep connection between Ikenna and Amaka; whether Ikenna accepts the goddess or not, Amaka is part of her heritage and genetic makeup. Ikenna later learns that her grandfather was killed because the republic needed an Accacian to test a new blood-gift dampening metal called iridium. Her best friend gives Ikenna a pendant made of iridium, but once Ikenna takes the pendant off, she is able to accept the blessing of Amaka to gain the magic she needs to save her friends and help them escape. Ikenna accepts Amaka's gift under duress, and she learns from Amaka's sister goddess Kissa that Amaka has her own agenda and cannot be trusted. Later, she sees gold running through her blood and remembers that the gods humans cast off the planet *"bled vivid gold."* Like Deka in *The Gilded Ones*, Ikenna is caught between her connection to questionable gods and her desire to help humanity survive. And although Amari's blood is red, it is tinged with gold and her blood-gift marks her body by turning her eyes red during blood moons. Ikenna and Deka are both portrayed as monstrous at first because of their gifts, and both feel shame because of their difference. However, when they eventually accept their gifts, whatever the reason, both main characters come into their power. Forna and Davenport employ blood magic and blood difference to link their Black character's lineages with powerful magic. Both characters "pass" to be accepted and are eventually outed and shunned. Yet both are also accepted by their friends and come into great power because of their difference. These characters demonstrate how blood magic can be utilized to offset the history of Black blood as a contaminant; Forna and Davenport both create blood magic systems that restore the power of Black blood and lineage.

"Black Magic"

The labeling of African-based spiritual and healing practices such as Santería, Vodun, and Juju as "black magic" by white colonizers was a specific practice designed to weaken Indigenous cultural knowledge and the practices that brought colonized peoples together in organized groups. Paravisini-Gebert and Fernández Olmos explain that "creolized religious systems, developed in secrecy, were frequently outlawed by the colonizers because they posed a challenge to official Christian practices and were believed to be associated with magic and sorcery" (3). They also note that among African slaves, ritualized practices such as Obeah allowed slave communities the "illusion of autonomy" and were often embedded in slave communities' healing, spiritual, and governing practices (156).

African-based religions often involve elements of secrecy—certain elements of knowledge and practices are only revealed to practitioners or religious leaders, such as Santos/Santeras or Obeah men/women, who have access to deities and their knowledge. The combination of public misunderstanding of African-based spiritual rituals and the criminalization of these practices by colonizing governments and Christian churches have led to these practices being labeled as "black magic" and associated with evil or devil worship, even among nonwhite peoples. Most Caribbean islands had or still have anti-Obeah laws, typically laws that banned practices like drumming or "pretend[ing] to use any occult means, or pretend[ing] to possess any supernatural power or knowledge" ("Strange"). One of the most famous contemporary examples of Western reaction to African-based religious ritual is the case of *Church of Lukumi Babalu Aye v. City of Hialeah* (1993), where the city of Hialeah, Florida, enacted ordinances designed to keep members of a newly formed Santería practice from sacrificing animals by describing such practices as animal cruelty ("Church"). The historical practice of labeling Indigenous cultural and religious practices as "black magic" is especially important when considering fantasy writing by authors of color. The authors discussed in this section deliberately include references to the colonial and internalized colonial fear of "black magic" and magic systems centered on African-based religious practices to engage in speculative and fantasy writing that links these practices with powerful, often reclaimed or recovered magical knowledge.

Magic based on African or other Indigenous practices and religions may seem like an easy transition; after all, there are often already ritual practices and objects imbued with power within these practices. But authors who choose to base their magic systems on Indigenous practices must be particularly careful to avoid reinforcing colonial and Christian beliefs in these practices as "primitive" or "black magic." Diana Paton explains that such depictions stem from the use of religion as a "race-making term":

> In the Roman Christian world *religio* (the root of the contemporary word religion) was a term that articulated truth claims, defining the boundary between "true" religion and "false" superstition and paganism. Since the European Enlightenment, this boundary-marking aspect of the term [religion] has continued in the frequent contrast made between religion and terms such as witchcraft, magic, superstition, and charlatanism, all of which have been applied to obeah. Thus, the concept "religion" has acted as a race-making category: a marker of the line between supposedly "civilized" peoples (who practice religion) and "primitive" peoples (who practice superstition or magic). (2)

Colonizers used references to slave belief in "magic"[11] to portray slaves as ignorant peoples and justify slavery. This labeling has been damaging to African-based and other Indigenous religious practices; many Black and brown postcolonial and diasporic communities still view African-based religious practices as evil or demonic. Adrienne Keene notes that the Indigenous communities of the United States have also been affected by depictions of Indigenous cultural practices as magical. In a blog post responding to J. K. Rowling's inclusion of the Native figures of medicine men/women and skinwalkers in her History of Magic in North America series, Keene explains why describing Native traditions as "magic" is problematic:

> The problem, Jo . . . is that we as Indigenous peoples are constantly situated as fantasy creatures. Think about Peter Pan, where Neverland has mermaids, pirates . . . and Indians. Or on Halloween, children dress up as monsters, zombies, princesses, disney [sic] characters . . . and Indians. Beyond the positioning as "not real," there is also a pervasive and problematic narrative wherein Native peoples are always "mystical" and "magical" and "spiritual"—able to talk to animals, conjure spirits, perform magic, heal with "medicine" and destroy with "curses." Think about Grandmother Willow in Pocahontas, or Tonto talking to his bird and horse in The Lone Ranger, or the wolfpack in Twilight . . . or any other number of examples.
>
> But we're not magical creatures, we're contemporary peoples who are still here, and still practice our spiritual traditions, traditions that are not akin to a completely imaginary wizarding world. . . . In a fact I quote often on this blog, it wasn't until 1978 that we as Native peoples were even legally allowed to practice our religious beliefs or possess sacred objects like eagle feathers. Up until that point, there was a coordinated effort through assimilation policies, missionary systems, and cultural genocide to stamp out these traditions, and with them, our existence as Indigenous peoples. We've fought and worked incredibly hard to maintain these practices and pass them on. (first and fifth ellipsis added)

This tension both within and outside of African diasporic and Indigenous groups means that an author who decides to write fantasy literature featuring African-based or Indigenous religious or cultural practices must take great care in how they employ the term "magic"; such awareness is currently leading to Oghenechovwe Donald Ekpeki's pantheology movement,

---

11. I use quotation marks here because while some African-based religions use the term "magic" in their practices, not all do. And the labeling of African-based religious practices as "witchcraft" or "black magic" was not based on an understanding of these religions or belief systems. For more information, see Murrell.

which he defines as "a way of thinking about stories, that aims to solve the existing problem of categorization, in genre fiction and beyond, and that the term fantasy is plagued with" ("OD Ekpeki"). What Keene's comments and Ekpeki's movement demonstrate is that there are fantasy authors and fans who are no longer willing to resign themselves to the stereotyped depictions of Indigenous peoples found in many popular Western fantasy works and, as a result, are pushing back against these labels and stereotypes. Many of the authors discussed in this chapter are writing in a cultural moment where non-Western fantasy, aided by the internet and fan funding, is beginning to redefine what constitutes "Indigenous magic."

Conjurers, Witches, and Brujas

Irene Lara notes that while all women of the Americas were suspect to accusations of witchcraft based on gender, "women of colonized groups were suspect on multiple grounds. Indian women, African-origin women, and racially mixed women—whether Indo-mestiza or Afro-mestiza—were suspect by virtue of being female, by virtue of deriving from non-Christian, or 'diabolic' religions and cultures, and by virtue of being colonized or enslaved people who might rebel and use their alleged magical power at any moment" (10). Much of the negative association of La Bruja, or witch, particularly regarding the use of "black magic," stems from the rejection of Indigenous or African identity in Black and Latinx/Chicanx cultures, a direct result of European colonization. Some ways that fantasy authors of color are combating Western views of brujas and other conjurers as evil are either by reworking the known Eurocentric witch figure or by writing characters who don't conform to Western stereotypes about "black magic" into their speculative works. As Maria Rodriguez-Morales notes, "When people, regardless of gender, decide to call themselves Bruja it is to embrace the other, the dark-side, the historically rejected and oppressed figure and simultaneously they call on their natural gifts to conjure a better reality." Since fantasy/fantastic genres already include the idea of "conjuring," these genres could be helpful in aiding authors of color who wish to depict the "better reality" that Rodriguez-Morales describes.

Authors of color who write fantasy or fantastic narratives are in a unique position to reclaim terms like "black magic" or "witch/bruja" through depictions of Indigenous-based magics and tensions between members of formerly colonized nations who have differing views about Indigenous practices. A good example of an author putting a twist on the Eurocentric fairy-tale witch is Clarence Young, who goes by the pen name of Zig Zag Claybourne. Claybourne's "The Air in My House Tastes like Sugar" turns the story of Hansel and Gretel being lured by an evil, child-eating witch into a story about acceptance of cultural difference. The story centers on a witch mother and her daughter Amnandi, from the country Afrela, who have recently moved into a shack near a small town named Eurola. Claybourne addresses Eurocentric witch stereotypes early on in his story: "The two witches traveled a lot because people believed extremely dubious things. Not a single child had ever died in a witch's home. Those stories of ovens and eatings, pure idiocy. Ovens and transporting, yes; a witch used many things as portals." Amnandi and her mother Khumalo have been driven from other towns because of the townspeople's fear of witches and superstitious beliefs. However, this time, there is another person originally from Afrela who has intermarried with a Eurolan woman twelve years earlier. This man, Jobam Imnahl, apologizes for his children's fear and works to keep the townspeople from burning Khumalo and Amnandi's home. In return, Khumalo helps him remember the culture he comes from and its belief that "magick" is not an evil thing. She also uses her abilities to mend Jobam's crops with her knowledge of plants. Eventually, Khumalo and Amnandi help the townspeople eradicate a changeling spirit who is killing children. They don magical masks to channel the abilities of the hyena and the hare, symbols of cunning and speed that feature in many African folktales.[12] The tension in Claybourne's story emerges because the people of Eurola resist learning about magic and allow their fear to lead to a foolish belief in superstitions. Khumalo uses her superior knowledge of magical portals and the natural world to help the townspeople, who will likely continue to live in ignorance and fear despite her efforts. Claybourne combines a well-known Western fairy tale with African-inspired practices of acknowledgment of other planes of existence and living attuned to nature to challenge the rational vs. primitive binary historically used by white colonizers to justify violence against African peoples.

Two authors who move away from the Eurocentric witch figure and invent magical systems based entirely on non-Western belief systems are Nnedi Okorafor and Kacen Callender. Okorafor includes a Juju-based magical system in her Akata Witch series and Callender includes the use of kraft in their Islands of Blood and Storm series. Okorafor frequently comments on the fact that she blends African belief with her imagination to challenge stereotypes about Africans both within and outside of African communities.

---

12. For examples, see Gaudet; Mandela.

The title of her series, Akata Witch, refers to two terms used as insults in African cultures: "akata," or a Black person not born in Africa, and "witch," a term Okorafor notes is often used as an insult against women who question African patriarchal systems (Okolo et al.). Okorafor has explicitly stated that she does not consider the Akata Witch series to be "fantasy" in the Western tradition because many of the fantastic elements that Westerners might associate with magic are actually part of African cultural beliefs.[13] Callender uses the US Virgin Islands as their inspiration and labels their magic system "kraft" after the Danish word for power (Cohen-Perez). However, the term "craft," or witchcraft in Western cultures, also refers to the practice of witches using magic for evil intent, which is significant to Callender's main character, a Black woman who uses her kraft to manipulate and kill. Callender has explained in interviews that they wanted to address issues of colonialism in this series, and that they were specifically interested in the ways that the colonial system might cause Black peoples to participate in the slavery and oppression of other Black peoples (Cohen-Perez). Because views of witchcraft and black magic in postcolonial spaces are tied to histories of slavery and internalized colonization, both series utilize magical systems to comment on the layers of racial and gendered estrangement their main characters experience. Okorafor and Callender each employ terms linked to witches and witchcraft and depict powerful main characters who are between cultures to comment on external and internalized racism/sexism in African and Caribbean cultures.

The first book of the Akata Witch series, *Akata Witch* (2011), follows the adventures of a twelve-year-old girl named Sunny, who lives in Nigeria but deals with racism and sexism because she is an outspoken, foreign-born girl with albinism. Sunny discovers that she is a "free agent Leopard Person," a person with a connection to the Leopard People, a secret society of magic-users, but who does not know about her connection because her parents are not Leopard People. When Sunny's friends, Orlu and Chichi, take her to a strong magic-user to be initiated, he explains the society to Sunny:

> In any case, you're what we call a free agent Leopard Person. You're in a Leopard spirit line . . . somehow. It's not a blood thing. Leopard ability doesn't travel in the physical. Though blood is familiar with spirit.

---

13. One reason for Okorafor's view may be her publisher's decision to label the Akata Witch series as "the Nigerian Harry Potter," which potentially downplays the influence of Nigerian cultural practices and leaves space for readers to paint Nigerians as "magical" people. For an example of Okorafor's views on her writing and African culture, see Okolo et al.

> . . . Most Leopard People are like your friends here, born to two sorcerer parents—strong ancestor connections. They are the most powerful. Those born to one parent can't do much of anything unless they have an especially expensive juju knife or something like that or if they come from an especially adept mother. It travels strongest from woman to child, since she's the one with the strongest spiritual bond with the developing fetus. (*Akata Witch* 52–53)

Okorafor chooses the name Leopard People because many Nigerians believe in the idea of shapeshifting people, in particular ones who can change into leopards. David Pratten notes that in the 1920s and 1940s, rumors of a secret leopard society of magical shapeshifters engaging in murders that looked like leopard attacks fueled white colonial officials to investigate, charge, and kill African men accused of being "leopard men." These incidents reinforced colonial stereotypes about Africans because "Africa represented a blank space in Europe's collective imagination and could therefore be populated by all manner of invented creatures, sometimes noble, sometimes monstrous, that were the visual and visceral products of European fears and desires" (9). Pratten notes that many of the leopard-men series of killings coincided with colonial restructuring of lineage-based Nigerian governing systems (22–23). Colonizers ignored Nigerian local governments and traditional knowledge in favor of enforced, reconfigured government structures and Christianity. Secret leopard societies may also have been one way that local Nigerians engaged in resistance against colonial interference. As a Nigerian American, Okorafor would likely know this history, and the name of her secret magical society honors both the history of Nigerian resistance to colonization and Nigerian beliefs in the supernatural. It is also significant that Okorafor makes matriarchal lineage the key to a Leopard Person's magical power, a move that nods to the history of African matriarchal cultures and female rulers that has been overlooked in many histories of the continent.[14]

Okorafor takes on powerful themes about racism and colonization in the worldbuilding of her series. Sunny's Leopard Person friend, Chichi, explains that there are Leopard People all over the world, but that some might be called by different names such as "witches, sorcerers, shamans, wizards." Leopard people can be any race and gender as long as they have the necessary "spiritual genetics" (*Akata Witch* 78, 96). However, she differentiates between Leopard People and "Lambs," a term used for nonmagical

---

14. For more information on the history of African female rulers, see Steady.

capitalists that has a clear connection to Christianity: "Leopard People—all our kind all over the world—are not like Lambs. Lambs think money and material things are the most important thing in the world.... Money and material things make you the king or queen of the Lamb world. You can do no wrong, you can do anything" (82). Chichi implies that all Leopard People are free of materialism, instead preferring to earn spiritual money, or *chittim*, through learning, but her friend Orlu corrects her and explains to Sunny that there are Leopard People who do care about amassing spiritual and material wealth. The distinction between Leopard People and Lambs nods toward a culture where knowledge is valued more than material goods, and where the hidden community of Leopard Knocks, only accessible to either people with two Leopard People parents or those who have been initiated, and which is built on "an island conjured by the ancestors," can exist without fear of another "great massacre" like the one that occurred after the death of Jesus Christ (*Akata Witch* 65, 6). Okorafor creates a magical world where all people with spiritual inclinations toward magic are equals, regardless of race or gender, but she also uses references to Lambs, an animal that is often linked to depictions of Jesus, to create a world where some non–magic users are viewed as ignorant followers, and African juju is considered a valuable knowledge system, reversing the stereotype of African cultural practices as "primitive." The Akata Witch series utilizes elements of worldbuilding and hidden magical communities to comment on the resilience of African peoples and beliefs in the face of Western stereotypes.

The first book of the Islands of Blood and Storm series, *Queen of the Conquered* (2019), is narrated by Sigourney Rose, a Black woman with kraft whose entire family was killed by the white Fjern colonizers who conquered her island nation. Sigourney grows up vowing to avenge her family by using her kraft ability to control and manipulate others with the goal of succeeding the current king and taking over the Fjern nation. To achieve her purpose, she serves the current king and refuses to grant her slaves their freedom, a promise made by her mother. Sigourney hates herself for participating in slavery and supporting the king, and she explains this hatred in Western fantasy terms after a young slave whom she sleeps with asks her why she doesn't run away to a different country where she can be happy: "He truly believes he loves me, but this love isn't real. It's imagined, a story he tells himself, and while he sees me as the princess in the fairy tales we heard as children, I'm nothing more than the wicked queen" (Callender 28). Sigourney sees herself as a villain, but Callender includes flashbacks of her family's murder and Sigourney's internal dialogue to ensure that readers sympathize with her position.

Sigourney uses her kraft to kill islanders and manipulate people for power, which makes her akin to a Dark Lord figure, but Callender complicates her situation to explore the ways that Black peoples were often forced to participate in systems of colonization and slavery to survive. Callender uses graphic descriptions of Sigourney's kraft to demonstrate her power. She can enter the minds of others, which is a powerful magic, but also one that forces her to experience her victims' pain as they die. During a slave rebellion on the island she rules, she is forced to enter one of the rebels to stop the fighting: "I enter another rebel, overtaken for a moment by his hopelessness as I see myself through his eyes, the traitorous island woman in my dress of white, my eyes fluttering as my kraft works through my veins, and he turns on his friends, cutting his fellow rebels down" (9). The fact that Sigourney is forced to see through her victims' eyes as part of her kraft links her great power to empathy as she experiences their fear, hatred, and eventual death. Callender does not give many details about how people obtain kraft in her worldbuilding, but Sigourney explains that the law of Fjern states that only nobility is allowed to have kraft and live. After the rebellion, she is forced to order the death of a young slave girl with kraft. This fact coupled with the description of kraft "working through her veins" implies that lineage may play a role in which people receive the ability. The Fjern consider kraft to be a "divine gift," but Sigourney's slave, Marieke, describes it as "evil's trickery" (35). Callender offers a complex depiction of magic that both embraces and defies the view of witchcraft as linked to evil.

Callender also describes the role of religion in the colonization of the native island peoples of their fantasy world. Sigourney's depiction of this forced colonization explains the differing systems and the islanders' ability to adapt to the new religious system: "The gods were brought to these islands by the Fjern many eras ago; gods to be worshipped instead of the spirits of our ancestors, as our people had done since the islands themselves rose from the waters. Islanders are no longer allowed to pray to the spirits. If we do, we are hung, so we learned the ways of the Fjern gods" (10). Callender's decision to call the island deities "spirits of our ancestors" and their depiction of the islanders' response to the Fjern gods is similar to depictions of Indigenous peoples of the Caribbean and Africa adapting to forced Christianity, which resulted in syncretic religious practices like Santería and Ifa. Author Nisi Shawl describes the adaptability of the West African system of Ifa in her essay "Ifa: Reverence, Science, and Social Technology":

> I'm not going to try to thoroughly define Ifa, but I'll tell you some things about it. It's animistic—that is, the Ifa universe lives and grows and

changes, and is full of subjects rather than objects. It's old. But also, it's new, because it's syncretistic—that is, it adapts itself to cultures it comes into contact with, adopting elements of them for its own purposes, thus co-opting Christianity, European paganism, and other philosophies. (222)

The religious system of the islands and its ancestor spirits, which Shawl might describe as "subjects" rather than gods, could be defined as a syncretistic system based on the islanders' decision to "learn" about Fjern gods for survival. Whether by choice or through forced colonization, syncretistic systems like Santería and Ifa are practices open to change and adaptation, a fact that puts these religions in opposition to the hierarchical systems of Christianity. Callender uses the topic of religion to demonstrate the ways that colonizers harmed native populations, but this depiction also demonstrates the islanders' intelligence and resilience; the fact that they can adapt by integrating their colonizing culture's religious practices and deities challenges the notion that Indigenous colonization was necessary to "civilize" native peoples.

Fantasy authors can also utilize tensions between rival magical users or clans to address issues of internalized colonization, tensions between generations, or tensions between a native group and its diaspora. Two fantasy works that employ this approach are Fonda Lee's *Jade City* (2017) and Ciannon Smart's *Witches Steeped in Gold* (2021). Both authors utilize tensions between magical factions to highlight conflict within communities of color, and the main characters in each novel face a conflict between their personal desires and a duty to avenge family members or communities. Lee and Smart create magical worlds that bring issues of internalized colonization to the forefront.

Jade City, the first book of the Green Bone Saga (2017–21), is set on the island of Kekon and depicts a conflict between rival gangs known as "Green Bones": families that train in martial arts and the six disciplines (Strength, Steel, Perception, Lightness, Deflection, and Channeling) to be able to control the power of a magic jade that is only found on the island. A conflict arises between the No Peak clan, traditionalists who believe that the jade should not leave Kekon, and the Mountain clan, who want to sell the ability to wield jade to foreigners now that foreign scientists have created a serum that allows non-Kekonese peoples to wear jade. After the Many Nations War, foreigners called the Espenians set up military bases on Kekon and devised the serum called SN1 or "shine." The major conflict of *Jade City* thus centers on a common problem for occupied but "independent" nations:

how to preserve a precious resource without angering foreign forces who are looking for an opportunity to come and forcibly take it.[15]

Within the larger conflict between clans and nations, Lee embeds a family conflict that addresses the tensions between family duty and the desire for younger generations to forge their own paths. One of the main characters is a young woman named Shae who is a former member of the No Peak clan. Shae has renounced her clan affiliation and no longer wears jade, but she returns home to the island of Kekon after getting a degree at a foreign university because her grandfather is dying. Shae has a vexed relationship with her Kekonese heritage. Foreigners believe that the Kekonese are a savage, uneducated people. Shae has internalized this belief and begins to distance herself from her family. She also doubts the main Kekonese religion, Deitism, a polytheistic religion that teaches that jade is a gift from the gods that should always be used for good so that humans can make peace with the gods and "return to the spiritually and physically divine state" (151). Despite her doubts, Shae explains that she still believes in the power of jade:

> She wasn't sure if she believed in the ancestor gods, or in the Banishment and Return, or even in the idea that jade came from Heaven. But every Green Bone knew that invisible energy could be felt, tapped, and harnessed. The world worked at a deeper level, and maybe if she concentrated hard enough, even without jade, she could communicate with it. (259)

Shae represents the younger, often diasporic, generations of occupied or colonized nations. She has internalized a foreign perception of her people and their polytheistic religion. But because of her family link to jade, she also understands that there are forces that cannot be explained by foreign science and rationality. Lee combines elements of Western and Chinese religious or philosophical belief systems to create the Kekonese religion of Deitism. The word Deitism is likely a combination of "Deism," or "a form of rational theology that emerged among 'freethinking' Europeans in the 17th and 18th centuries" and "Daoism/Taoism," which is "the oldest indigenous philosophic–spiritual tradition of China and one of the most ancient of the world's spiritual structures" (Staloff; Littlejohn 16). One of the "highest numinal powers" of Daoism is a figure called the Jade Emperor (Yuhuang Shangdi) (Littlejohn 16). However, Lee also includes an element

---

15. For more information on colonization, the exploitation of natural resources, and the ongoing effects of such exploitation, see Reid-Henry.

of "Banishment and Return" that is not a part of the Deist theology and was not a part of Daoist teachings until the addition of the idea of "universal salvation" between the twelfth and fourteenth centuries, which fostered "contradictory yet compatible religious elements" such as the contradiction between the idea of individual salvation and the more family-oriented, lineage-based Daoist teachings (Liu). The reference to a fall of mankind and a desire to reconcile with God can thus be considered an influence of Christian principles, principles that Lee questions with the addition of Deism, which is based on the idea of religion being "subject to the authority of human reason rather than divine revelation" (Staloff). However, the presence of multiple deities and Shae's understandings of "invisible energy" and "deeper workings" stem from Daoist views about Dao, or "the energizing process that permeates and animates all of reality to move in its ongoing process" (Littlejohn 16). Lee's choice to combine Western and Indigenous Chinese religious and philosophical principles in her worldbuilding helps her to show the historical effects of Western belief systems on Chinese culture and the ways that internalized colonial views can exist even in a country that was never formally colonized.[16]

Ciannon Smart's *Witches Steeped in Gold*, the first book of the series that shares the same name, is centered on a conflict between the Alumbrar, a group of witches, and the Obeah, a different group of witches/maji who were forcibly conquered during an uprising called the Viper's Massacre (12). The Obeah are treated as savage peoples and are imprisoned until age eighteen, after which they are forced to receive their ancestral magic and complete twenty years of compulsory service to the crown (11). Smart depicts a fear of the Obeah peoples in her novel to reflect the fear that white colonizers and some colonized peoples had and have toward Obeah. Tracey E. Hucks explains that "throughout the British Atlantic, the colonial imagination perceived Obeah as an illusory threat encompassing African sorcery, witchcraft, revolt, divination, poisoning, fetishism, superstition, and supernatural weaponry" (52). Hucks notes that the term "Obeah" lost its association with West African healers and the social context of Obeah practitioners as leaders of their communities and, instead, became a term linked to witchcraft and imbued with fear. White colonizers practiced "punitive legalized torture and juridically authorized amputations of the extremities of accused Africans" that "reflected deliberate colonial obliteration of competing social power and demonstrated colonists' performance of policing perceived

---

16. For more information on the effects of British colonization and trade on China, see Columbia University's page "China and Europe: 1780–1937."

religious deviation and heterodoxy" (53). Smart utilizes this colonial history of fear and suppression of Obeah to portray conflict between differing magical factions and to speak to the ways that oppression can lead to internal conflicts within communities of color.

The religion of Smart's world centers on "Anasi, the great spider god and brother to our matriarchal pantheon of gods and goddesses, all housed in our Supreme Being, the Seven-Faced Mudda" (18–19). Smart's description employs the well-known trickster-god figure Anasi, who is present in multiple Indigenous cultures. Trickster figures are often known as boundary crossers: "The trickster crosses both physical and social boundaries—the trickster is often a traveller, and he often breaks societal rules. Tricksters cross lines, breaking or blurring connections and distinctions between 'right and wrong, sacred and profane, clean and dirty, male and female, young and old, living and dead'" ("Tricksters"; Hyde 7). By combining a trickster figure with a multifaceted female god, Smart creates a religion that pays homage to the ways that Indigenous teachings account for transgressive figures and polytheistic viewpoints. The fact that the religion is also a matriarchy speaks to an African history of matriarchal societies that were often disrupted by European colonization.[17]

The fantasy genre also allows authors to explore differing views toward Indigenous practices that often exist in diasporic communities. In Alex Temblador's "Curanderas on the Ceiling" (2021), Daniel José Older's *Ballad and Dagger* (2022), and Zoraida Córdova's Brooklyn Brujas series (2016–19), the young protagonists are each caught between wanting to fit into mainstream US culture and accepting the Indigenous practices of their families, which they eventually discover are linked to powerful magics. Each of the protagonists attempts to ignore the gifts of their heritage, and they each suffer some difficulty or loss as a result. Temblador, Córdova, and Older each utilize speculative or fantasy elements to address the tension stemming from mainstream US culture's belief that science is more "rational" than Indigenous healing or belief. The protagonists each discover that their Indigenous heritage accounts for fantastic happenings that cannot be explained by Western science, a narrative device that allows these novels to address the consequences of colonization on Latinx and Chicanx populations.

"Curanderas on the Ceiling" captures the tension between generational thinking about brujeria in a Mexican/Chicanx family through the internal monologue of the main character. The narrator, a college-aged Chicana undergoing treatment for HPV, has a mother who insists on bringing a

---

17. For a detailed account of precolonial matriarchies in Africa, see Farrar.

curandera, or Indigenous healer, to the procedure. Her mother believes in the curandera's, Doña Maria's, ability to heal her daughter. But her father calls Doña Maria a "bruja" and wants his daughter to only trust "white American doctors" (201). Temblador uses the narrator's internal musings about her parents' differences in opinion to draw attention to the ways that internalized colonization produces differing views in Chicanx/Latinx families regarding Indigenous knowledges. The narrator is unsure of her own opinions about Doña Maria; this uncertainty combined with the fact that she is medicated allows Temblador to fashion a story where readers can never be sure if Doña Maria is actually a bruja, allowing readers to consider their own views about curanderas and brujas.

The story reaches a climax when Doña Maria curses the English-speaking Chicana doctor for cauterizing the narrator's surgical wound:

> *I curse you and all these doctors. Hurting women with your medicines, your burning instruments. You will burn in hell with the devil. White man's whore! Manditos!* And then she spat on the ground. Twice. To seal the curse.
>
> I hear Mamá gasp as Doña Maria claps twice and disappears. (207; emphasis in original)

In this scene, Temblador reverses the assumption that Western medicine is superior to Indigenous knowledge. Doña Maria tells the narrator that she could have healed her without all the pain she is currently going through in the operating room and compares the doctor to a "devil" because of her decision to burn the narrator's flesh. By comparing Western doctors and their medicines to "bruja mala," or black magic, Temblador draws attention to the fact that Indigenous healing and healers were labeled in similar ways, often with deadly consequences. The influence of colonization is shown through the phrase "White man's whore"—a reference to colonial figures like Malinche, the Nahuatl female slave who served as translator for Cortez and whose name is often used in Mexican and Chicanx communities to indicate a traitor.[18] By describing a Western-trained doctor, who also happens to be Chicana, as a Malinche, Temblador is asking readers to think about the consequences such labels have had on views of Indigenous peoples and practices in Mexican/Chicanx cultures. Whether Doña Maria actually disappears, or whether this is a medically induced vision on the narrator's part, is irrelevant; the figure of la bruja and the idea of bruja mala

---

18. For more information on the legacy of Malinche, see Cutter.

serve as metaphorical reminders of the costs of colonization and Indigenous culture's ability to account for "irrational" happenings.

Older's *Ballad and Dagger* centers practices of Santería in a fictional diasporic Latinx community in New York City. The main character, a young boy named Mateo, wants to become a musician and tour with his hero Gerval, a member of his community who went viral and is currently a star musician. Mateo lives with his aunt, a Santera, and her ghost wife; he discusses his tenuous relationship to Santería at the beginning of the novel:

> I'm still not totally used to all this spirit stuff she's got going on. Mom and Dad are doctors, science people. They love data, facts, things that can be proven. . . . But Tía Lucia's santos (or orishas, they're also called)—I don't really go in for all that stuff. And I know what you're thinking: Mateo, you literally live with a dead woman. But the dead are one thing, and santos are a whole other. They're like supercharged spirits, got all kinds of powers and complicated backstories and intertwined connections and stuff. It's beyond me. (22)

Mateo describes the difference between his parents' household, which is Western science–based, and his aunt's household, where Santería and the Santos are embraced; Older's description is a metaphor for differing views toward Indigenous practices and beliefs in many diasporic Caribbean and Latinx communities. Mateo accepts the presence of a ghost in the house, a fantastic element that is normalized in his culture. But his insistence that Santos are too "complicated" and "intertwined" highlights the difficulties younger Latinx people have combining mainstream US culture's belief in the superiority of "rational" thinking and Latinx cultural heritage, which is often composed of complex histories, beliefs, and cultural practices that make room for other planes of existence and fantastic happenings. Mateo wants to ignore his heritage and focus on his goal of being a musician, but like many Latinx people, he is unable to distance himself completely from his community. Eventually, he learns that he was initiated to a spirit of the island of San Madrigal as a child, and that he is fated to fulfill a prophecy that will raise the sunken island and allow his diasporic community to return home. Mateo must come to terms with the spirits of San Madrigal and claim the gift of his heritage to come into his healing powers. Older uses Indigenous ideals of balance and healing to portray a fictional island with its own mythology and magic based on the Indigenous practices of the Caribbean.

In her Brooklyn Brujas series, Zoraida Córdova ties brujeria to family tradition and lineage. In the first book of the series, *Labyrinth Lost*, the narrator, a young bruja named Alex, rejects her magic and through this rejection, her family and Latina/bruja heritage. Alex's choice causes her family to be pulled into another plane of existence, where Alex is forced to accept her magical gifts to save her family and heal the rift caused by her spell of rejection. Alex describes her burgeoning magic as something she fears and feels compelled to hide: "I can feel the secrets pushing against my veins, and in turn, I push right back—hiding them deep inside, where I hope one day even I won't be able to find them" (16). Córdova equates Alex's knowledge of her emerging magic with a "secret" and describes the magic as "pushing against [Alex's] veins." The first description is linked to a common trope of fantastic literature by authors of color. Secrets that eventually emerge as ghosts or spirits are common in fantastic writings such as magical realism, fantastic horror, and neo–slave narratives; novels like Toni Morrison's *Beloved* (1987), Angie Cruz's *Soledad* (2001), Rivers Solomon's *An Unkindness of Ghosts* (2017), and Tananarive Due's *The Reformatory* (2023) each include ghostly figures that serve as a metaphor for hidden family or community secrets often linked to the horrors of slavery, colonialism, and racism. Alex's hidden magic is thus connected to her family and community history, which is made even more clear by Córdova's description of the magic as existing in her veins. Blood becomes a marker of lineage and is an integral part of the bruja ceremonies (which are Santería-based and involve human blood and animal sacrifice) she rejects out of fear.

Córdova's worldbuilding of the magical realm of Los Lagos includes references to Greek mythology, classical literature, and Indigenous beliefs. The title of the first book in the series, *Labyrinth Lost*, combines the Greek myth of Theseus and the Minotaur with John Milton's *Paradise Lost* (1667), fitting because much Western fantasy writing has been influenced by Greek and European literature and mythology.[19] Córdova structures *Labyrinth Lost* as a typical portal-quest fantasy[20] and even includes recognizable fantasy

---

19. While I cannot go into the entire history of fantasy literature and media influenced by European literature and mythology, fantasy works from *Clash of the Titans* (1981) to the Percy Jackson series (2006–23) to the recent mainstream success of Madeline Miller's *Song of Achilles* (2011) and *Circe* (2018) demonstrate how many fantasy creators have long been inspired by Greek mythology. Fantasy stories such as Steven Brust's *To Rein in Hell* (1984) and Philip Pullman's His Dark Materials series (1995–2000) are also heavily influenced by Milton's *Paradise Lost*.

20. In *Rhetorics of Fantasy* (2008), Farah Mendlesohn defines the portal-quest fantasy as a work where "a character leaves her familiar surroundings and passes through a portal into an unknown place. Although portal fantasies do not have to be quest fantasies the overwhelming majority are, and the rhetorical position taken by the author/narrator is consistent" (1).

figures such as adas (fairies), avianas (harpies), giants, imps, and duendes (trolls). However, the center of Los Lagos is defined by the presence of the Tree of Souls, which "recalls the world tree, a trope that appears not only in the stories of Maya, Aztec, Itzapan, Mixtec and Olmec cultures, all of which are indigenous to Abya Yala (so-called Central and South America) but also features in Baltic, Persian, Norse, Greek and Roman mythologies as well as Abrahamic religious traditions" (Drumright). Los Lagos is also polytheistic with two main creation deities: La Mama (the sun) and El Papa (the moon). The balance fostered by the equal status of the two creation deities and the fact that the sun is a goddess diverges from European mythology and moves toward African-based belief systems like Santería, which are based on a belief in multiple gods called Orishas[21] and are practiced throughout Latin America, Central America, and the Caribbean. Indeed, Córdova herself states this fact in her author's note at the end of *Labyrinth Lost*: "Alex's ancestors come from Ecuador, Spain, Africa, Mexico, and the Caribbean. Her magic is like Latin America—a combination of the old world and new" (318). By combining European and Latin American fantasy traditions, Córdova offers a recognizable fantasy series that highlights the rich history of the fantastic within these traditions and those of their diasporas.

Alex must eventually come to terms with her magical lineage to defeat the Devourer, a Dark lord figure who is trying to drain the realm of Los Lagos of its magic. Rather than positing another good–evil binary, Córdova uses her heroine/Dark Lady characters as metaphors for the effects of colonization; Alex and her family represent the peoples of the Americas who were displaced through slavery and colonization, and the Devourer, her antithesis, represents the greed and destruction of European colonization. The Devourer explains the magic/blood/family link when Alex confronts her at the Tree of Souls: "You don't know the way of Los Lagos Alejandria Mortiz. Power comes at a great cost, yes. But what is the price of banishing it? Did you stop to think that your power is connected to your blood—the living and the dead that are tied to you?" (203). When Alex finally accepts her magical lineage, she channels it to defeat the Devourer: "My family channels their power through me all at once. I can see the lifelines twisting like sinew, like DNA, like roots in the earth. When I can breathe again, I direct the flow of magic. It floods in prisms of color that can only exist between the realms. It is pure, undiluted power, and I fire it at the Devourer" (302). Córdova combines references to science and magic in this description, which challenges the idea of Indigenous practices as a "primitive" alternative to

---

21. Córdova explains this influence in the author's note for *Labyrinth Lost*: "The Deos [gods] represent all aspects of nature, creation, and everyday life, similar to the Orishas of Santeria and the Gods of Greek mythology" (320).

science. Alex's power comes from her family, and like many stories in the history of Latinx literature, she cannot escape her family and community because her existence and power in the world stems from her family/cultural connection. However, Córdova makes sure to also address issues within the Latinx community by making her world (both the "real" world of the story and Los Lagos) more accepting of strong women and nonbinary relations. Alex feels attracted to her male guide, Nova, and to her female friend Rishi during her journey. She is also the most powerful bruja in her community, even though brujos are also present. For Córdova and Temblador, embracing la bruja and brujeria becomes a way to both embrace the rich Indigenous history of Latinx/Chicanx cultures and challenge views of la bruja that often use fear of social transgression to silence Latinas/Chicanas.[22]

A New Legacy

This chapter speaks to the ways that fantasy authors of color are reimagining Western fantasy tropes of black magic and blood magic by combining these tropes with Indigenous knowledges to challenge the hierarchical and binary thinking of Western fantasy that makes darkness akin to evil. While there are Western fantasy authors challenging the Dark Lord trope, the choices made by the authors in this chapter to include multiple levels of estrangement and Indigenous knowledges add layers of meaning to the idea of dark magic users and the significance of blood ritual. The worldbuilding choices made by each author in this chapter create spaces that move away from a light–dark binary and, instead, depict complex internalized cultural beliefs that highlight the effects of colonization on postcolonial groups and their diasporas.

Further Reading

Aliette de Bodard, Obsidian and Blood series (2016–17)
Silvia Moreno-Garcia, *Gods of Jade and Shadow* (2019)
Meg Xuemei X, Half-Blood Academy series (2019–20)

---

22. Córdova references this cultural view in the author's note for *Labyrinth Lost*: "The word [bruja] has both negative and empowering connotations. . . . Since all these countries [in Latin America] have a large Catholic population, it's easy to place a bruja, or witch, in a negative light. I've seen Latin women all over the Internet take back the word 'bruja' with pride, from the Latina skate crew in the Bronx (The Brujas) to the contemporary young women who practice nondenominational brujeria" (318).

Chloe Gong, These Violent Delights Duet (2020–21)

Alaya Dawn Johnson, *Trouble the Saints* (2020)

C. L. Clark, Magic of the Lost series (2021–23)

Zoraida Córdova, *The Inheritance of Orquídea Divina* (2021)

J. Elle, Wings of Ebony series (2021–22)

Alex Hernandez, Matthew David Goodwin, and Sarah Rafael García, *Speculative Fiction for Dreamers: A Latinx Anthology* (2021)

T. L. Huchu, Edinburgh Nights series (2021–present)

Liselle Sambury, Blood Like Magic series (2021–22)

Cadwell Turnbull, The Convergence Saga (2021–23)

Isabel Yap, *Never Have I Ever: Stories* (2021)

E. G. Condé, "Somnambulist" (2022)

Lauren T. Davila, *Where Monsters Lurk & Magic Hides: A Latine Anthology* (2022)

Deborah Falaye, *Blood Scion* (2022)

Veronica G. Henry, Mambo Reina series (2022–23)

Simon Jimenez, *The Spear Cuts Through Water* (2022)

Shingai Njeri Kagunda, Yvette Lisa Ndlovu, "H. D." Hunter, and LP Kindred, *Voodoonauts Presents: (Re)Living Mythology* (2022)

Vanessa Len, Only a Monster series (2022–23)

Leslye Penelope, *The Monsters We Defy* (2022)

Kylie Lee Baker, The Scarlet Alchemist series (2023–24)

A. J. Locke, *The Vanish Witch* (2023)

Premee Mohamed, *No One Will Come Back for Us* (2023)

Eden Royce, *Who Lost, I Found* (2023)

Wole Talabi, *Shigidi and the Brass Head of Obalufon* (2023)

Bethany Baptiste, *The Poisons We Drink* (2024)

Yangsze Choo, *The Fox Wife* (2024)

Yvette Lisa Ndlovu, *Drinking from Graveyard Wells* (2024)

CHAPTER 3

Patriarchy

Reimagining Gender Roles in Fantasy

The Encyclopedia of Fantasy notes in the entry for "feminism" that "providing Genre-Fantasy women with adequate roles as protagonists, mages or rulers has not been—given the medieval fixity of Fantasyland as a venue—a task very plausibly accomplished." Given the fact that the "medieval fixity" described is in large part the result of the Oxford school of fantasy, particularly the members of the all-male writing group the Inklings, it is worth noting the influence of Christianity's patriarchal views on the fantasy genre. Taylor Driggers notes in *Queering Faith in Fantasy Literature: Fantastic Incarnations and the Deconstruction of Theology* (2022) that religion, Christianity specifically, is embedded into the genre of Western fantasy literature, leading to the exclusion of certain groups:

> Yet if fantasy's religious speech is often spoken in Christian registers, what remains to be examined is how it may do so for those of us who are marginalized by, or within, Chrisitan traditions and institutions because of our genders, modes of presentation, or sexual desires. How might the creation of fantastical alternate realities ... speak good news to those excluded and abused by the preachers of the Gospel in this world? (15)

Driggers's question addresses a major issue for Western fantasy literature: Christianity's focus on the heteronormative male as the pinnacle of its gendered hierarchy, a focus that was brought to many cultures through colonization and missionary efforts, has negatively affected Western fantasy literature's depictions of gender and sexuality. While there are ongoing efforts in fantasy literature to make room for stronger female characters and protagonists, the genre's tendency to privilege white, heteronormative narratives and its portrayal of gendered violence as necessary for historical accuracy continues to influence depictions of gender and sexuality in fantasy works. Fantasy has the potential to create worlds that reorient toward more complex visions of gender and sexuality, but Christianity's historical exclusion of specific racial and gender groups means that fantasy authors have much work to do if they want to avoid perpetuating the hierarchical views of gender and negative portrayals of sexuality reinforced by Christian theology.

I cannot discuss the effects of Christianity on gender without also discussing the racialized narratives used by colonizers to depict Indigenous women of color as indecent or overly sexual, a direct contrast to the ways that Christian missionaries portrayed the Virgin Mary. Marcella Althaus-Reid uses the example of a missionary mocking "unclean" Indigenous female street vendors in Peru as an example of this history to highlight the shift away from Indigenous religious practices, which she calls "the destruction of the Grand Meta-narratives of Latin America," to a more Christian, sexually constrained version of women and sexuality:

> These women may still speak their indigenous language apart from Castilian Spanish and may also still respect the faces of La Pachamama (the Goddess Earth of the Incas) in their lives, but their epistemological and theological universe collapsed centuries ago. It lost its public credibility with the Conquista of Latin America, with Christianity and European rule. Other discourses of the sacred had come to sustain other laws and justice, and forms of love in their countries. . . . The daughters of the Inca Empire lost their narratives. They now worship the medieval dressed figurine of the Virgin Mary with its oversize crown and God-prince in its arms. Few of them may be able to decode the intricacy of the Virgin Mary's ancient European dress and mantle. . . . The Virgin Mary is overdressed, and contrary to the lemon vendors the smell of her sex (even if statues were alive) would be difficult to perceive.

The ideal of the pure, chaste Virgin Mary was brought to many colonized cultures through Christian missionary efforts and often used to portray Indigenous women as primitive, overly sexualized beings. Negative responses to practices of fluid gender acceptance and polygamy among some Indigenous groups were also used to justify colonization efforts.[1] Since Western fantasy is a genre that often uses depictions of fantasy worlds to reinforce the beliefs of the culture it was produced in, it stands to reason that it has absorbed the gendered, racialized hierarchies of Christianity; Althaus-Reid's depiction of Mary's "medieval" clothing, which fully covers the body and rewards Mary's chasteness with a "crown," and of Jesus as a "God-prince" goes to the heart of the entanglement of Christianity and Western fantasy; the "medieval fixity" of fantasy means that heterosexual male characters are often placed at the forefront of its heroic tales while female and gender-nonconforming characters are regulated to limited, marginal roles or villainized. Male characters often become godlike or royalty while female characters are rewarded for their purity through marriage to a king or prince. I will give an example of gender hierarchies in Tolkien's Lord of the Rings series and then move to discuss issues of sexuality in George R. R. Martin's A Song of Ice and Fire series to show how fantasy, past and present, still struggles to move away from Christian views of gender and sexuality. I will then discuss ways that authors of color are using fantasy narratives to make space for more complex depictions of gender and sexuality.

It is no accident that the fellowship Tolkien's Lord of the Rings series centers on and the hero of the series, Frodo, are all male. In *Women among the Inklings: Gender, C. S. Lewis, J. R. R. Tolkien, and Charles Williams,* Candice Fredrick and Sam McBride note that the all-male literary group Tolkien was a member of, the Inklings, specifically excluded women (6). They also note the influence of early twentieth-century British school systems on male social groupings; these schools excluded women and encouraged male students to bond through shared interests (7). The Lord of the Rings series is therefore an example of Tolkien's participation in and acceptance of all-male social groups. Christopher Hansen notes that Tolkien's depictions of monstrous female spiders in the Lord of the Rings series shows his gender positioning, which adheres to views of Christianity:

> Their monstrosity is because of their sexual freedom, which violates the [sic] Tolkien's natural order. Their lack of subservience to men and their

---

1. For more information on the link between the restriction of polygamy and colonial control, see Rutherdale and Pickles.

lack of strict monogamy makes them monstrous, not their outward appearance. As such, the monstrous feminine is a manifest instance of "woman" in Tolkien's work. It is the form the "evil woman" is embodied in, while the "proper woman" is defined by her acceptance of Catholic binary gender norms: subservience to the husband, monogamy, sexual restraint only for procreative activity, etc.

Tolkien's Christianity and his participation in social groups that specifically excluded women influence his depictions of women and sexuality in the Lord of the Rings series and makes women who move outside of the gendered expectations of Christianity dark, monstrous characters.

Fredrick and McBride provide multiple examples of writings by Lewis, Tolkien, and Williams that featured idealized versions of women based on women the authors knew or had relationships with, which often led to strained relations with these women. The three main female characters of the Lord of the Rings series, Galadriel, Arwen, and Éowyn, represent this gendered ideal of the pure woman; although they are powerful in ways, the female characters of Tolkien's series mainly serve to aid Frodo in his quest and are relegated to the background of the story by the end of the series. All three women are described as beautiful by Western standards, Arwen and Éowyn end the series married to royalty, and no sexual relations are described in the series. Tolkien's descriptions of his main female characters and the ways they interact with male characters make these characters flat, chaste, idealized women who follow traditional Western womanly roles of mother, helper, or good daughter. And unless you count the spider Shelob, there are no women of color in this series. The Lord of the Rings series places men at the forefront and gives a handful of white and monstrous women limited roles.[2]

Although fantasy's depictions of gender and sexuality are not always as chaste as Tolkien's writings, problematic depictions of gendered violence are still present. Sylwia Borowska-Szerszun explains that some Western fantasy authors shifted from the more chaste relations of Tolkien to a more violent representation of gender and sexuality:

> The motif of rape in fantasy fiction can probably be traced back to Stephen R. Donaldson's *Lord Foul's Bane* (1977), the first novel of *The Chronicles of Thomas Covenant* (1977–2013), . . . featuring morally ambiguous, troubled characters and rejecting the asexual atmosphere of The Lord of the Rings,

---

2. I give a more detailed description of The Lord of the Rings and race in the introduction and Envy chapters. For a detailed account of this series' racial depictions, see Mills.

Donaldson's fiction has provided a significant counterpoint to Tolkien's paradigm of fantasy and inspired later writers to follow the path. With the emergence of the so-called "gritty" or "grimdark" fantasy in the late twentieth century, sexual violence and rape have become one of the genre's most distinctive components. Usually set in quasi-medieval worlds and peopled with characters whose moral code is typically quite questionable, novels by such writers as Glen Cook, Steven Erikson, Joe Abercrombie, and George R. R. Martin are frequently considered less escapist and more "realistic" than epic fantasy fiction, due to their emphasis on the brutality of war and political machinations, as well as graphic depictions of violence and sex. Yet, the employment of the motif of rape is not limited to grimdark fantasy and also features in other areas of the genre, including the more female-oriented writings of Anne McCaffrey, Mercedes Lackey, and Robin Hobb. (1)

The fact that fantasy writing that includes scenes of sexualized violence against women and members of the LGBTQIA+ community is viewed as more "realistic" creates a problematic association where authors may feel the need to include sexual violence in the name of "historical accuracy" or "grittiness." Lenise Prater notes that fantasy literature often "depoliticize[s] the patriarchal structures featured in the fantasy world which engender sexist representations of sexual violence" (149). Fantasy authors may, consciously or unconsciously, reinforce patriarchal views of dominance and sexuality through their choices to include male savior and female victim stereotypes. And the antitrans comments made by J. K. Rowling, where she accused trans advocates of promoting the notion that "sex isn't real,"[3] demonstrate the fears of some women who identify as "feminist" that gender fluidity is an erasure of their gender identity. It seems odd that those who create fantasy, which is often viewed as the opposite of "reality," would continue to uphold conservative views of gender and sexuality. However, these views stem from Western fantasy's "medieval fixity"—the influences of Chrisitan views of gender and sexuality and Western culture's obsession with gender binaries and hierarchies.

Because of its popularity across mediums, I will use George R. R. Martin's A Song of Ice and Fire series (1996–present) as one example of the problematics of gendered violence in contemporary Western fantasy. Martin, whose series was adapted for the popular *Game of Thrones* TV series (2011–19), has defended his use of sexualized violence as necessary for a more accurate portrayal of the class systems of the Middle Ages and as a

---

3. Rowling made this comment on her *Twitter*/X account on June 6, 2020.

way to distinguish his world from the "Disneyland Middle Ages" versions of Tolkien's imitators (Poniewozik). Martin's fans have mostly accepted this rationale; in a study of the main *Game of Thrones* fan site, *Westeros.org*, Helen Young notes that fan comments mostly highlight an acceptance of sexism in Martin's books and the *Game of Thrones* TV adaptations as part of the patriarchal, medieval world the stories are set in (740). However, many of the rape scenes in Martin's A Song of Ice and Fire series are designed to either emphasize the moral depravity or further the development of the male characters, while leaving the female characters to serve as helpless, invisible victims who suffer from a lack of strong male protectors (Borowska-Szerszun 6–7).[4] The portrayal of female nudity and rape in the *Game of Thrones* TV series resulted in several online criticisms of the show's portrayal of women and LGBTQIA+ characters.[5] Young notes that "a common response to criticisms of racial representation in Martin's work is to suggest that the textual Eurocentricity is not racism, but history" (741). A similar argument can be made for representations of gender and sexuality in this series: fantasy fans are more likely to not question violence against women and queer people in medieval-set fantasy series because of the assumption that these groups were mostly subordinate in the medieval period. While medieval Europe was a patriarchal society, historians have documented numerous instances of women in the Middle Ages serving as midwives, explorers, warriors, playwrights, and many other powerful roles; they also engaged in same-sex and other forms of marriage.[6] The issue with the contention that rape narratives are historically accurate or an inevitable part of a gritty setting in Western fantasy narratives is that such statements do not leave room for a more complex depiction of gender and sexuality; the fantasy of the necessity of gendered violence in the fantasy genre is thus similar to the racial fantasy of an all-white medieval Europe.

Colonial violence against women of color and domestic violence in past and contemporary communities of color are well documented by revisionist historians and social activists, and the presence of such issues is important

---

4. I will note that some scholarly criticisms of violence in Martin's series, such as Tobi Evans's *Reimagining Masculinity and Violence in "Game of Thrones" and "A Song of Ice and Fire,"* make a counterargument that heteronormative males who use violence for their own gains end up punished in some way—typically by no longer being able to participate in patriarchal reproductive systems. I think this is an interesting argument about violence in Martin's series, but I question whether fans of the book series and TV shows would be picking up on such nuances. I also worry that the popularity of Martin's work serves to normalize the idea of gendered violence for contemporary fantasy fans.

5. For examples of this conversation, see Bruney; Gilbert; Shunyata.

6. For more information, see Morrison; Karras.

to acknowledge.[7] Fantasy authors of color are in a strong position to discuss these issues because magic can be used as a tool of intervention in racist and patriarchal systems, a way to metaphorically give marginalized peoples their power back. However, it is important to note that communities of color are not only defined by racism and violence. When racialized and gendered violence situated alongside narratives of poverty and victimhood are viewed by publishers as the only acceptable narratives for authors of color to write, these expectations can inevitably produce barriers for authors of color who choose to include narratives of radical joy.[8] Literary publishers have a history of encouraging authors of color to write "realist" narratives that portray the poverty and violence of the ghetto to create "authentic" racial narratives.[9] It would be unwise to assume that the genre of fantasy has not been influenced by mainstream-publishing views of racial minorities, especially given the history of associating peoples of color with violence and evil in mainstream fantasy works. Several of the authors discussed in this chapter choose to combine humor with multiple speculative genres to create fantasy works that serve as counternarratives to stereotypical depictions of racialized and gendered violence through portrayals of radical joy.

But there is great potential in fantasy literature to move beyond Western, Christian views of gender norms and heteronormative relationships. José Esteban Muñoz notes that pro–gay marriage activists often make arguments that address the desires of a specific, often privileged, section of the queer community; he identifies such efforts as representing a troubling "pragmatic" politics and "an erosion of the gay and lesbian political imagination":

> The aping of traditional straight relationality, especially marriage, for gays and lesbians announces itself as a pragmatic strategy when it is in fact a deeply ideological project that is hardly practical. . . . Irrationality flourishes in "established institutions"—marriage is perhaps one of the very best

---

7. For a comprehensive guide to issues of colonial violence against peoples of color, see Washington. For more information on domestic violence and communities of color, see "Domestic Violence in Communities of Color."

8. Addie Shrodes defines "radical joy" in "Humor and Oppression: The Queer Work of Radical Joy in Critical Literary Education" as "joyful resistance in the face of oppression" (22).

9. Matthew Clair gives an overview of the history of Black authors being encouraged to write about oppression as "indigenous interpreters" for white liberal audiences in "Black Intellectuals and White Audiences" (2016). Author Percival Everett's satire of the publishing industry's expectations for Black "authenticity," or Black stereotypes of ghettoization, *Erasure: A Novel* (2011), was recently adapted into the film *American Fiction* (2023).

examples of an institution that hampers rational advancement and the not-yet-imagined versions of freedom that heteronormative and homonormative culture proscribe. (64, 81)

Muñoz reminds us that marriage has always been an "irrational" tool of social control; bans on interracial and gay marriage have been used to keep specific populations under state control, all the while maintaining the idea that marriage is a rational, natural, and desirable state of being. The happy endings of Western storytelling reinforce Western cultures' belief that marriage and heteronormative relations are the natural conclusion to a fantasy tale. While Muñoz finds the answer to the identified lack of imagination in queer communities in futurity and utopia, fantasy and fantastic literatures are also qualified to move audiences away from "pragmatic" or "natural" versions of reality, often defined in terms of Western "rationality," toward a more imaginative view of gender and sexuality.[10] Authors of color writing fantasy have the potential to go further and depict fantasy worlds that utilize non-Western belief systems, which often allow room for more fluid gender depictions, to destabilize Western assumptions about race and gender. Sara Ahmed reminds us in *Queer Phenomenology: Orientations, Objects, Others* (2006) that orientation can apply to sexuality or to a body's inhabited space and effect on other bodies. Fantasy literature already includes many orienting features in its worldbuilding. As such, this genre affords authors the ability to reorient the orienting features of Western fantasy, such as landscape descriptions and maps, toward more diverse, queer spaces where the goal is less to "find our way" than to "feel at home" (Ahmed location 146). While such writing is not necessarily new (Delany's Tales of Nevèrÿon series is an example of late-1970s fantasy writing that queers ideas of gender and sexuality; I briefly discuss this series in chapter 1), fantasy by authors of color that goes against the Western, patriarchal, heteronormative structures of the genre is doing critical work in the reimagination of fantasy worlds. The authors discussed in this chapter offer alternatives to the chaste fantasy of Tolkien or the helpless victim of sexual violence present in Martin. Whether the authors are writing a new take on an old story or a contemporary, mixed-genre representation, they each find ways to make room for

---

10. I am aware that there are many great feminist utopian novels, fairy-tale retellings, and fantasy novels with female main characters. Some examples include Kelly Barnhill's *When Women Were Dragons* (1950), Anne McCaffery's Dragonsong series (1976–78), T. Kingfisher's *A Wizard's Guide to Defensive Baking* (2020), and Tori Bovalino's *Not Good for Maidens* (2022), among others. There are fantasy novels and series with strong female representation. However, I am arguing that strong, well-developed female characters and nonheteronormative characters are still not the dominant representation in fantasy.

complex depictions of identity. They also address issues of consent, an idea often linked to sexual violence in Western cultures that holds a deeper, more significant meaning in many Indigenous cultures.[11]

Revising Legends

One interesting way that fantasy authors of color are redefining the tropes of the chaste female helper or the evil woman who creates obstacles for the hero is by rewriting epic tales that include these tropes. Shelley Parker-Chan's Radiant Emperor series (2021–23) and Vaishnavi Patel's *Kaikeyi: A Novel* (2022) each employ legends—the Chinese legend of Hua Mulan and the South/Southeast Asian epic *Ramayana*—about women who step out of traditional gender roles, women who are then either vilified or honored, to create powerful narratives that upset traditional gender hierarchies. Both works include main characters who discover magical powers based on tenets of interconnectivity in Confucianism and Hinduism, which moves these works away from Christian gendered expectations. The main characters of Parker-Chan and Patel's works are strong individuals seeking power and simultaneously members of a larger web of connection that includes other planes of existence. While they would not necessarily be considered "virtuous" or "heroic" by Western, patriarchal standards, their ability to utilize vital forces, forge connections, and relate to marginalized others makes them powerful heroic figures in their own right. Parker-Chan and Patel each look to the values of non-Christian religions to combat the limited gender roles of epic tales and Western fantasy literature.

She Who Became the Sun, the first novel of the Radiant Emperor series, is promoted as an epic fantasy story based on the Chinese legend of Hua Mulan. And yet, anyone familiar with the epic tale (or even those who have seen the Disney film version) will quickly realize that Parker-Chan's story takes a sharp turn away from the traditional legend early in the series. Lan Dong explains that while the minor story details may differ between retellings, the overall message of the legend of Hua Mulan centers the transgression and restoration of gender hierarchy:

---

11. I would like to credit Indigenous scholar Kyle Powys Whyte in the online talk "Bridging the Divides: Yomaira Figueroa-Vásquez & Kyle Powys Whyte on Apocalypse and Indigenizing Futures" for giving me the idea of consent being fundamental to Indigenous cultures and a necessary element to avoiding future apocalypse.

Certain elements of the story are consistent in its many retellings: a young woman takes the place of her elderly father in war, serves her country valiantly in disguise as a man, and returns home with triumph and honor to resume her womanly life. Mulan's tale, despite its journey across time, geography, and cultures, continues to be about a young woman's successful transgression. (1)

Dong notes that the legend of Mulan is one of many early Chinese accounts of female transgressors; other examples include tales of female knights-errant, mercenaries, and martial artists. What each of these examples has in common, Dong argues, is that the oral and written accounts are designed to overlook the gender transgression of the woman by aligning these women's motivations with the patriarchal values of Confucianism:

> In examining historical records of women's involvement in warfare, I find that the potential conflict between the heroines' violation of gender roles and their conformity to Confucian doctrines is often neutralized. Their transgression usually is rooted in central values of Confucian ethics, such as filial piety and loyalty, and occurs in exigent circumstances. (30)

The gender transgressions committed by Mulan and other female warriors—generally, cross-dressing, moving outside of the domestic sphere, and assuming positions of power—are downplayed or overlooked as a necessity in times of conflict or upheaval. Because these female transgressors were viewed as loyal subjects who only stepped out of their gendered roles due to filial piety, any power that these women accumulated by transgressing becomes voided and depicted as in service to the patriarchy. The oral and written accounts of female transgressors served to maintain gender roles and made for entertaining stories; women warriors like Mulan could exist as thrilling tales but did not ultimately challenge or change the patriarchal order.

Although there are some depictions of Mulan that shift the story to make her a feminist icon, such as the version found in Maxine Hong Kingston's *Woman Warrior* (1976), most of the retellings maintain the ideals of familial duty and loyalty to the ruling powers that are found in the original. What makes Parker-Chan's retelling interesting is that it begins as a retelling but quickly reorients toward a space of queer empowerment. *She Who Became the Sun* utilizes depictions of gender nonconformity to present a new version of the Mulan tale; the main character, known only as "girl" at the beginning of the novel, takes on her brother's identity for survival and to escape her fate of nothingness. Chan takes a story linked to the moral restoration of order and patriarchy—a story that would fit well with the moral universe of many Western epic fantasy stories—and shifts away from feminine ideas of filial obedience and the restoration of patriarchy. Rather than returning to her expected feminine role, the main character of the Radiant Emperor series decides to create a new world—one that she will rule.

Vaishnavi Patel also chooses to revise an epic tale to redefine a female character who has been labeled as an envious villain by her patriarchal culture. *Kaikeyi* is loosely based on the epic story *Ramayana*, a text considered to be foundational to the Hindu religion. Patel explains in her author's note at the beginning of the novel that the idea for this novel came from an argument between her mother and grandmother over the actions of Queen Kaikeyi toward her stepson Rama:

> My mother stepped in to add that Kaikeyi had actually *helped* Rama. Without Kaikeyi, my mother pointed out, Rama would never have achieved his destiny by slaying the demon king Ravana, his main adversary in the *Ramayana*. My grandmother disagreed, arguing that it was cruel to exile your child, no matter the circumstance. (location 87; emphasis in original)

The fact that Patel's text stems from an argument between two female family members about moral duty within a foundational Hindu text shows the strong influence of family, culture, and religion on Patel's writing. In a post on the *Goodreads* page for *Kaikeyi*, Patel writes a short explanation of her religious views:

> I am a Hindu. It's the religion that I love. I do not believe it to be above criticism. . . . My Hinduism is one that can be critiqued, put through the wringer and come out stronger for it. I wrote this book for the Hindus who question their place in this religion because of patriarchy or fundamentalism, and for myself, because I love my religion and want to see it become better. ("Kaikeyi")

Patel considers herself to be Hindu but does not condone specific practices within her religion that serve to reinforce patriarchy. Vaishnavi Pallapothu notes in "The Role of Patriarchy in Hinduism" that while several ancient Hindu scriptures and words seem to allow for a more fluid depiction of gender and sexuality, these descriptions have been subsumed by patriarchal laws and cultural practices that result in harm to women and members of the LGBTQIA+ community.[12]

One reason that the *Ramayana* is an ideal text for Patel to revise is because the main character, Prince Rama, is often described as an incarnation of Vishnu, the preserver god (one of the three aspects of Brahman, the supreme god, and considered by some Hindus to be the greatest god) and is also considered to be an ideal man ("Hinduism" and "Vishnu"). While early Hindu scriptures might describe gods as gender-fluid and make references to third-gender individuals (Dokras 3; Rhude), Rama is clearly depicted as a typical heterosexual male hero; he is a virtuous man who is exiled through the plotting of his stepmother Kaikeyi. He marries Sita, a princess considered to be the epitome of female purity—she even walks through fire to prove her chastity after being kidnapped (*Rámáyan* 9, 1750–55). The *Ramayana* is a foundational epic tale that reinforces patriarchal views, particularly depictions of evil vs. good women. By looking back to "premodern" belief systems, Patel and Parker-Chan present more fluid and complex depictions of both gender roles and heroic figures.

Patel and Parker-Chan take different approaches to the idea of the virtuous hero in their epic works. Patel reverses the gender roles of her main male and female characters to make Kaikeyi more virtuous than Rama, even though Rama is a reincarnated god. Kaikeyi is given two boons by her husband, the Raja, after she saves his life in battle, and she decides to use her boons to save her kingdom by using the first to banish Rama, who is hellbent on cleansing the world and restoring patriarchal norms, and the second to put her birth son, Bharata, on the throne. Kaikeyi does so not to consolidate her power, but to save the kingdom from war. She is labeled as a traitor by god and man at the end of the novel, yet her self-sacrifice to save her kingdom makes her "the best of us" according to her son, Lakshmana, whom Kaikeyi saved from Rama and his influence. Kaikeyi gives up her reputation as a "good" woman and fills the role of envious villain to save her people. Patel reverses the gendered roles found in many epic narratives; the virtuous male god/man becomes the villain, while the "evil" woman Kaikeyi becomes an unsung hero.

Parker-Chan makes their protagonist, Zhu, a much less virtuous character by Christian standards. Zhu discovers at key moments in the novel that

---

12. The most extreme cultural practice that caused harm to women was Sati, where women were encouraged to kill themselves after their husband's death, a practice that, though not the norm, was enough of an issue that the Indian government passed new legislation in 1987 to ban it.

the feminine experiences of her youth give her skills that her male compatriots lack and allow her to empathize with other women and the eunuch general Ouyang; this empathy gives her the ability to rally groups of overlooked or oppressed peoples and use all the resources at her disposal to achieve her desires. Zhu would not be considered a hero by Christian standards; she kills a child to eliminate a rival for the throne despite the fact that the child poses no immediate threat. When confronted about the killing, Zhu tells her lover, Ma, that she is willing to sacrifice many more people to achieve her ends (*She* 407–8). The idea of sacrificing others, especially an innocent child, is not considered virtuous or heroic; however, Zhu's ability to empathize and connect with oppressed peoples and her desire to establish a society accepting of difference means that by the standards of interconnectivity, she is taking on ethical responsibility for her community. These traits are the main reason that the people closest to Zhu are willing to give their lives to help her realize her vision for a new world, despite her morally questionable actions. Patel and Parker-Chan each revise the idea of the lone virtuous male hero to portray characters who engage in questionable acts, but who also form connections with overlooked others and work to make their societies better.

Parker-Chan purposely goes against traditional depictions of gender and sexuality in the Radiant Emperor series to push back against the tropes of the chaste woman and female victim. They play with the many meanings of desire in their novel through depictions of the relationship that blossoms between Zhu and Ma, the widow of a general who is the embodiment of toxic masculinity. Ma marries her husband out of loyalty and believes she cannot escape her limited female role. But when Zhu shows Ma her naked body, Ma's reaction is one of hope; she sees "the rigid pattern of her future falling away, until all that was left was the blankness of pure possibility" (*She* 254). Challenging the depictions of chastity and virtue found in many women warrior tales, Parker-Chan reveals Zhu's asexuality while also describing scenes of Zhu pleasuring Ma to challenge the assumption that asexual individuals don't engage in consensual sexual activity. Zhu is often described in the novel as ugly or unattractive; she does not have the beauty or femininity of a typical female transgressor. However, she wins Ma over and pleases her through the force of her desire and her refusal to accept the limited gender roles of her society. It is interesting that contemporary fantasy authors like Parker-Chan, Patel, and Nghi Vo choose to make their female-bodied fantasy characters asexual. One reason for this connection may be the authors' decision to focus on bonds of connection over sexual tension. Being asexual does not mean that the main characters cannot have sex or desire bonds with others ("Understanding"). In fact, the main characters of these novels form many bonds that strengthen their ability to wield their magic and solidify their positions. In the works of Parker-Chan, Patel, and Vo, connectivity is valued over hierarchy and the maintenance of patriarchy.

Parker-Chan also takes on the Western trope of the female fantasy victim in the second novel of her series, *He Who Drowned the World*. When Baoxing, the overlooked son of the Prince of Henan, becomes the next Great Khan, Zhu asks Ma to sleep with him to get close enough to kill him despite knowing that Ma will not want to do so. Baoxing knows that Ma is not sexually interested in him, but, in a moment of anger, he decides to force her to have sex and tells her that she will hate him afterward. Ma refuses to be labeled as a victim, stating, "You can't ruin me" and choosing to see "new paths, new choices" outside of the gendered view of a woman who has lost her "purity" as ruined (435–36). By giving agency to Ma and Zhu to formulate their own gendered views, Parker-Chan reorients the trope of the helpless victim of sexualized violence found in many Western fantasy portrayals to one where the victim is given agency to see "new choices." Ouyang's betrayal of Zhu when he discovers that she is female also speaks to the internalized sexism that keeps him from being able to live to see Zhu's new world. Zhu is more than an underdog character; she is not simply hindered by a lack of knowledge or a poor background. In her society, a woman is nothing and should not be able to live let alone change her fate. The choice to place readers in the position of characters viewed as impure and disgusting, along with Zhu's willingness to kill to achieve her ends, has the potential to create a new level of gendered self-awareness for the reader as they participate in the dismantling of Zhu's patriarchal, heteronormative society. Parker-Chan reorients her reader toward a world where people who are marginalized because of their gender orientation or sexuality band together to force a patriarchal society to make space for them.

Parker-Chan and Patel highlight how the rewriting of epic tales can make room for authors of color to challenge patriarchal and heteronormative expectations. By reworking gender tropes found in patriarchal epic tales and Western fantasy texts, these authors depict complex characters who challenge readers to rethink assumptions that female and queer victims cannot have agency. Parker-Chan and Patel's protagonists own their asexuality and represent strong characters who are not afraid to claim their desires and achieve their goals. This embracing of desire provides an alternative to Christian moral codes and creates space to reimagine gender roles in the fantasy genre.

Magic as a Return of Power

While the Western fantasy genre has a history of upholding Christian and colonial views of racial and gender hierarchies, authors of color are finding ways to utilize fantastic happenings and magic to reverse Western, patriarchal hierarchies of power. The fantastic interventions that occur in Karlo Yeager Rodriguez's "Up in the Hills, She Dreams of Her Daughter Deep in the Ground" (2023) and Ezzy G. Languzzi's "Soledad" (2021) address connections between colonization and gendered violence in Latinx and Chicanx communities. Another avenue of resistance to gendered, colonial norms is through depictions of liminal characters like shape-shifters; relationships between humans and shapeshifters featured in Celu Amberstone's "Guardians of the Bright Isles" (2022) and Suzan Palumbo's "The Pull of the Herd" (2023) reimagine the civilized–primitive binary through depictions of strong female characters who reclaim magical inheritances. Magic in these stories becomes a way to right historical injustices and to give power back to women who have suffered from the colonial, patriarchal rule of "civilized" societies.

Among the often-unacknowledged violence against colonized women of color are the practices of medical experimentation inflicted on Black, Chicanx/Latinx, and Indigenous women. In *Medical Apartheid: The Dark History of Medical Experimentation on Black Americans from Colonial Times to the Present* (2006), Harriet A. Washington documents the many ways that enslaved and colonized peoples in the Americas were subject to medical experimentation and eugenic efforts. She explains that justifications for medical experimentation on Black peoples were often linked to moral judgments of inferiority and fear of Black peoples spreading diseases to white colonizers:

> We have seen that scientific racists successfully promoted several necessary medical fictions that made blacks attractive as experimental subjects. Most physicians of the day also believed that blacks had low intellectual capacities and were sexually promiscuous, that diseases manifested differently in blacks, and that blacks could not be trusted to take medicines, follow treatment, or maintain basic standards of hygiene without white supervision. (58)

This combination of fear of Black contamination[13] and an infantilization of Black peoples as children in need of medical supervision led to centuries

---

13. See my discussion in chapter 2 of the "one-drop rule," which portrayed Black blood as a contaminant.

of overlooked forced medical procedures. In 2018 a statue of James Marion Sims, long considered the "father of gynecology," was removed from Central Park after protests brought to public attention the fact that Sims experimented on Black enslaved women and children without anesthesia (Washington 61–68; Domonoske). The twentieth-century US eugenics movement led to the sterilization of Black, Chicanx/Latinx, and Indigenous women in the United States and the US territory of Puerto Rico. Paola Alonso explains that "Puerto Rico had some of the highest sterilization rates of women in the twentieth century. The island has had a long history of reproductive regulation, which tied to ideas of female 'decency.'" Beliefs in the inferiority of peoples of color, and specifically moral judgments about female hygiene, decency, and sexual deviance created opportunities for white colonizers to sterilize one-third of Puerto Rican women by 1960 and at least twenty thousand Latinx and Chicanx people in the state of California throughout the twentieth century (Alonso; Stern 1128).

While Western cultures tend to define the idea of consent in terms of sexual violence against women, one of the reasons that the effects of colonization have been so severe for Indigenous populations is because to many of these populations, the idea of consent and kinship—between peoples, but also between humans, animals, inanimate objects, and other planes of existence—is a foundational practice. It should be stressed that each Indigenous population has its own unique teachings and practices, and that I am in no way trying to homogenize Indigenous communities into a simplistic grouping. I am, however, noting that kinship practices are a system of knowledge taught in many Indigenous communities. Enrique Salmón, a member of the Rarámuri tribe of Mexico, describes the experience of being introduced to healing plants:

> The plant knowledge I learned from my family was one aspect of a trove of culturally accumulated ecological knowledge. When my relatives introduced me to individual plants, they also introduced my kinship to the plants and to the land from where they and we emerged. They were introducing me to other relatives. Through this way of knowing, especially with regard to kinship, I realized a comfort and a sense of security that I was bound to everything around me in a reciprocal relationship. ("Grandma's 'Bawena'")

Salmón's description of the healing plants speaks of them as "relatives" and describes his learning as a recognition of mutual responsibility and a grounding in place. He later notes that "it is understood that a person who harms the natural world harms themselves" ("Grandma's 'Bawena'").

Colonization and settler-colonial practices have disrupted many Indigenous communities' ability to teach and learn kinship practices through forced assimilation and relocation. Colonial dismissal of Indigenous teachings has ultimately resulted in a missed opportunity to learn ideals of kinship and the responsibility needed for truly consensual relations.

Authors of color today are utilizing the idea of magical intervention to address the history of violence and erasure toward Indigenous communities, particularly Indigenous women. The presence of magic in these stories serves to disrupt colonial gendered hierarchies and the narrative of women of color as helpless victims in the face of community and colonial violence. Rodriguez's "Up in the Hills" directly references eugenic efforts in Puerto Rico. The story is set in San Juan and the main character, a woman named Gloria, marries a man named Pedro to avoid becoming a spinster. Gloria finds herself having a recurring dream of her belly swelling and sprouting an ají plant, a plant native to the island that forms the base of many Puerto Rican dishes. The dreams cause her insomnia, so her husband takes her to see a doctor who talks them into signing paperwork to be part of a clinical trial. The doctor assumes that Gloria and her husband cannot read or write, and Gloria feels uneasy about going in without her husband because the doctor treats him with more respect. Gloria awakens to find that "an angry red smile had been cut into her, inches below her navel" and realizes that her womb has been cut out without her consent. Pedro wants to hire a lawyer to sue, but Gloria is hesitant to speak out about the violence she has experienced:

> She knew Pedro expected her to want to do something, to act so what had happened to her didn't happen to other women, but that might mean letting others—who knew almost nothing about her—see her as a victim. It would mean she would have to think of herself as a victim. Then again, maybe Pedro didn't want to see himself that way, either. So used to believing he was in control, he thought he was owed justice, and misunderstanding there are blows so devastating there was no hope of redress. One could only try to live with the aftermath.

Gloria's comments speak to the dilemma that women who are victims of violence often face; to attempt to seek justice against their perpetrators, they must subject themselves to public scrutiny. Many women who are victims of sexual assault find themselves being painted as immoral or promiscuous, similar to the moral judgments made against women of color that allowed the state to depict them as unfit mothers deserving of eugenic control.[14] The emotional, social, and monetary costs of litigation can often be higher than remaining silent. Rodriguez's story helps readers understand that victims of state violence are often unable to seek justice due to structural racial and gender barriers.

"Up in the Hills" utilizes magic to give Gloria justice, but readers are never sure if the fantastic events of the story are actually taking place. Gloria begins to have dreams or visions of her daughter calling out from under the ají plant. She begins spending all her time by the plant singing songs to calm her daughter. The ají plant thus becomes a magical representation of kinship; the plant becomes a member of her family. When Pedro comes home drunk one night, he tries to dig up the plant, and Gloria hits him on the head with his flashlight. He drives off and dies in a car crash. Gloria does not regret Pedro's death and even finds comfort in her outcast status as a widow. But her daughter will not come back. While readers may assume that Gloria imagined the child under the ají plant, Rodriguez uses uncertainty to force readers to rethink their assumptions about reality and rationality. The end of the story finds Gloria receiving a mysterious gift of a new ají pepper and planting it in hopes that her daughter will return to her. Rodriguez's story uses magic tied to reproduction to give agency back to the victims of state and colonial violence. If the magic of the ají plant is real and gives Gloria a daughter, it would restore her reproductive ability without the help of a man and create a matriarchal line of magic-users with the potential to restore both native plants and the next generation of Puerto Ricans. The magic of the story disrupts traditional patriarchal gender hierarchies and restores lost power and resources to women and Indigenous populations.

"Soledad" utilizes a magic agave plant, passed down through a matriarchy, to address cycles of domestic abuse in Chicanx communities. In the story, Soledad suffers under the control of her lazy husband, who is putting her family's restaurant, and their legacy, in danger by taking out loans against the restaurant offered by a white American man. Soledad recalls the story her grandmother told her about a magical agave plant. In the story, a woman ran away from her abusive husband into the mountains. When Soledad asks why the husband was unkind, her grandmother states, "No se, mi amor. Perhaps his own Papi had been mean and he did not know any better" (379). The woman receives a gift of nectar from a magical agave plant.

---

14. For accounts of victim blaming in sexual assault cases and violence against women of color, see Cusmano; Crenshaw.

Readers have already been told how Soledad's mother gave her a bottle of mescal on the day of her wedding and explained that this gift, passed from mother to daughter or female relative, allows the women of their family one wish. She also explains that this magical gift should only be used by Soledad once. This information, combined with the story of the magical agave, creates a magical matriarchy of women that began with the woman of the grandmother's story, likely the grandmother herself, who utilizes the gift of the magic agave to escape an abusive situation. It is worth pointing out that the agave is a native plant of Mexico and the southern United States that has been a significant part of the Indigenous cultures and economies in these regions even in precolonial times.[15] The magical mescal is thus the product of Indigenous female knowledge and serves to disrupt the gendered violence that stems from views of machismo[16] found in many Spanish-speaking cultures and their diasporas.

Soledad is the product of generations of domestic abuse, a common issue in postcolonial cultures. She remembers hearing her parents fight because of her father's alcoholism and infidelity and seems to be stuck on a similar path with her husband, so she drinks the magical mescal and offers some to him as well. Soledad knows that the mescal is not supposed to be consumed by men, and the effect of the magic is that her husband is turned into a pig. The end of the story finds Soledad serving the American businessman some tamales and a shot of the magical mescal. At this point, Soledad has taken her power back from the two men who attempted to destroy her matriarchal inheritance. Soledad also makes references to her husband caressing her the previous night and states that one day, her own daughter would sit and watch her work in the kitchen as she did with her mother. The end of the story sees the continuation of a line of powerful women who utilize their Indigenous, matriarchal inheritance to survive gendered violence. The fact that the story is written from the point of view of someone who could be viewed as a victim of patriarchy, but who also taps into matriarchal, Indigenous ways of knowing to take back her power, highlights the ways that point of view and magical intervention can be used together to create gendered self-consciousness.

---

15. For more information on the significance of agave in Indigenous Mexican cultures, see Godoy.

16. Nuñez et al. define machismo as "a set of values, attitudes, and beliefs about masculinity, or what it is to be a man" that "encompasses positive and negative aspects of masculinity, including bravery, honor, dominance, aggression, sexism, sexual prowess, and reserved emotions, among others." They go on to explain that "endorsement of traditional male gender role beliefs has been associated with detrimental emotional health outcomes, such as higher depression, anxiety, and anger" (204).

Shapeshifters and Gender Fluidity

Shapeshifters feature prominently in Indigenous folklore and literature; from the skin-shedding or body-ripping *soucouyant* to the animal-human hybrid *lagahoo*,[17] Caribbean oral stories are full of characters who straddle the boundaries between human and monster. What is interesting about these depictions is that they often represent "a relational mode of thinking foregrounding the diversity, fluidity, and dynamic state of the archipelago, disrupting binarism, dichotomies, and the static form" (Su and Grydehøj 689). Caribbean folklore is representative of its cultural beliefs. While some of these beliefs foster problematic depictions of women, the fact that shapeshifters are integrated into Caribbean culture demonstrates an acceptance of multiplicity and the Other not typically found in Western cultural thinking. For fantasy authors of color, the shapeshifter serves as both a connection to oral storytelling cultures and a liminal figure that can represent multicultural or gender-fluid experiences. Celu Amberstone and Suzan Palumbo utilize the shapeshifter in their works to add additional layers of estrangement by making their shapeshifter characters representative of Indigenous cultural acceptance of the Other, including othered sexualities, and issues of consent.

While all Indigenous cultures do not hold the same beliefs, it is important to note that there are many Indigenous cultures that have a more fluid representation of gender than the hard male–female binary found in much of Western culture. Many North American Indigenous groups such as the Cherokee and Diné (Navajo) did not have hard boundaries between genders before European colonization:

> The idea that an individual might blend multiple gender identities into their conception of self is an alien concept in virtually every Westen culture. But when Europeans began invading the Americas during the late fifteenth century, most Native communities did not connect gender to anatomical concepts of "sex" in the way we do today. Instead, Indigenous people blended occupational roles, physical characteristics and clothing, speech pattern and jewelry, and spiritual and ceremonial participation into dynamic and ever-changing identities. (Smithers 23)

By returning to oral folktale traditions and utilizing characters such as shapeshifters, authors of color can reclaim a more fluid depiction of gender

---

17. For examples of such stories, see Elswit.

and sexuality to subvert Western, colonial binaries. This work is critically important because the legacy of colonialism has produced harmful depictions of the LGBTQIA+ community, particularly in the Caribbean, where antigay laws and homophobia have led to unsafe environments for queer peoples.[18] While contemporary Indigenous activist groups are reclaiming the idea of the "two-spirit" person, fantasy authors of color can serve to remind readers that gender fluidity is a concept that was already present in many precolonial cultures.

Amberstone's "Guardians of the Bright Isles" utilizes a shapeshifting figure to break down the civilized–primitive binary. The story centers on the relationship between Mara Burke, the newly returned heir of the Bright Isles, and Ronfear, a selkie who must convince Mara to stay in Scotland and claim her heritage and familial duty to become a coguardian of the land. Mara is influenced by her mother, Gormla, who went to a convent school and became convinced that "her own kin were soulless spawn of the devil" (49). Gormla wants Mara to marry her fiancé, Adam, and return to Boston. Throughout the story, Mara struggles with her duty to the peoples of the Bright Isles and her attraction to Ronfear. At the beginning of the story, she tells Gormla that "no evil fairies or hobgoblins are going to kidnap me" (60). But later in the story, as she begins to believe, she meets her uncle's spirit at a fairy pool in a dream and seeks guidance from an Undine, a water-spirit. The Undine reveals that Mara has an affinity for water that will allow her to summon its magic in a forthcoming time of great need. She also allows Mara to look into her mirror, where Mara learns that her mother can summon deadly monsters that she intends to use to "save" Mara's soul. When Mara is attacked by the monster, she uses water magic to call on Ronfear for help. She then realizes that the scene she witnessed in the magical mirror was real and finally accepts that Ronfear is a selkie guardian. When Mara balks at the idea of being just another of Ronfear's conquests, he offers her his sealskin, which would prevent him from turning into a seal and force him to stay on land. Mara realizes that she does not wish to bind Ronfear and chooses instead to engage in a mutual, consensual relationship with the shapeshifter.

Amberstone, an author of Cherokee and Scots–Irish ancestry, uses the common Western fantasy practice of creating characters who serve a metaphorical purpose, but instead of the more archetypal hero vs. villain of Western conceptualization, Amberstone makes the antagonists of her story, Ronfear and Gormla, metaphors for the maintenance of Indigenous connection to the land vs. views of internalized colonization. Gormla represents the

---

18. For more information, see Henao.

influence of Christianity on Indigenous cultures; she believes that the people of the Bright Isles are "heathens" and "sinners" because she has been taught this lesson at the convent she attended. Even when Gormla is using magic to call on monsters, she is doing so for the stated purposes of salvation. Gormla fears the elemental magic of the Bright Isles because of her internalized colonial, Christian beliefs. Even Mara's fiancé, Adam, represents the Christian, patriarchal ideals that Gormla is being influenced by. As a selkie, Ronfear represents Indigenous connection to place, but he is also the antithesis of Gormla: a liminal being who tells Mara when she questions the rationality of her choices: "The world is a place of wonder; don't cage its enchantments within the narrow walls of rational thought and social convention" (104). By accepting Ronfear, Mara chooses to overcome her internalized beliefs, and she and Ronfear will become the new guardian pair of the Bright Isles, ensuring its continued survival. The use of a shapeshifting character helps the reader accept the idea of a more fluid depiction of both cultural belief and sexual relations.

Palumbo's "The Pull of the Herd" follows a shapeshifting doe named Agni, who decides to put away her doeskin and live as a human in a relationship with a human woman named Diya. Agni has never been able to comfortably wear her doeskin, and she leaves her herd after the death of her mother. Like Mara, Diya accepts Agni for the being she is and chooses to enter into a consensual relationship with her. Agni returns to her herd after sensing that the other shapeshifters are in danger from a man who has come to steal a doe hide and claim the owner as his wife. The idea of a shapeshifter being bound to the one who has possession of their animal skin is similar to selkie and other shapeshifting tales, but instead of the shapeshifter consenting and offering their hide or pelt, like Ronfear, Palumbo offers a more common Western fantasy scene where a male character tries to steal the doeskin because he feels he is entitled to it, making him the embodiment of patriarchal views. After Agni and the other shapeshifters catch the skin thief and save their fellow doe, the men in town begin to create stories painting the shapeshifters as monsters that human men need to be protected from and plan a hunting party. Diya and Agni work together to get word of the hunting party to Agni's herd, but the hunters manage to kill three of the herd and drive off the rest.

Palumbo uses the figure of the shapeshifter as a connection to her Trinidadian culture and also to comment on the harms of forced gender and cultural roles. Agni comes from a herd of female-presenting shapeshifters being hunted by men, and yet these beings refuse to accept that she is not comfortable in her doeskin, a symbol of the gender and societal role she is expected to fulfill. Agni struggles between a longing for acceptance and the knowledge that she cannot force herself to wear an ill-fitting skin for the rest of her life. Her relationship with Diya is one where her identity is accepted, but Diya cannot understand her cultural needs, the "pull of the herd." Palumbo creates empathy for a figure that could be viewed as monstrous, and her story combines Caribbean folklore with gendered violence to expose the ways that women of color are often forced to choose between gender freedom and cultural acceptance in postcolonial communities. At the end of "The Pull of the Herd," Agni decides to continue her herd's ritual of welcoming the sun, a decision that shows a continuity of Indigenous practice. Although Agni has lost her connection to her herd, she does not assimilate into the human community and become "civilized." Palumbo's story highlights the cultural resilience of Caribbean peoples, who were often forced to hide their Indigenous cultural practices or integrate them into European religious ritual.[19]

Authors of color are making important contributions to the fantasy genre by utilizing Indigenous knowledges to portray magical interventions. This culturally linked magic draws attention to issues of violence and abuse against women of color and gender-nonconforming peoples without feeding into stereotypes of these groups as powerless victims of men. Magic in these stories is linked to knowledge and empowers those suffering from the effects of colonialism and the rigid gender roles of patriarchal societies.

Genre/Gender-Bending Fantasy

In "Humor and Oppression: The Queer Work of Radical Joy in Critical Literacy Education," Addie Shrodes argues that LGBTQIA+ youth are using online humor to combat the feelings of shame and anger that often dominate discussions of reactions to homophobia: "Anger and resistance are important tools in dismantling oppressive structures. Yet . . . marginalized youth may also need other feelings to nurture livability in the face of persistent experiences with hate. Young people also need humor and radical joy" (22). Shrodes is specifically speaking about the needs of young LQBTQIA+ people dealing with intersectional issues of racism and homophobia, people who are most vulnerable to oppression and violence in contemporary patriarchal, white-supremacist societies. One way that fantasy authors of

---

19. Caribbean belief systems such as Santería, Ifa, and Vodun are examples of syncretic religious practices.

color are contributing to such efforts is through a combination of humor and genre-mixing that I identify as "genre/gender-bending" fantasy. This term is a play on the phrase "gender bender," which refers to people who subvert traditional notions of gender, either by combining or blurring elements of "masculine" and "feminine" presentation or through exaggerated or humorous representations of gender.[20] It is important to note that the term "gender bender" has been used as both a negative slur and a means of resistant self-identification; my interest in this term is that it describes a use of gender-fluid representation in combination with humor and radical resistance. Three fantasy texts that would fall under the category of genre/gender-bending fantasy are Ryka Aoki's *Light from Uncommon Stars* (2021), Anna-Marie McLemore's "Reign of Diamonds" (2022), and Xiran Jay Zhao's *Iron Widow* (2021). Each of these texts employs a combination of science fiction and fantasy genres along with irreverent humor to bring radical joy to the hardships of being a gender-nonconforming individual in patriarchal, homophobic societies.

Aoki combines elements of science fiction and fantasy in *Light from Uncommon Stars* to produce a text that utilizes humor to discuss the ridiculousness that immigrants and LGBTQIA+ people face in a society that believes in strict gender representations the same way that it believes that aliens and demons are not real. Aoki, a Japanese American trans activist, has discussed her use of humor and genre-bending in her writing as connected to her desire to undermine the binary of a homophobic vs. posthomophobic representation:

> The trick for me doing this was to not sacrifice my family, my chosen family, my neighborhood in order to reach for the stars. Rather than think of a future where either, one, everybody's queer, so it doesn't really matter, or two, everything is the same and we all have to be careful because it's still a very cisgender and very patriarchal society—I wanted to cut against both of those things. The way I did that was to combine some very out-there premises—Vietnamese donut shop, aliens coming in from across the galaxy who are plum-colored—with the very real sense that sometimes when you're a trans woman of color, you're doing sex work, and it's not good or bad, it's how much you're getting paid. (qtd. in Tu)

---

20. The *Cambridge Dictionary* defines "gender bender" as "a person who dresses or behaves in a way that is not considered typical of their gender." For more information on performance and gender bending, see Egner and Maloney.

104 • CHAPTER 3

Aoki's "out-there premises" deftly combine common tropes from Western fantasy and science fiction to create a text that is just as fluid as its trans and queer main characters. These tropes also work to dismantle the "rational" vs. "primitive" binary of Eurocentric cultures. While the presence of demons doesn't always guarantee that a text is fantasy, Aoki makes the demon in her novel, Tremon Philippe, a suit-wearing Francophone/Anglophone man with Eurocentric views about what makes people "cultured" and contrasts this figure with technologically advanced alien refugees who disguise themselves as Asian immigrants (their true forms are multicolored with additional joints). The two main characters, a queer violin teacher named Satomi Shizuka and her student, a trans woman named Katrina, create magic through their music. Aoki uses humorous representations of demons and aliens to achieve one of the hallmarks of Western fantasy literature: a hidden, secret fantastic world beyond the understanding of mundane humans. But the handful of peoples who can see this fantastic world are Asian, disguised as Asian, or Latinx.

Aoki's decision to make the most magically inclined character in her novel trans allows her to depict the sexism Katrina faces without making this character a helpless victim of sexual violence. The first time that Satomi, nicknamed the Queen of Hell, hears Katrina play the violin, she recognizes the special quality of her magical gift:

> What the girl held was . . . a mere beginner's instrument—but echoes of hatred, of insanities, of melodies one sings only when one has survived emanated from her just the same.
>
> . . . Most people would have heard a tone. A trained musician might hear A440.
>
> And a very special musician would hear the violin waking up, saying good morning, once again coming to life. (36–37)

Shizuka has agreed to send a certain number of her students' souls to hell in exchange for the return of her magical gift for music. She is a mature queer figure with hell's gift of intimidation and while she is at times socially awkward, she has no issues dating the female owner of a Vietnamese donut shop named Lan and immediately accepts that Lan is an alien once this fact is revealed. Katrina, on the other hand, is sexually abused and rejected because of her trans identity. She is attacked by her father and forced to leave her abusive home; she ends up engaging in sex work to survive. Katrina internalizes feelings of shame for being trans and views herself as ugly. She is also constantly on the alert for people who might attack her or call the police on her because of her transness. Aoki depicts two queer characters who are connected by their magical, musical gifts but also highlights the differences between these two characters, who come from different social and economic backgrounds. Aoki is not interested in creating one narrative of queer experience in her novel or writing one token queer character. Her novel is a joyful explosion of queer community and multicultural experience.

The humor of Anna-Marie McLemore's "Reign of Diamonds" comes from its whimsical premise: it is a story about dueling queer space princesses with magical abilities. The two princesses have opposing magics: the narrating princess has ice magic while the opposing princess, Ignacia, can control fire. The narrator describes Ignacia as her opposite; while the narrator is dark-skinned and curvy with wavy hair, Ignacia is fair-skinned, tall, and thin with straight hair (7). Through flashbacks and a conversation between the princesses, readers learn that they fell in love years ago. They hid their relationship for a time, and then Ignacia ended the relationship because she feared their families would use it as an excuse to have the princesses duel sooner. McLemore's story could be considered a whimsical romance; however, she infuses her genre-bending work with colonial and patriarchal significance. Ignacia pleads with the narrator to not "play by their rules" and reveals that she planned for the day when they would finally be alone together with access to a spaceship and could escape the traditional, heteronormative societies that have kept them from being together. The fact that Ignacia, who is lighter-skinned, is described as fitting people's vision of a queen shows that even in space, the societies of the two warring planets have still maintained views of colorism in addition to their traditional gender roles. But the magical abilities of the two princesses keep them from being portrayed as helpless, and their decision to run away together in defiance of both planets shows them as characters with agency. McLemore's whimsical premise becomes a story of two strong queer women who defy cultural and social expectations to take back their happy ending.

Xiran Jay Zhao's *Iron Widow* might not, at first glance, appear to be a humorous fantasy work. However, Zhao has an irreverent humor that is present not only in their writing, but also in their online presence. Zhao's author photo is a picture of them posing in a cow costume, a choice they note is the result of a bet they made with friends to wear a cow costume if they ever became a published author. This choice shows that Zhao is embracing radical joy in their success, a fact that they infuse into *Iron Widow* through the representation of a main character willing to laugh as she burns down the patriarchal culture that killed her sister. The main character, Zetian, vows to avenge her sister who died serving as a concubine for a Chrysalis pilot.

Zhao's Chrysalis, a term referring to a butterfly's transforming cocoon, is a war machine similar to a Gundam, or giant robot first featured in Japanese science fiction stories, and is powered by one or two human pilots. What sets Zhao's Chrysalis apart from past Gundam depictions is that the pilots use their qì, described in the novel as "the vital essence that sustained everything in the world," to power the craft (1). While the idea of qì or utilization of qì is not at all fictional, the idea of being able to power a machine with qì energy and the added idea of "spirit metal," or "qì in pure, crystallized form" are fictional notions that become the fantasy elements of Zhao's novel (53). The culture of the novel is a future China that has retained some of the practices and structures of ancient China, including the foot-binding of women and the presence of emperors. Zetian lives in a patriarchal culture; she has been taught that only male pilots have enough qì to be able to pilot the Chrysalis machines, but she discovers that this claim is a lie when she is able to overpower her first assigned male pilot and gain control of the Chrysalis he was piloting, killing him in the process. Zetian laughs "uncontrollably" as she stabs her male pilot in their shared spirit realm and "hysterically" as cameras record her carrying out her male pilot's dead body, which she discovers makes her an "Iron Widow" (81, 86). Zhao is using laughter to play with the idea of hysteria being used as an excuse for control and violence against women in many patriarchal cultures.[21] Combining the terms "Iron" and "Widow" is a move that makes widowhood, typically depicted as a socially negative status in patriarchal cultures, into a source of power.

Zhao offers an alternative relationship structure to the love triangles found in many popular YA fantasy series, including Suzanne Collins's Hunger Games series (book series 2008–20, film series 2012–23), J. K. Rowling's Harry Potter series (book series 1997–2007, play 2016, film series 2001–11), and Stephenie Meyer's Twilight series (book series 2005–15, film series 2008–12). Zhao puts their twist on this common YA fantasy trope by creating a throuple relationship in *Iron Widow*. Rather than two males fighting over a female character, who eventually chooses one of them to be in a relationship with, Zhao portrays a relationship between Yizhi, the "pretty" young man whom Zetian leaves behind to avenge her sister, and Li Shimin, a pilot nicknamed "Iron Demon" who is haunted by the memory of killing his family, an event which occurs after he discovers his brothers raping a woman. For a brief time, all three characters engage in a polyamorous relationship until Li Shimin sacrifices himself when the other Chrysalis pilots are ordered to kill him and Zetian. Zhao creates a brief moment of radical joy for their

---

21. For more information on the treatment of hysteria in women, see Scull.

characters in a world that views gender nonconformity and bisexuality as evil, a view similar to Christian views of sexuality. Zetian and Li Shimin are both forced to kill because of their refusal to accept the gender norms of their culture, and yet they are both still able to participate in a loving relationship and find happiness. Zhao's irreverent humor creates moments of hope in an otherwise bleak landscape.

Radical Resistance

Some authors of color have reversed the idea of radical joy and, instead, utilize horror and gothic elements in their fantasy works to disrupt the notion of women of color as helpless victims of gendered violence in an act of radical resistance. Silvia Moreno-Garcia's *Mexican Gothic* (2020) and Isabel Yap's "Good Girls" (2021) combine elements of gendered violence with vampire-like figures to disrupt the idea of gendered violence as natural. Moreno-Garcia portrays white vampiric figures connected to themes of colonization, while Yap chooses the Filipino figure of the Manananggal to address the ways that women of color are punished for refusing to conform to patriarchal, heteronormative cultural expectations.

In *Mexican Gothic*, Moreno-Garcia reverses the sense of uncanniness found in nineteenth-century Eurocentric travel narratives such as Joseph Conrad's *Heart of Darkness* (1899), which depicts a white traveler descending into the heart of "darkest Africa."[22] *Mexican Gothic* follows a recognizable gothic plot where a young woman comes to a manor house and experiences strange events. The main character, Noemí, is sent by her father to visit her cousin, Catalina, after her father receives a strange letter claiming that Catalina's new husband, Virgil Doyle, is poisoning her. As Noemí travels to her cousin, she describes the forest as a place she has only experienced through fairy tales:

> When Noemí was a little girl and Catalina read fairy tales to her, she used to mention "the forest," that place where Hansel and Gretel tossed their breadcrumbs or Little Red Riding Hood met a wolf. Growing up in a

---

22. Depictions of the interior of Africa as a "dark" continent were popularized by nineteenth-century expedition tales by authors like Henry Morton Stanley and W. D. Cooley. This phrase has not left the Eurocentric imagination; there is a book titled *In Darkest Africa* by erotic author JJ Argus (2011) that features a white, blond woman who is captured by Africans and eventually becomes a sexual slave. For more information, see Mitsein.

large city, it did not occur to Noemí until much later that forests were real places.... Even after she grew up, the forest remained in her mind a picture glimpsed in a storybook by a child, with charcoal outlines and bright splashes of color in the middle. (15)

Moreno-Garcia utilizes references to European fairy tales to help readers understand that they are entering a dark and untamed place where childhood innocence often encounters evil creatures or magic users. Any reader familiar with these fairy tales will recognize that Noemí is on a dangerous journey, but the fact that she is a darker-skinned adult character traveling to a house full of unfamiliar white people changes the dynamic of the reference.

Moreno-Garcia evokes a sense of strangeness in *Mexican Gothic* that is linked to depictions of uncanny whiteness. When Noemí first meets one of the Doyles, a young man named Francis, she describes him as unnaturally pale: "He was fair-haired and pale—she didn't realize that anyone could be *that* pale; goodness, did he ever wander into the sun" (16; emphasis in original). When Noemí arrives at the Doyle manor, she describes a hall of paintings full of Doyle ancestors as a sea of pale faces: "Pale, fair-haired, like Francis and his mother. One face blended into another. She would not have been able to tell them apart even if she'd looked closely" (22). Moreno-Garcia uses these descriptions of whiteness to reverse the common racial trope of the horde of dark savages found in texts like *Heart of Darkness*[23] and, instead, make the white faces all blend together in a disturbing and unnatural way. The depictions continue with the food that Noemí is served, an "unappealing creamy white sauce with mushrooms" (28). But it is the patriarch of the family, Howard Doyle, whom Noemí describes as truly frightening: "*Old* would have been an inaccurate word to describe him. He was ancient, his face gouged with wrinkles, a few sparse hairs stubbornly attached to his skull. He was very pale, like an underground creature. A slug, perhaps. His veins contrasted with his pallor, thin, spidery lines of purple and blue" (28; emphasis in original). Moreno-Garcia uses descriptions of uncanny whiteness not just to indicate which characters are the villains. She specifically uses these descriptions about the men in the Doyle family—who represent generations of patriarchy and colonization—also as a play on depictions of evil crones in European fairy tales.[24] In *Mexican Gothic*,

---

23. For examples of passages from Conrad's *Heart of Darkness* that objectify African bodies, see Snyder.

24. For examples of gender stereotypes of women in fairy tales, see Warner.

it is a young dark-skinned woman who judges the attractiveness (or lack thereof) of the decaying white men and their manor that she must endure to save her cousin.

Noemí discovers that the strange effects she and Catalina are experiencing in the Doyle manor come from a mushroom that runs under and throughout the house. The fungus was first discovered by an Indigenous group who taught Howard Doyle about its properties, and he killed them for this knowledge once he realized that the fungus could make him nearly immortal. Francis eventually reveals the secret of the fungus, and Noemí's reaction is one of horror: "Whatever this *thing's* nature was, she couldn't begin to understand it. A nightmare. That's what it was. A living nightmare, sins and malevolent secrets fastened together" (211; emphasis in original). Moreno-Garcia gives Howard Doyle dialogue throughout the novel that makes it clear he is a racist who believes in eugenics. Howard's decision to kill an Indigenous community so he could be the sole possessor of the mushroom, along with his choice to intermarry with his relatives to keep the secret of immortality in his family, have corrupted both the mushroom, a symbol of uncanny whiteness and the natural world, and the Doyle family, who believe Howard is akin to a god. Moreno-Garica utilizes the corruption of the Doyle family to critique many of the assumptions European colonizers made about Indigenous peoples, particularly those tied to their purity, religion, and primitive status. The Doyles are an incestuous, racist family that has destroyed and warped multiple populations and landscapes to achieve their ends. Noemí's disgust, coupled with a disturbing sexual scene where Virgil Doyle forces her to lie in bed with Howard so she can be infected by the fungus faster, creates a gothic nightmare centered on the horrors of colonization.

Moreno-Garcia connects Noemí and Catalina's survival to Indigenous cultural knowledge. Noemí discovers that Catalina went to see a local healer to help her overcome the effects of the Doyle manor; she is surprised by this fact because she and Catalina have been raised to dismiss and fear such knowledge:

> Noemí knew there were healers who made all sorts of remedies, gathering herbs for hangovers and herbs for fevers, and even tricks to cure the evil eye, but Catalina had never been the type to seek such cures. The first book that had gotten Noemí really interested in anthropology had been *Witchcraft, Oracles, and Magic Among the Azande,* and when she tried to discuss it with Catalina, Catalina would not hear of it. The mere word "witchcraft"

gave her a fright, and a healer of Duval's sort was two steps removed from witchcraft, not only handing out tonics but also curing the susto by placing a cross of holy palm on someone's head. (65)

Moreno-Garcia takes on the stereotypes found in many Spanish-speaking cultures about Indigenous healers to highlight the effects of internalized colonization. Catalina's negative response to the idea of "witchcraft" and her love of European fairy tales and novels such as Emily Brontë's *Wuthering Heights* demonstrates that she has absorbed ideas of European superiority. The fact that Noemí is open to learning about the Azande, a people located in Central Africa, shows that Noemí is more receptive to Indigenous knowledge, a fact that is reinforced when she learns that she is more "compatible" with the fungus than Catalina.

The end of the novel finds Noemí, Catalina, and Francis fighting to escape the Doyle manor. Again, Noemí describes their situation in terms of fairy tales:

> The fairy tales Catalina had shared with her always had good endings. The wicked were punished, order was restored. A prince climbed a tower and fetched down the princess. Even the dark details, such as the cutting of the wicked stepsisters' heels, faded into oblivion once Catalina declared that everyone lived happily ever after.
>
> Catalina could not recite those magical words—happily ever after—and Noemí had to hope the escape they had formulated was not a tall tale. (246)

Moreno-Garcia makes women the key to defeating Howard Doyle and his corruption. Noemí saves Francis from becoming a vessel for Howard, and during their escape she discovers the most horrifying Doyle family secret: Agnes Doyle, Howard's wife, was buried alive so her mind could feed the fungus. Agnes is the reason that Howard was able to achieve immortality; she is "the creation of an afterlife, furnished with the marrow and the bones and the neurons of a woman, made of stems and spores" (284). Noemí also describes Agnes in religious terms; she depicts the uncanny mushrooms as growing all over her naked body, including her head, "creating a crown, a halo, of glowing gold" (282). Agnes becomes a symbol for female archetypes in Eurocentric fairy tales and literature; she is a wronged innocent, a monster, and a virginal Madonna figure all at once. She is also a victim of patriarchal violence and the cause of the downfall of the Doyle family line. Noemí states that Agnes is "the manifestation of all the suffering that had been inflicted on this woman" and describes her only desire as: "Simply to wake up. But she couldn't. She couldn't ever wake" (289). Noemí tells Agnes "Time to open your eyes" and throws a lantern at her corpse, igniting the mushrooms (290). The damage done to the mushrooms is enough to allow her, Catalina, and Francis to escape. All three surviving characters have "woken up" by the end of the novel. Catalina, the fairy-tale lover, ends up stabbing Howard and Virgil Doyle in the face, which demonstrates her awaking from the idea that she needs a male savior. Noemí discovers the hidden secrets of the fungus and saves Agnes from centuries of additional pain. Francis confronts his complacency and defies the role his family has planned for him. All three characters overcome the systems of patriarchal, colonizing oppression that have placed them in roles of colonizer and colonized.

Isabel Yap addresses themes of monstrousness in her story "Good Girl," but rather than depicting her monstrous character as a creature who needs saving or release through death, Yap embraces the contradiction of empathizing with a monster who eats organs and unborn children. The Filipino figure of the Manananggal, like many tales of monstrous women, comes from a cultural fear of female jealousy and rage. Like the figure of La Llorona in Mexican/Chicanx cultures, the Manananggal is a woman who experiences loss—either by being left at the altar or through the loss of a child—and becomes a vampire-like monster. The Manananggal seeks revenge for her abandonment by praying on grooms-to-be and pregnant women (Chen). She serves multiple purposes for a patriarchal culture; she is a reminder of the fate of unmarried women, she is a symbol of a female who is ruled by her emotions, and her tale is often told to deter women and children from challenging their place inside a patriarchal family structure. The fact that the monster has trailing organs and eats fetuses uses the idea of female bloodlust to induce fear. The Manananggal thus embodies cultural revulsion toward women who challenge patriarchal norms.

Yap does not shy away from visceral descriptions of her Manananggal character, Kaye, in "Good Girl." The first lines of the story describe Kaye's physical transformation: "You've denied the hunger for so long that when you transform tonight, it hurts more than usual. You twist all the way round, feel your insides slosh and snap as you detach. Your wings pierce your skin as you leave your lower half completely. A sharp pain rips through your guts, compounding the hunger" (4). The graphic descriptions and use of the second person produce a story where the reader finds themselves experiencing a painful transformation into a monstrous creature. The knowledge that it causes you/Kaye pain to transform, and the explanation of a hunger that is involuntary, create the type of empathy for the Dark Other that Thomas calls for in *The Dark Fantastic*. Thomas argues that "would-be story tellers must somehow liberate the Dark Other from her imprisonment and impending doom, not only in the text itself, but also in the imaginations of his or her readers" (29). Yap's choice to use the second person achieves this goal by forcing the reader into the position of the Dark Other, a Manananggal who is forced to disguise herself as a young girl and whose survival depends on her being able to integrate with humans while also satiating her hunger for organs and unborn children.

The setting of "Good Girl" is the Bakersville Good Girl Reformation Retreat, a place where "troubled" girls are sent to reform their behaviors. Kaye tells her roommate, Sara, that she eats organs and unborn babies, but tells the other girls in her support group that she was brought to the United States from the Philippines as a mail-order bride and that her much older husband died of a drug overdose. In either story, Kaye represents the very real experiences of violence that women of color face in patriarchal cultures. And yet, Yap is good at finding humor even in the pain and violence of Kaye's monstrous existence; her use of humor as radical resistance becomes apparent in a scene where Kaye comes across a white, rich teenage girl who has just realized she is pregnant:

> She is pregnant, the private-school princess in her immaculate bedroom . . . you imagine the taste of her child in your mouth; you consider sucking it up and sparing her the agony of waking tomorrow. Wouldn't that be a mercy to this child? . . .
>
> Then she starts playing a Taylor Swift song. It's blaring from her iTunes and she is wailing on the bed, and suddenly it's so hilarious that you can't bear to end it. (11)

Yap uses the contrast between Kaye, a monster disguised as a woman of color who has likely experienced sexualized violence as a mail-order bride and who is now in a detention center for girls, with the "private school princess" in California, one of the wealthiest states in the United States, and also a reference to the many white princesses found in Western fantasy literature and fairy tales. The humorous reference to Taylor Swift, a pop princess who has amassed a fortune by writing songs about her feelings,[25] combines humor with racial criticism; the two "princesses" in this story are as far removed from the lives of women of color as a fairy-tale princess locked in

---

25. As of October 30, 2023, Taylor Swift's net worth was estimated at $1.1 billion. For more information, see Mercuri.

her tower. Yap finds radical joy and resistance in the intertwining of humor and horror, which highlights the ridiculous contrast between the privileged white teen mother and the lives of Kaye and Sara.

The end of "Good Girl" finds Kaye transforming in front of Sara and taking her for a flight. Sara has confessed to suicidal ideations after she accidentally dropped her sister's baby. Sara tells Kaye that when others asked her what her "problem" was, she couldn't explain her feelings and simply stated, "I want to fly" (10–11). The idea of flight as connected to freedom is found in many tales, from the Greek myth of Icarus flying too close to the sun to the Myth of the Flying African, where slaves could grow wings and return to Africa.[26] Yap employs a flying monster to multiple ends: Sara accepts that Kaye is a monster, and, in return, Kaye helps her by helping her realize her desire to fly. But Kaye is conscious of their difference; she knows that Sara is going to return to her family, while Kaye will be forced to find somewhere else willing to take her in. Kaye is also subject to the US penal system because she came to the United States with falsified papers; she could end up imprisoned. The differences between Kaye and Sara allow Yap to comment on the layers of violence and privilege women of different backgrounds face. While Kaye and Sara are in a similar position for a brief time, Sara's whiteness allows a return to safety while Kaye will likely once again be subjected to violence and oppression. Yap and Moreno-Garcia each combine layers of gendered estrangement with horrific characters and settings to create texts that utilize fear (and in Yap's case, humor) to engage in radical resistance.

A Less Chaste or Violent Fantasy

The legacy of the Inklings relegates women in Western fantasy to two roles: the chaste helper or the evil obstacle. Men become depraved sadists or heroic protectors while women become a plot device that serves to move the male figure forward. Gender-nonconforming peoples either don't exist or they are made monstrous. It is no accident that Ebony Elizabeth Thomas uses "she/her" pronouns to describe the figure of the Dark Other;[27] just as dark-skinned peoples are often linked to evil, gender-nonconforming characters are frequently linked in Western fantasy narratives to sexual deviance and

---

26. To read these myths, see Giesecke; Allison.
27. Thomas states, "Although the Dark Other elicits both fear and desire, her continuing presence is necessary for creating and sustaining these 'playgrounds for the imagination'" (27).

sinfulness. Fantasy needs new ways of thinking about gender and sexuality, and while authors of color are not the only contemporary fantasy authors thinking about such issues, they are uniquely posed to highlight intersectional[28] issues of race and gender in their fantasy texts. By depicting various levels of estrangement in their writing and themes of radical resistance and joy, fantasy authors of color are offering texts designed to break the Dark Other free from her/their bonds.

Further Reading

Nalo Hopkinson, *Skin Folk* (2001)

Rosalie Morales Kearns, *Virgins and Tricksters* (2012)

Carlos Hernandez, *The Assimilated Cuban's Guide to Quantum Santeria* (2016)

Carmen Maria Machado, *Her Body and Other Parties* (2017)

Sosuke Natsukawa, *The Cat Who Saved Books: A Novel* (2017)

K. S. Villoso, The Chronicles of the Wolf Queen series (2018–21)

Silvia Moreno-Garcia, *Gods of Jade and Shadow* (2019), *The Daughter of Doctor Moreau* (2022)

Kalynn Bayron, *Cinderella Is Dead* (2020), *This Poison Heart* (2021), *This Wicked Fate* (2022)

Nicole Givens Kurtz, Kingdom of Aves Mystery series (2020–21)

Darcie Little Badger, *Elatsoe* (2020), *A Snake Falls to Earth* (2021)

Roselle Lim, *Vanessa Yu's Magical Paris Tea Shop* (2020)

Aiden Thomas, *Cemetery Boys* (2020)

Kimberly Lemming, Mead Mishaps series (2021–23)

Sangu Mandanna, *The Very Secret Society of Irregular Witches* (2022)

Nghi Vo, *Siren Queen* (2022)

Chikodili Emelumadu, *Dazzling* (2023)

Brent Lambert, *A Necessary Chaos* (2023)

Eliza Chan, *Fathomfolk* (2024)

Van Hoang, *The Monstrous Misses Mai* (2024)

Justinian Huang, *The Emperor and the Endless Palace* (2024)

Esmie Jikiemi-Pearson, *The Principle of Moments* (2024)

Rosalie M. Lin, *Daughter of Calamity* (2024)

K. R. S. McEntire et al., *Once Upon a Realm: Remixed Fairy Tales by Diverse Voices* (2024)

---

28. I am using this term, originated by Kimberlé Crenshaw, to refer to "the interconnected nature of social categorizations such as race, class, and gender as they apply to a given individual or group, regarded as creating overlapping and interdependent systems of discrimination or disadvantage" ("Intersectionality").

CHAPTER 4

Salvation
Rescuing the Dark Other from the White Savior

Christian notions of salvation played a critical role in European colonizers' justifications about the need for "civilized" peoples to save the "savage" Indigenous populations of Africa and the Americas. In *The Christian Imagination: Theology and the Origins of Race,* Willie James Jennings points to the example of Prince Henry of Portugal's 1444 ritualistic welcome of 235 African slaves to the port of Lagos as an important documenting of the ways that European powers utilized narratives of salvation to justify the expansion of their colonizing efforts. Citing the official chronicle of the event by Henry's royal historian, Zurara, Jennings explains the ways that Christian doctrine became intertwined with the rhetoric of racial salvation:

> Zurara deploys a rhetorical strategy of containment, holding slave suffering inside a Christian story that will be recycled by countless theologians and intellectuals of every colonialist nation. The *telos* and the denouement of the event will be enacted as an order of salvation, an *ordo salutis*—African captivity leads to African salvation and to black bodies that show the disciplining power of the faith. (20)

Conversion of the slave also allowed white slaveowners to argue that the slave had no need for freedom or financial compensation because the

Providence of being able to have their souls saved was worth the costs of enslavement. A quote from a nineteenth-century priest argues that "these cares the Slave has not—he has no property, no business, no reputation to care for.... It is manifest therefore, that the *circumstances* of slavery, in which Providence has placed the Negro, are most *favorable* to his conversion and religious enjoyment" (Lyon qtd. in Wander 58; emphasis in original). The conversion of African slaves to Christianity was thus linked to the idea of the benevolent white owner "caring" for the Black slave, who is fortunate in their exploitation because they can become "civilized" and eventually receive salvation. The references to Providence, or God's perfect and divine plan, enable the rationalization that the Black slave was always fated to become a slave because of their need for salvation. Rhetorics of salvation, therefore, served to link Christianity with white supremacy, and dark skin with religious inferiority. They have also led to the death of the sacred, a suppression of Indigenous beliefs dismissed by colonizers as "paganism" or a marker of inferiority.[1] I would argue that this type of Christian religious rhetoric is one of the "habits of whiteness"[2] found in Western fantasy storytelling; the works of Tolkien, Lewis, and the other Inklings formed the basis of a male "white savior" figure that is still present in much Western fantasy literature. The works discussed in this chapter serve as a counterbalance to the idea that white heroes are needed to save fantasy worlds from darkness. By using non-Christian elements such as "civilized" slave characters, polytheistic religious structures, liminal characters, anticolonial viewpoints, and non-English languages, the authors in this chapter provide alternatives to the white savior vs. Dark Other Western fantasy binary.

The "Civilized" Slave

C. L. Clark's *The Unbroken* (2021) and Thea Guanzon's *Hurricane Wars* (2023) are both romantic fantasy novels that address the unequal power structures of colonization. By changing the perspective of the narration, Clark and Guanzon are able to tell stories of oppression from the perspective of

---

1. The phrase "the death of the sacred" has been used by religious and ethnic studies scholars for many different purposes, but I am using this phrase to refer specifically to a suppression of Indigenous cultural beliefs. I first heard this term from scholar Yomaira Figueroa-Vásquez in an online talk titled "Bridging the Divides: Yomaira Figueroa-Vásquez & Kyle Powys Whyte on Apocalypse and Indigenizing Futures."

2. See my discussion of this term as it is discussed in Helen Young's *Race and Popular Fantasy Literature: Habits of Whiteness* in the introduction.

the enslaved and colonized, which disrupts the white-savior tropes of Western fantasy literature. In Clark and Guanzon's worlds, the darker-skinned enslaved or colonized narrators find themselves in situations where they must form relationships with white or lighter-skinned royalty to ensure their survival and the survival of their communities. The novels employ an added layer of racial self-consciousness to highlight the narrators' struggle with feelings of attraction and hate directed at one of the privileged people responsible for their oppression. The narrators of these stories are not only not "saved," they experience trauma as they are forced to navigate relationships with both colonized and colonizer, a position similar to the female native informers who served as translators to European colonizers and were often villainized in historical narratives of colonization.[3]

Clark's *The Unbroken* tells the story of Lieutenant Touraine, a soldier of the Balladairan army who travels with her regiment to occupy the desert colony of Qazāli. Readers find out in the first few pages of the novel that Touraine and the other members of the Balladairan Colonial Brigade were desert children, labeled with the pejorative term "Sands," stolen from their homes and conscripted by the Balladairan forces. Some of the brigade members are old enough to remember their desert home, while Touraine and the other children too young to remember only know Balladaire as home. Touraine has internalized the belief that desert peoples are "uncivilized" and is surprised upon viewing the desert city of El-Wast for the first time that it is "surprisingly big. Surprisingly bright. It was surprisingly . . . civilized. A proper city, not some scattering of tents and sand" (3). Touraine has internalized colonial thinking about her homeland as primitive, but even after witnessing evidence that the city of El-Wast is "civilized," she continues to be more focused on being promoted in the Balladairan forces than on reconnecting with her lost heritage. Touraine and her fellow brigade members are ultimately being used to communicate with and spy on native populations to strengthen Balladairan colonial interests.

Touraine does not identify with the Qazāli because of her experiences as a conscripted child soldier. Betancourt et al. note that the trauma inflicted on child soldiers does not entirely come from their treatment or exposure to violence; there is an additional component of social stigma upon return, especially for women because of their already low status in patriarchal societies and because of a perceived sexual impurity for female child soldiers (17, 28). These facts are reflected in Touraine's return to El-Wast after she

---

3. I have discussed the example of the native informer Malinche in previous chapters. For more information, see Downs; Jager.

saves the Balladairan princess from an assassination attempt and is asked to help with the execution of the Qazāli rebels. Even as she readies herself to place nooses on the rebels' necks, Touraine believes what she is doing is right. She can't understand the Qazāli language but describes it as "rocks rattling in a cup" and recognizes that she has been brought to the desert as an example of a "civilized" desert person. Clark begins their narrative from the perspective of a Black queer colonized woman who has internalized Eurocentric beliefs in her people's inferiority. Touraine's internal narrative, and its eventual shift as she learns more about the history behind Qazāli colonization, creates an additional layer of racial estrangement in the novel. Touraine is in a liminal position; as a Black female soldier and informant who has suffered a loss of family and language, she receives violence, negativity, racism, and sexism from Qazāli and Balladairan peoples.

Clark also uses Touraine's reaction to gods and magic to highlight the ways that Indigenous communities are often labeled as primitive: "Uncivilized. It meant they kept a god close. Touraine had never believed in magic. It was the sort of crutch the Tailleurist books urged the Sands away from. Gods were myths, and holding them close was the sign of a weak mind. Touraine has honed her mind against them" (25). Clark presents this scene to remind readers of the history of European colonizers creating narratives of Indigenous peoples as irrational, and therefore unfit to rule themselves. By connecting gods to magic, Clark shows how Indigenous communities make way for beliefs that go beyond Eurocentric rationality, an ability that Clark links to power.

Touraine's relationship with the Balladairan princess, Luca, highlights the inequalities of slavery, even when slaves are treated well. Luca repays Touraine for saving her life by getting her out of a treason charge and taking her on as an assistant and spy. When Touraine is allowed to go to the funeral of one of her fallen comrades, she is accused by one of her fellow soldiers of being a traitor, and when she is asked by another, her friend Pruett, if she is sleeping with the princess, she says no but adds "What could I do if she did want me?" (118). At this point in the novel, Touraine has escaped death and rape threats from her white superior officer, but she is still subject to the whims of Princess Luca while also being branded a traitor by Qazāli rebels and soldiers. Touraine is being forced into the role of native informant to avoid death, but in doing so, she has become someone hated by Balladairans and Qazāli. Touraine's sudden shift to outsider status forces her to interact with the Qazāli, which eventually leads to her reconnection with her mother and her decision to fight with the rebels to force the Balladairans out of Qazāli. The end of the first novel in the series finds Touraine struggling to rebuild a broken Qazāli while grappling with her feelings for Luca. The second novel in the series, *The Faithless* (2023), finds Touraine and Luca forced to work together again to ensure Luca's ascent to the throne and Qazāli's security. Clark does not provide an easy, happy restoration of order in her fantasy series. Instead, she uses the complicated relations between a colonizing nation and its colonized peoples to demonstrate that the process of postcolonial rebuilding is not a happy ending.

Guanzon's *Hurricane Wars* introduces readers to Talasyn, a young girl recruited by the Sardovian army after the wartime destruction of her city. The army is attempting to keep the Kesath nation and its Night Emperor from colonizing the entire continent. When Talasyn is attacked by Kesath forces during a battle, she reveals her abilities as a "lightweaver," a person who manipulates aether, the force that connects dimensions, and engages in battle with the Night Emperor's son, Alaric. Alaric can also manipulate aether, but his powers come from the Shadowforge, a different dimension. Talasyn is tasked by the Sardovian army leader, the Amirante Vela, to sneak into the wealthy island nation of Nenavar and access a powerful nexus of the lightweaver dimension, a Light Sever, to boost her lightweaver abilities and help the Sardovians win the war. However, Talasyn's quest is thwarted when a traitor warns Alaric of the Sardovians' plans. Talasyn and Alaric battle at the site of the Light Sever, but they are captured by Nenavar forces before she can access the Light Sever. The two outsiders are imprisoned together and escape after Talasyn discovers that she is the lost heir to the throne of Nenavar. *The Hurricane Wars* utilizes the trope of a Dark Lord figure (the Night Emperor) and a binary of light–dark magic familiar to Western fantasy fans. However, Guanzon includes the internal dialogues of Talasyn and Alaric to complicate the idea of clear good and evil forces in her series.

Fans of Western fantasy may come into this novel expecting Talasyn and the Sardovians to fight valiantly and, after hardships, win the overall war and defeat the evil Night Emperor. However, Guanzon quickly dismantles the typical hero's-journey narrative by allowing the Night Emperor's forces to defeat the Sardovians less than halfway through the novel. The remainder of the defeated forces travel to Nenavar to bargain with its Dragon Queen, Talasyn's grandmother, for sanctuary. The queen agrees to hide the fleet only if Talasyn takes up her family position as heir to the throne of Nenavar, which she agrees to do. But lest readers think this story has become a "long-lost princess lives happily ever after" fairytale, Guanzon has Alaric, who has been promoted to Night Emperor by his father, threaten to go to war with Nenavar for its resources. The queen decides to forge a strategic alliance, and Talasyn finds herself forced to marry Alaric to avoid a war that would decimate both her war comrades and her newly recovered family. The stakes become even higher when the Dragon Queen reveals that the Voidfell, a nexus of void aether that allows the Nenavar to devise advanced ships and weapons, is volatile and about to erupt and create the "Dead Season," a period that occurs every thousand years where the Voidfell breaks free and destroys everything in its wake. The queen reveals that the Voidfell eruptions are growing larger every cycle, so unless Talasyn and Alaric can learn to merge their abilities and create a shielding magic to contain the Voidfell, this time Nenavar and the entire continent that is home to Sardovia and Kesath will be destroyed. Guanzon offers an interesting storyline that calls to mind the chosen-one Western trope of fantasy, but also complicates this familiar storyline by forcing Talasyn to make ethical compromises. Talasyn is never a free individual and her lack of available choices adds additional levels of racial and gender estrangement to the narrative.

The Hurricane Wars, like many contemporary fantasy novels, does not shy away from portrayals of sexuality. However, Guanzon's treatment of Talasyn and Alaric's sexual encounters moves away from the male-dominant rape scenes of novels like George R. R. Martin's A Song of Ice and Fire series. Alaric does not force himself on Talasyn; in the first novel of the series, he pauses when she asks him to and, most interestingly, never penetrates her. Instead, he and Talasyn engage in mutual masturbation, a choice that places them on equal sexual grounds. Sexual penetration in patriarchal societies is often portrayed in pornography as "framed to signal male dominance and female subjugation" (254). Because this type of sexual narrative is the most common among pornographic videos (a third of all videos according to a study by Wright et al.), it is not hard to imagine that men in patriarchal societies become indoctrinated to the idea that sex must involve dominance and penetration. Western fantasy literature reflects the societal beliefs of the cultures that produce it; submissive, pure women and virile, dominant men feature frequently in Western fantasy narratives. But texts like the *Kamasutra*, an Indian work written for men and women that advocated for the proper treatment of women in sexual encounters (Doniger 96), demonstrate that the narrative of male dominance in sexual encounters is not present in all cultures; the idea of sex for mutual gratification goes back centuries. The fact that authors like Guanzon are imagining alternatives to the violent, male-dominant sex scene—even in a fantasy narrative set in a world with kingdoms and social hierarchies—is a unique approach that defies the "It's historically accurate" defense of Western fantasy authors by refusing to use the sexual subjugation of a woman to further the narrative.

Toward the end of the novel, Guanzon moves away from themes of oppression to question the stories countries tell themselves to justify wars. During an argument, Talasyn and Alaric uncover differing accounts of which nation was responsible for starting the Hurricane Wars. Guanzon connects the idea of differing historical accounts to folklore after Talasyn and Alaric each share their differing myths explaining the phenomenon of the Night of the World-Eater: "Perhaps it was all the same, in the end. Stories to tell around the fire and put children to bed the world over. Perhaps more than one thing could be true at the same time, when they were the folktales that made a nation" (406). Guanzon references the idea of oral storytelling to acknowledge the universality of mythmaking. But instead of a formula that Western and non-Western cultures are forced to fit, Guanzon's words acknowledge the differences that occur when myths travel from one culture to the next. In the world of *The Hurricane Wars*, there is room for difference and contradiction. Instead of arguing over whose myth is correct, Talasyn and Alaric trade knowledge and come to a better understanding of the cultures that produced such knowledge. Guanzon's narrative demonstrates that oral storytelling and myths are not the hallmarks of primitive peoples; they are different cultures' attempts to make meaning. Like Clark, Guanzon refuses to allow readers a simple binary of good and evil, hero and villain; instead, she writes scenes where Talasyn and Alaric trade stories—of their childhood, their myths, and their histories—to show readers that there is no true villain in this story. The end of *The Hurricane Wars* leaves the contradictions unresolved, but Guanzon's use of a foreshadowing argument between Talasyn and Alaric where each accuses the other of being manipulated by their rulers hints that both characters are going to have to engage in compromise to end the war.

Multiple Imperfect Gods

Another way that fantasy authors of color may choose to combat narratives of salvation is through worldbuilding strategies that include polytheistic religious structures with untrustworthy god or trickster characters. N. K. Jemisin's *Hundred Thousand Kingdoms* (2010) and Aiden Thomas's *Sunbearer Trials* (2022) both utilize the idea of mortal–god mixed-race humans engaging in celestial conflicts while Karen Lord's *Redemption in Indigo: A Novel* (2010), Jemisin's *Broken Kingdoms* (2011), and Joshua Uchenna Omenga's "The Phial of Olodumare" (first published in 2021) each discuss themes of godly redemption and revenge. These stories step away from a Christian pattern of an all-powerful, monotheistic God/Christ figure and, instead, feature a more complex relationship between mortals and gods and between the gods themselves.[4] But while most Western fantasy texts that include multiple gods tend to focus on Greek or Norse mythology, the stories in this chapter draw on African, Caribbean, and Mexican cultures to create narratives that challenge the Christian ideal of a hierarchy of power that moves from an all-powerful God/Christ to a flawed mankind in need of salvation. The gods featured in this chapter are powerful, but also flawed and a nuisance to humanity at times. The authors in this chapter make use of what Taylor Driggers describes as the "defamiliarizing strategies of fantasy" that he explains can "help us re-figure God as the devalued and dehumanized 'other' against which dominant Western Christian subjectivity constructs and asserts itself" (16). While Driggers is speaking to a monotheistic depiction of God, the stories in this chapter ultimately use flawed and unequal relations between gods or between gods and mortals to similar effect. These texts also employ god–human relations to critique the ways that colonial societies alter historical and cultural narratives to justify past and present atrocities.

Thomas and Jemisin each create worlds with specific social or racial hierarchies mixed with flawed or jealous gods. In *The Hundred Thousand Kingdoms*, nineteen-year-old Yeine discovers that she was implanted with the soul of a murdered goddess after conception. Her mother was the heir of the Arameri people until she married a man from Darr, which is considered a "barbaric" country, and was disowned. When Yeine's grandfather, the current ruler of the Arameri peoples named Dekarta, calls her to the city of Sky and names her a potential heir, Yeine knows she is likely to be killed by one of the two other named heirs. Yeine's status as a Darr outsider forces her to find unlikely allies like her servant cousin T'vril and the enslaved gods who roam the palace. Her othered position and the fact that she holds a god's soul in her body allow her to overcome death, take over the role of the goddess Enefa, and fix the broken system that the god Itempas has created through his jealousy. Itempas, the god of light, killed Enefa, the goddess of dawn and creation, causing a breakdown in the balance of the universe. Because Yeine understands suffering and loneliness, she can empathize with Itempas and see that the solution to his acts is not to kill him, a deed that would keep the world unbalanced, but to allow him a chance at redemption. Yeine convinces Nahadoth, the god of darkness and death whom Itempas

---

4. Examples of the self-sacrificing God/Christ figure include Aslan the lion in C. S. Lewis's Chronicles of Narnia series or Harry Potter in J. K. Rowling's Harry Potter series. Examples of contemporary fantasy series stepping away from this paradigm include Rick Riordan's Percy Jackson series or Neil Gaiman's American Gods series.

imprisoned for centuries, not to kill Itempas but, instead, to sentence him to live as a mortal helping to alleviate the suffering of humanity, which becomes the plot of the second book of the series, *The Broken Kingdoms*. *The Hundred Thousand Kingdoms* teaches readers to look beyond the god–human and savior–saved binaries by creating a situation where a mortal who is considered barbaric by other mortals becomes a god and ends up saving the world from the gods and followers who would "civilize" it. It is interesting that Itempas, the god who most likes order and rationality, did not think about how killing Enefa would affect the relationships between the gods and the overall balance of the universe. Jemisin's story ultimately shows how Western civilization's obsession with order, hierarchy, and rationality has negatively affected Indigenous communities by eradicating knowledge of kinship and balance.

Thomas's *Sunbearer Trials* introduces readers to Tio, the newly transitioned son of the "Diosa," or goddess, Quetzal. Tio is a Jade semidios, the son of a minor goddess who is not as powerful as the Gold semidioses, the children of the major, more powerful gods. Tio and Quetzal attend the ceremony that decides which semidioses are chosen to participate in the Sunbearer Trials, combat games held every ten years where ten champions between thirteen and eighteen complete dangerous challenges. The winner of the trials must kill the loser in a sacrificial offering to Sol that keeps the world of Reino del Sol safe. Typically, the champions are Gold semidioses, who train in an academy to prepare for the trials. But when Tio and another Jade, Xio, the son of the dios Mala Suerte, find themselves chosen, the two untrained Jades must figure out a way to survive and avoid becoming sacrifices to Sol. Thomas creates tension in the novel through the depictions of class differences between Gold and Jade semidioses. While Tio has a friend who is a Gold, Niya, the child of the earth dios, Tio was not permitted to attend the training school for the Golds because of their "lower" status. The upper-level dioses have accepted the trials and sacrifice as part of their history, but the comments and interactions of Tio and Xio throughout the novel demonstrate that not all the dioses and semidioses accept the systemic issues of Reino del Sol.

Thomas depicts a polytheistic world filled with flawed relations and actions. Through the telling of a creation story, Thomas demonstrates that the gods of this story are not considered more worthy than humanity: "Eventually, Sol and Tierra grew tired of shaping gods. . . . Sol's heartsblood mingled with the humble dirt and, unexpectedly, humans were born. . . . By nature of their short existence, the humans held more compassion and empathy, loved more fiercely, than any god could through an eternity" (1). Mortals are at the top of Sol's hierarchy, so much so that the destructive Obsidian dioses become jealous and seek to rule humanity. The dioses involved in the trials also fail to recognize that Xio is the child of an Obsidian, which allows Xio and Mala Suerte to achieve their goal of bringing back the Obsidian gods when Tio refuses to perform the sacrifice that recharges the sun stones. Sol sacrificed himself to create the sun stones that protect the world of Reino del Sol, which paints him as a savior figure, but the stones are not a perfect solution because they involve the sacrifice of a semidios. When the current system of sacrificing one to protect all breaks down, the semidioses end up tasked with retrieving the Sol Stone from Los Restos in the hopes of bringing Sol back to banish the Obsidians. Sol and the other gods are not all-powerful beings; in fact, the gods need the semidioses to retrieve the Sol Stone because of their lower status, which allows them to avoid detection by the Obsidians. It is also interesting that the protagonist and antagonist of the novel, Tio and Xio, are both transgender individuals whose transgender status is accepted without question. While the presence of the Obsidians does nod to a use of darkness to indicate evil, Thomas creates a world where class status does not depend on skin color or sexuality, and where Gold and Jade semidioses come together to save the world when their god parents cannot. While Western fantasy fans might see influences of series like The Hunger Games or Percy Jackson in Thomas's story, it is important to note that these series still center on a white-savior figure despite being lauded for their inclusion of characters of color. Such depictions are described by scholars like Ebony Elizabeth Thomas and S. R. Toliver as reinforcing racial hierarchies where minority figures are brought into the fantasy world to serve a specific purpose—often as emotional support, love interest, or sacrifice—and then returned to the periphery so the white hero can emerge victorious.[5] Western fantasy publishers frequently point to these "diverse" popular series to claim that fantasy is now diverse, which allows them to avoid allocating resources to supporting fantasy authors of color. The fact that Thomas has created a fantasy world based on Mexican mythology with nonwhite, trans heroes pushes back against the white-savior trope of Western fantasy literature and media while also challenging systemic issues of gender and sexuality in Western and Mexican/Chicanx cultures.

While the idea of flawed gods is not new in literature and mythology, authors like Lord and Jemisin convey themes of learning and compromise rather than relying on an exceptional male hero to bring the gods to their senses. *Redemption in Indigo* and *The Broken Kingdoms* each offer plot lines where a mortal woman serves as a moral compass for gods who have angered their brethren with their arrogance and are subsequently stripped

---

5. For more information, see E. Thomas; Toliver.

of a portion of their godly powers and forced to interact with mortals as a means of redemption. This humbling of male god figures inverts Christian and gender hierarchies and fosters narratives where Black women act as equal-helper figures while serving as the focus of the narrative. The gods in these stories are not all-powerful heroes come to save humanity; they are flawed figures who are educated by their female mortal counterparts.

Lord writes *Redemption in Indigo* in the style of an oral tale, and from the beginning, sets her readers up for a text that will challenge Western fantasy and fairy-tale narrative structures:

> Once upon a time—but whether a time that was, or a time that is, or a time that is to come, I may not tell—there was a man, a tracker by occupation, called Kwame. He had been born in a certain country in a certain year when history had reached that grey twilight in which fables of true love, the power of princes, and deeds of honor are told only to children. (1)

Lord plays with the idea of the Western fairy tale by using the phrase "Once upon a time" but then points out that "time" can refer to many different times, a view that aligns with Indigenous teachings of nonlinear time. Aleksandar Janca and Clothilde Bullen note the varying differences between Western cultures' linear view of time and some Indigenous cultures' views of time as cyclical:

> Perception of time differs across cultures. In the Judeo-Christian culture time is perceived as having a "linear" form (i.e. past–present–future). People from this culture often "visualise" linear time categories as follows: the past is "behind us," the future is "in front [of] us," and the present time is "where we are (right) now." . . . Many Indigenous people and a number of non-Indigenous cultures do not perceive time as linear and describe it as having a "circular" or "cyclic" form. According to such a conceptualisation of time, time is perceived as "static" and the individual person is "in the centre of time" (i.e. surrounded by concentric "time circles"). Life events are placed in time along and across the "time circles" according to their relative importance to the individual and his or her respective community. (S40–S41)

Lord uses the opening of her novel to critique Western storytelling that insists on a linear time structure. She refers to the idea of Western fairy tales as being children's stories, a common pre-Tolkien view of fantasy literature, and, instead, presents readers with a messy, nonlinear tale where the characters are often unsure whether their actions are morally right. Lord offers a story rooted in Caribbean and African oral storytelling techniques that defies Western fairy-tale conventions. She moves away from tales of "true love" and "the power of princes" to present a narrative centered on a Black woman being tracked down for escaping her unhappy marriage who finds herself caught in the middle of a power struggle between gods.

The djombi, or gods, in *Redemption in Indigo* are in conflict because a powerful djombi has given up on humanity. Lord indicates this djombi's status in the novel by referring to him as the villain of the story: "This one was the unknown danger. He had switched sides. He had started with benevolence, with the belief that there is a fine potential in humankind waiting only to be tapped. He now viewed the whole stinking breed as a pest and a plague. We may view him as a villain, but he would see us as cockroaches" (54). The narrator's explanation serves multiple purposes: It teaches readers that the gods of this story are not in a clear good–evil binary and can instead be located on a spectrum of good or evil. The gods can even play the role of trickster, a figure described in the novel as a god who utilizes choice and tricks to amuse themselves at the expense of mortals (42), but who can also serve as a liminal figure or boundary-breaker. Lord's description also gives us the perspective of the Dark Other, in this case the god of chance, and provides his perspective of humanity as "cockroaches" to create a tale where neither god nor human is presented as morally superior. When a more powerful goddess, Patience, decides to steal Chance's chaos stick and give it to Paama, a mortal woman, she finds herself kidnapped by Chance as he attempts to take back his power. Eventually, he realizes that he must convince Paama to give him back his power, and in his attempts to help her understand why she should forgo the power of chaos, he begins to see, once again, that humanity has redeeming qualities. After Paama returns the chaos stick, Patience tells Chance that his revelation is only the first step in his rehabilitation; he needs to go further and live as a human to be fully redeemed. Lord thus offers a narrative where two women, goddess and mortal, redeem a male god to restore balance in the world of the story. *Redemption in Indigo* employs Caribbean and African oral storytelling techniques to create a fantasy narrative that shifts the redeeming figure from white to Black and male to female.

Jemisin's *Broken Kingdoms* shows readers the actual process of godly rehabilitation that Lord's narrative ends with. In this novel, the main character, a blind woman named Oree with the power to see magic who is later revealed to be a demon, or child of a mortal and a god, finds the god Itempas in a dumpster and brings him into her home. At the beginning of the novel, Itempas has no regard for Oree or his own mortal life. He refuses to speak to Oree and kills himself multiple times because he cannot care about anything enough to live. Oree eventually gets him to stop killing himself by pointing out the inconvenience of cleaning his blood each time. She also decides to name him "Shiny" because he glows every morning. Jemisin's macabre humor shows Oree teaching Itempas good manners, as one would teach a child, and giving him an endearing nickname. This scene is a clear reversal of the god–mortal hierarchy of Christian narratives.

Oree eventually finds herself imprisoned by an unauthorized sect of the order of Itempas called New Lights. The New Lights are run by a demon scrivener named Dateh and his wife, Serymn Arameri. Dateh and Serymn feel that mortals, particularly the Arameri family, are worse off after the loss of "The Bright," or the time where Itempas ruled the world without the other two members of "The Three," the goddess Enefa (who has now given her powers to the former mortal Yeine) and the god Nahadoth. Dateh and Serymn have created the New Lights to worship Itempas and also to fund and obscure their experiments on how to murder gods and their immortal children, or godlings. Oree discovers a dead godling's body at the beginning of the novel, and this death causes Nahadoth to threaten to exact revenge for his child's murder unless the murderer is found and brought to justice in thirty days. Dateh and Serymn plan to use Oree's blood to kill Nahadoth, an idea based on Itempas's murder of the goddess Enefa. Jemisin uses humor and irony to show the ridiculousness of Oree's situation. The New Lights actually want the old light, the hierarchy of Itempas that gave the Arameris total dominance over other peoples. And yet, Dateh cannot see that Oree's friend Shiny is actually the god Itempas in mortal form. One of the reasons Dateh and Serymn do not recognize Itempas is because his mortal form is Maroneh, a dark-skinned people that Arameri view as a lesser people. Jemisin thus creates a situation where the people who are trying to bring a god back to power end up dismissing and torturing their god as the result of their racial prejudice. *The Broken Kingdoms* continues working through themes of imperfect gods and the fanatics who worship them. Jemisin's novels highlight the ways that religious indoctrination often aligns with the racism and sexism of the people in control of the religious narrative. Dateh and Serymn also serve as the viewpoint of the colonizer; they try to "save" Itempas but because they refuse to see dark-skinned peoples as worthy of salvation, they end up damning themselves.

Joshua Uchenna Omenga's "Phial of Olodumare" takes a different approach to the portrayal of gods by depicting a goddess who gets revenge on the mortal man who betrayed her. When contractors from China discover a statue they describe as a "traditional relic," one of the men, Wang Wu, suggests they invite a "native" to see if it has cultural significance. The lead contractor, Jun Li, has Wang Wu cut a valuable phial made of blue stone from the statue's neck, then leaves the site abruptly. Wang Wu watches him drive away on an electric boat and thinks about what he just witnessed: "He felt that Jun Li had just cheated in this transaction, and it seemed to him that it was not only the government of Lagos that Jun Li had cheated, but also him. Was he not entitled to the dividend of their discovery? He was gripped by a premonition that he would never see that flask again" (Ekpeki and Omenga 37). Omenga uses this passage to discuss a form of cultural erasure that has occurred for centuries. Sarah Van Beurden notes that colonial "collecting" or "looting" in Africa was a practice that involved colonizers at all levels who took "cultural objects, human remains, and art" resulting in "the removal of collective memory and a sense of self." She also notes that colonizers often viewed African artifacts as evidence of primitiveness and justification for "the need for a colonizing 'civilizing mission.'" Omenga's choice to make the contractors Chinese speaks to contemporary development efforts in Africa that are the result of Chinese–African agreements and are being described as a potential "new colonization" (Van Mead). "The Phial of Olodumare" is a story about revenge against those who have and would continue to take cultural artifacts and resources from the African continent; the fantastic element of the statue beginning to bleed and come to life as it kills Wang Wu makes the cultural damage literal and draws attention to the colonial violence that continues to rob African peoples of the truth of their histories.

After the Orisha, or goddess, Olokun tracks Jun Li and the phial to the plane he is traveling on as he attempts to get to China and sell the phial, he suddenly remembers another life, the life of Enaisan, the mortal man who was tasked with retrieving the phial after Olokun stole it from Obatala the craftsgod. Obatala had been ordered by Olodumare, the Supreme God, to use the phial to part the ocean and create land for the race of men. Olokun was angry that the other gods had intruded into her domain and she tricked Obatala by giving him palm wine to render him senseless. Olodumare does not want to attempt to take the phial back by force, so Eshun the trickster recruits Enaisan to trick Olokun and retrieve the phial.

The fact that none of the male gods want to attempt a direct battle with Olokun highlights her great power. Olokun is the goddess of the seas, and she is often portrayed as one of the more powerful and complex Orishas in the Yoruba religion. Sometimes depicted as male or male–female, Olokun represents all that the seas offer mankind: wealth, abundance, fertility, and healing (Badejo 490). Omenga's decision to make Olokun a powerful, redemption-seeking character highlights the need to restore communities and resources being destroyed through colonization and "development." In enacting her revenge, Olokun is not necessarily playing the role of vindictive goddess; her decision to use the phial to restore her oceans is made necessary by the harmful acts of the other gods. "The Phial of Olodumare" is a reflection on the effects of colonization on African cultures and one author's attempt to restore what was lost through the creation of a fantastic story featuring cultural figures that were often dismissed by colonizers and labeled as "primitive" or "magical." Omenga's story includes fantastic elements, but the Orishas depicted are not "magical," as noted in the introduction to *Between Dystopias: The Road to Afropantheology*, the story collection by Omenga and his coauthor Oghenechovwe Donald Ekpeki:

> Is *Revelation* in the Bible a work of fantasy? If one believes that it stemmed wholly from the imagination of John the Apostle as he sat on the Island of Patmos, then perhaps. But not if one believes that John wrote what was revealed to him by "God" or His delegates. So are the stories presented in *Afropantheology* and contemplated under the label: they are fantasy only insofar as the channels of their passage are dismissed, as has unfortunately been done for centuries now, when the continent's jugular was slashed with the swords of slavery and colonialism, and its history and culture and stories poured into the arid sands of theft and erasure. But not anymore. *Afropantheology* has been born to cauterize that wound, our words to sing to life what was lost. (2)

The gods of Omenga's story are a representation of the rich heritage and power located within a culture that is often dismissed by Western cultures. By combining the fantastic element of a statue come to life with depictions of Orishas using their power to restore, Omenga is able to write a work of Afropantheology that avoids portraying African gods and religious beliefs as "magic" while using godly interventions to imagine justice for the harms of colonization.

Fantasy, Language, and Erasure

Fantasy authors of color often utilize tropes of warring nations and political intrigue to portray the effects of colonization. Rather than depicting epic battles between clear good and evil forces, these stories are more likely to focus on how war and colonization affect individuals and communities of color. Maya Motayne's *Nocturna* (2019), R. F. Kuang's *Babel* (2022), and Moses Ose Utomi's *Lies of the Ajungo* (2023) each utilize stories of conflicting nations to address colonial erasure and exploitation. Through discussions of alternate histories, language loss or manipulation, and exploitation of natural and community resources, Motayne, Kuang, and Utomi highlight the rhetorics that nations use to justify the lies that eventually become history.

Nocturna tells the story of Prince Alfie, who is set to become the heir to the throne of the kingdom of Castallan after the assassination of his older brother, Dez. Alfie is haunted by the idea that his brother may still be alive because he was trapped in a magical void and his body was never found; Alfie risks his own life to collect illegal Englassen magic that may help him locate his brother but that is banned because of the history of the Englassen colonization of Castallan. Early in the novel, Alfie uses his elemental magic to animate a mural depicting his people's history:

> At his command, the mural moved with life, swirling above his head in bursts of color. The magic poured life into the images, showing his people swathed in bright colors, prospering and using magic freely. Then the mural slowly darkened as Englassen conquerors appeared on the shores. They chained his people, and Alfie watched the enchanted chains glow as his people's magic was drained from them and transferred to their Englassen masters so that they could perform more magic. The Englassen regime destroyed all the tomes of their language, forcing them to forget the tongue that connected them to their heritage—to their magic. (8)

Motayne's description of the conquering of Castallan employs magic as a metaphor for both resources and cultural knowledge. The enchanted chains are a marker of slavery, and the depletion of the Castallans' magic references the ways that Indigenous communities suffered great economic and cultural losses through European colonization and enslavement. It is important to note that even when discussing such historical horrors, Motayne diverges from the typical light–dark Western binary and, instead, describes the Castallans as "swathed in bright colors" rather than depicting them in white. The "darkness" of the Englassen makes the invaders the "evil" of the story, but because the Castallans are not connected with the color white, a Christian marker of purity, the colonization is instead portrayed as a leeching of a native culture's "brightness" and "color," a portrayal that clearly shows the connection between colonization and native cultural erasure and that marks the Englassen invaders as an evil, greedy force far removed from the benevolent "saviors" depicted in European colonial accounts. The Englassen are only defeated after one of the Castallan people uses a magical cloak of invisibility to steal back magic books written in Castallan; with these books, the Castallan people relearn their language and restore their lost magic.

Motayne relegates the Englassen invasion to the past to focus on the main conflict of the story between Prince Alfie and Finn, a thief who can change her appearance, and the dark magic Alfie sets free to save his cousin. This magic serves the god Sombra, an evil god who was exiled by the other gods for sowing strife and war among mankind. If Sombra returns, he will bring about Nocturna, an "unravelling of all things good" (224). Motayne avoids the light–dark binary of Western fantasy by portraying a conflict between two natives of Castallan and a dark, ancient Castallan magic known only through ancient tales and children's rhymes. Alfie and Finn's journey of self-discovery is both personal, as they each overcome past trauma and learn to become better people, and a metaphor for the Castallan people's mastery of magic, a magic that allows them to avoid Nocturna and come into their own as a global force. Motayne's story is a depiction of Indigenous restoration, a difficult process under which Indigenous peoples who have suffered the losses of colonization attempt to relearn languages, oral histories, and cultural practices.[6] Like Guanzon and Clark, Motayne teaches readers that surviving colonization is only a first step in a long process of restoration and reinvention for postcolonial peoples.

R. F. Kuang's *Babel* also addresses colonial erasure through language use. However, instead of having European colonizers eradicate foreign languages, Kuang makes non-English languages a key component of the magical system of her novel. In the world of *Babel*, languages can be mastered and used to inscribe silver bars to create magical artifacts. The narrator, Robin Swift, is brought from China to England by his mentor (and, as later revealed, father), Professor Lovell, because of his Chinese language skills. Once he arrives at Babel, the home of language-learners who produce the magical silver bars that run England's economy, he meets Ramy, a student with knowledge of Urdu, Arabic, and Persian languages, Victoire, a student of French and Haitian Creole, and Letty, a student from a wealthy English family who knows French and German. Babel recruited Robin, Ramy, and Victoire because it needs more diverse languages to power the silver bars; Romance languages are becoming less effective as they grow more similar over time. At this point, Robin begins to question whether he is being exploited, a question that is intensified when he meets Griffin, his brother who was brought to Babel years before him and who now aids a clandestine organization called the Hermes Society, which is dedicated to bringing silver-working magic to non-European countries. Griffin explains to Robin in their first meeting the underlying work that Babel is engaged in: "The professors like to pretend that the tower is a refuge for pure knowledge,

---

6. For examples of ongoing Indigenous restoration practices, see Dickson-Hoyle et al.

that it sits above the mundane concerns of business and commerce, but it does not. It's intricately tied to the business of colonialism. It *is* the business of colonialism" (100; emphasis in original). Kuang uses the exploitation of Robin, Ramy, and Victoire's language knowledge to address the uneven power structures fostered by European colonization. Professor Lovell tells Robin that language is "not a commercial good, like teas or silks, to be bought and paid for" (117), an allusion to a history of unequal colonial trade and European encroachment in China,[7] but Robin realizes that he is still aiding Babel in exploiting a resource that the Chinese people could be using to their advantage if it weren't for these uneven relations.

Kuang and Clark both create multiple layers of estrangement in their novels by giving their narrators an internal dialogue that shifts from views of assimilation and internalized colonial beliefs to an awareness of how non-Western cultures have been affected by Western colonization. Robin expresses his doubleness after he witnesses the effect of opium on the Chinese population:

> He had become so good at holding two truths in his head at once. That he was an Englishman and not. That Professor Lovell was his father and not. That the Chinese were a stupid, backwards people, and that he was also one of them. That he hated Babel, and wanted to live forever in its embrace. He had danced for years on the razor's edge of these truths, had remained there as a means of survival, a way to cope, unable to accept either side fully because an unflinching examination of the truth was so frightening that the contradictions threatened to break him. (319)

As Robin awakens from the fantasy that Babel is a tower out of time where issues of the present don't affect the rest of the world,[8] Kuang takes on the fantasy of Oxford as the seat of enlightened educators and authors. Instead of the Inklings' tales of chivalry and Christianity, Kuang contrasts the reified image of an English seat of learning with the stark reality of the colonialism it helps to bolster. Readers are never taken out of the world of *Babel*; there is no questioning of Kuang's worldbuilding or the validity of the silver bars and their magic. And yet, in giving us Robin's internal conflict between fantasy and reality, Kuang evokes an awareness of how depictions of places like Oxford in fantasy literature have been designed to reinforce habits of whiteness for fantasy readers.

---

7. For more information on the history of European–Chinese relations, see "19th Century."

8. See my explanation of fairy-tale language in *Babel* in the introduction.

Utomi's *Lies of the Ajungo* takes a radically different approach to the idea of cultural erasure by depicting the ways that corruption and historical lies within black and brown nations can lead to a breakdown in kinship practices. Utomi's story tells the tale of the "City of Lies," a city that trades the tongues of its peoples to its colonizer, the Ajungo, in exchange for the water the city's people need to survive. The narrator, a young man named Tutu, explains that the Ajungo's demand serves multiple purposes: "It was a twofold price, a price of blood and a price of history: an untongued people cannot tell their story" (1). Tutu's comment outlines the dual consequences of colonialism; colonized peoples suffer the loss of their people as well as their link to their culture and history. This act of colonial erasure sets the tone for the rest of the story. Tutu is about to turn thirteen, the age when his tongue will be cut out. He decides to take on the challenge of leaving the city to look for water in exchange for enough water to keep his dying mother alive. None of the young people who went out have ever come back. Oba Ijefi, the leader of the City of Lies, tells Tutu that she will give him one year of water for his mother in exchange for his attempt, but if he does not find water within a year, his mother will not receive more. Tutu goes out into the world in the hopes of becoming a hero to his people.

During his search for water in the desert, Tutu encounters three women from another city where people trade their ears to the Ajungo for iron to protect themselves. One of the women, Lami, explains the Ajungo's reasoning: "'They said they took our ears because we were mad and heard evil whispers,' she said. 'They said they gave us poor iron because we were violent. Savages. And after the bastards had served up this nonsense to all who could hear, they named us so that none would ever believe if we told them otherwise'" (30). Utomi utilizes Lami's dialogue to address the ways that colonizers justify their treatment of colonized peoples. By stereotyping black and brown peoples as "savage," "mad," and "violent," colonizers can depict themselves as helpers or saviors of colonized peoples. The fact that this town is watched over by a goddess also alludes to the ways that Indigenous cultures with nonpatriarchal and non-Christian cultures were viewed as inferior; the people of Lami's town are obviously "mad" if they don't adhere to Western cultural and religious beliefs and practices. Eventually, Tutu learns that the women's city is also called the "City of Lies," a reference to the ways that dominant cultures twist depictions of Indigenous peoples and their interactions to fit a historical narrative of white supremacy.

Eventually, Tutu, the three women, and a blind man who hails from a third City of Lies, one that trades their eyes for magic to stop the city's flooding, discover that the Ajungo are a made-up people, a cover for the greed of the officials of their three towns. He returns to his city for vengeance and is attacked by Oba Ijefi's guards. Tutu explains in this scene why his newly acquired seeing abilities can defeat seasoned magic users:

> None of the elites of the three Cities of Lies really understood the world. They knew the big secret, of course. They knew that all of history was a lie told to instill fear in those whose fearlessness could have rewritten it. They knew the only Ajungo were themselves. They knew power.
>
> But they didn't know powerlessness. They didn't know what it meant to have your gods stolen from you, leaving you blind to your own past. They didn't know what it was to be deprived of iron, waiting helplessly for monsters to come ruin everything you loved. They didn't know how it felt to live in a world with no friends, no heroes. A world of never-ending thirst.
>
> And their ignorance made them weak. (81)

Utomi uses Tutu's vengeance to discuss the evils of internalized colonization, but also broadens his scope to challenge the narrative of the ignorant "savage." The leaders of the three cities of lies have learned how to use narratives of colonization to hoard power and wealth. Tutu can defeat them because colonizers often become complacent and underestimate the peoples they have colonized. Utomi is ultimately arguing that when colonizers begin to believe their own lies about Indigenous groups, this ignorance causes them to become the weak peoples. *The Lies of the Ajungo* is a story about what happens when humanity rejects the lies of colonization in favor of community building and kinship.

"We Don't Need Another Hero"

I'm being a little cheeky with the title of this concluding section, but Tina Turner's song "We Don't Need Another Hero (Thunderdome)," written for the soundtrack of the *Mad Max Beyond Thunderdome* film (1985), a work that focuses on themes of life after apocalypse, well encapsulates the viewpoint of many of the authors in this chapter. The lyrics, written by Graham Lyle and Terry Britten, refer to not needing a hero figure who would lead people back to the mistakes of past generations by making promises that are "castles built in the air" (Turner line 15). Fantasy authors of color who are disillusioned with the white-savior rhetoric present in many Western fantasy narratives may find themselves looking for a different tale to tell. Or as Turner sings, "I wonder if we are ever gonna change, change" (line 7).

The authors in this chapter, like the authors I discuss throughout this project, are creating fantasy works with narratives that don't assume the need for the salvation of black and brown peoples, that refuse to believe the lies that colonizers tell and, instead, question what life after colonization looks like. These narratives don't shy away from hard truths about postcolonial recovery. The wounds of internalized colonization run deep and continue to affect community-building and kinship efforts. For texts that are supposed to be "fantasy," these stories employ multiple levels of estrangement in their narratives to help readers question whether there really is a line between reality and fantasy, or whether some of us have just been living in our dominant culture's fantasies all along. Fantasy authors of color often employ magic and godlike powers as an inheritance, a powerful knowledge passed down through generations, and as a way to shift binaries and hierarchies of power. They prove that authors looking to write non-Eurocentric fantasy texts need only look at their cultures' lived experiences for a world of possibilities.

Further Reading

Michelle West, The Sun Sword series (1997–2004), The House War series (2008–19)

David Anthony Durham, Acacia series (2007–11)

Saladin Ahmed, *Throne of the Crecent Moon* (2012)

Zen Cho, Sorcerer to the Crown series (2015–19), *Black Water Sister* (2021)

Victor LaValle, *The Changeling: A Novel* (2017)

R. F. Kuang, The Poppy War series (2018–21)

Roseanne A. Brown, *A Song of Wraiths and Ruin* (2020), *A Psalm of Storms and Silence* (2021)

Suyi Davies Okungbowa, The Nameless Republic series (2021–23)

C. M. Lockhart, Wrath of the Gods series (2022–23)

Tahereh Mafi, This Woven Kingdom series (2022–24)

R. R. Virdi, Tales of Tremaine series (2022–24)

Vajra Chandrasekera, *The Saint of Bright Doors* (2023)

Sara Hashem, The Scorched Throne series (2023–present)

João F. Silva, The Smokesmiths series (2023–present)

Keshe Chow, *The Girl with No Reflection* (2024)

Kamilah Cole, *So Let Them Burn* (2024)

Premee Mohamed, *The Butcher of the Forest* (2024)

Phillip B. Williams, *Ours* (2024)

CONCLUSION

Decolonizing the Imagination

In *The Dark Fantastic*, Ebony Elizabeth Thomas explains that Western fantasy must overcome the binary racial thinking that has led to the dark fantastic, the portrayal of darkness in fantasy literature that is never "natural" or "neutral," and the figure of the Dark Other, the endarkened symbol of evil in fantasy literature that is often linked to peoples of color in disturbing ways. She notes that the solution to the issue of the Dark Other will be found in the creation of fantasy counterstories that refuse to rely on the same tropes and assumptions as their predecessors:

> This is why taking a supposedly "neutral" or "objective" approach to theorizing the dark fantastic is problematic; the default position is to allow those who are used to seeing themselves as heroic and desired the power and privilege of naming, defining, and delimiting the entire world and everything that is in it. We never notice that monsters, fantastic beasts, and various Dark Others are silenced because we have never been taught the language that they speak. Critical race counterstorytelling provides both translation and amplification for these subsumed narratives. (23)

The stories discussed in *Dispelling Fantasies* are some of the contemporary fantasy narratives engaging in the counterstorytelling that Thomas calls for. And the need for such narratives is critical for closing the "imagination gap" Thomas identifies in children and young adult readers whose ability to imagine has been affected by the limited number of diverse fantastic stories available to them. I would argue that this imagination gap also occurs in adults; it is present in every college-age student and adult who, upon learning that I am a fantasy researcher, tells me they "just don't like fantasy." I hope this project proves that there is a sizable collection of fantasy texts now available from a diverse group of authors, but the damage has already been done. Young readers who grew up with only white fantasy options have given up on the genre, and the result becomes that they are not paying attention to the ways that fantasy has begun to include new voices. So what is the solution to our current imagination gap in fantasy literature? I will begin by discussing current efforts to market diverse fantasy stories and then discuss what is still needed.

Diverse Fantasy and Visibility

I remember going into my local bookstore as a teenager and heading straight for the fantasy section. Although I loved browsing and reading the fantasy shelves, I never saw any books by authors of color. I now know that Octavia E. Butler, Samuel R. Delany, and a number of other authors of color were writing at this time, and yet their works were not prominently displayed and, even if they were on the shelves, didn't have covers that reflected the diversity of the authors or the worlds they created.[1] Fantasy authors of color were also not reflected in awards like the World Fantasy Awards, which originated in 1975 but did not have consistent representation of authors of color among the award recipients until the early 2000s.[2] There has been change in the visibility of fantasy authors of color in recent years; I now see authors like Octavia E. Butler, Nnedi Okorafor, Tomi Adeyemi, R. F. Kuang, Fonda Lee, Marlon James, and Kalynn Bayron visible on shelves and being recommended by store employees. And authors like Okorafor, Nalo Hopkinson, Sheree Renée Thomas, Sofia Samatar, Tananarive Due, C. L. Polk, Nisi Shawl, Ken Liu, Tochi Onyebuchi, Silvia Moreno-Garcia, and Oghenechovwe Donald Ekpeki have received World Fantasy Awards. While this visibility is exciting, it is important to note that there are a whole

---

1. For an example of publishers' tendencies to whitewash covers of BIPOC speculative authors, see Mitchell.

2. To research past winners, I used this list of winners by year on the World Fantasy Convention's website: https://worldfantasy.org/awards/winners/.

host of authors of color still not present in fantasy-literature spaces. And there is still a history of authors of color being harassed by other authors or fan groups, especially when they are the first person of color to achieve certain successes. From N. K. Jemisin and the Sad Puppy debacle of 2013[3] to the recent 2023 Hugo controversy where authors R. F. Kuang and Xiran Jay Zhao may have been purposely omitted despite receiving enough nominations,[4] speculative awards still reflect the biases of the groups organizing and voting for the awards.

Traditional avenues of publishing can be difficult for fantasy authors of color to navigate. In a public blog post on her author's site posted in July 2021, fantasy author Michelle West (also known as Michelle Sagara) discusses in detail her struggles to publish her fantasy writing. The difficulties she describes include a lack of visibility and sales. She doesn't detail what steps her publishers took to market her books, but she does say that, in the end, the books were considered too risky because they were long (typical for fantasy novels) and did not have large sales numbers. West reminds her fans that publishing is a business, and that fantasy authors of color who fail to reach publishing sales goals find their books or sequels being dropped by publishers who are looking for guaranteed success. West then addresses alternate publishing routes like self-publishing and fundraising, noting that self-publishing a longer fantasy work is often prohibitively expensive and explaining that authors who don't have the funds to produce and market print copies must rely on fan willingness to read online texts or eBooks. In the end, West elected to start a *Patreon* account to make some money from her writing, but her post identifies a major hurdle for fantasy authors of color who wish to publish their books:

> Revenue neutral activity is, essentially, a hobby. It makes no money, but you do it for love. If the costs are higher than the income coming in it becomes an expensive hobby. We work to earn money and we pour it into our hobbies because we love our hobbies, right? But . . . for most of us, a hobby is distinctly separate from work. ("State of the Author")

---

3. For more information, see Newkirk.
4. For the full story, see Hawkins.

It's bad enough that the average fantasy author doesn't make a living from their writing,[5] but when fantasy writing becomes an expensive hobby only available to those who can afford to take a financial loss, then fantasy authors of color become even more excluded from the genre. Overall, West's publishing difficulties highlight the major impact publishing has on both the fantasy genre and scholarly production; if an author's books are not available to read, or are available in a difficult-to-access or limited form, they don't make the fantasy recommendation lists that fans and scholars often rely on to find new publications.

One way that publishers are trying to market fantasy authors of color is through media campaigns. In 2018 Macmillan marketed Tomi Adeyemi's debut African-based fantasy novel, *Children of Blood and Bone,* so well that it was a *New York Times* bestseller for 122 weeks and was optioned for film before it was officially published. Articles about Adeyemi's novel also appeared in spaces other than fantasy publications; visibility in popular publications like *Oprah Magazine, W Magazine, Teen Vogue,* and *Writer's Digest,* among others, likely contributed to the success of her debut work. Although Adeyemi has since been criticized for her loose interpretation of African culture in the series,[6] her successful sales demonstrated a demand for written fantasy works featuring Black characters and paved the way for other young diverse fantasy authors. One example is debut YA fantasy author Kamilah Cole, who explained the effect of seeing Black authors like Adeyemi achieve large-scale success: "When I finished my first book, *Black Panther, The Hate You Give,* and *Children of Blood and Bone* were all out. I was seeing Black authors and creators who took off and had huge success. And it wasn't that I didn't know you could write Black characters in stories like these, but I thought they'd never be bestsellers" (qtd. in Elison). Considering

---

5. In 2022 Australian fantasy author Jed Herne posted a *YouTube* video with transparent details on how much he earned for the year. He makes a very good point in this video that advances, if the author is offered one, are paid in installments over years and that most authors are required to "sell out" their advance to be eligible for royalties. His fantasy writing brought in a total of $5,567.51 for 2022 and his total salary, including side jobs in online content creation and editing, brought in $9,457.73, well below the poverty line by Australian and US standards. Author Xiran Jay Zhou has also revealed that she supplements her author income with *YouTube* videos. She received a 14K royalty for her first novel, *Iron Widow,* in 2020 and an additional 4K in 2021. Zhou states on her *Twitter/X* account, "I've emphasized many times that my payment talk is not a dig at my publishing team; it's industry critique. My situation would've been the same no matter where I'd gotten a deal of my size."

6. See my discussion of such criticisms of Adeyemi in the introduction.

that Adeyemi has stated in interviews that she struggled as a young author to depict Black characters in her fantasy works because of a lack of examples of this type of writing,[7] Cole's statement reflects a measure of progress.

Publishers are also looking to online marketing strategies to offset bookstores' hesitation to stock hardcover copies of lesser-known or debut authors.[8] In 2022 Harper Voyager began running targeted *Facebook* ads for several fantasy authors of color, including Sue Lynn Tan's *Daughter of the Moon Goddess* (2022), R. F. Kuang's *Babel* (2023), Thea Guanzon's *Hurricane Wars* (2023), and Ehigbor Okosun's *Forged by Blood* (2023). The ads include staged photos of the hardcover books that highlighted their custom cover art along with book descriptions and positive blurbs. Harper Voyager also maintains a *Facebook* page where they post pictures and video ads of their fantasy authors, as well as posts about book signings, pictures of their books in bookstores, and other details. Guanzon, an author who lives in Manila, Philippines, began her writing career as a Star Wars fanfic author and has stated in interviews that her fanfic writing helped her achieve her dream of becoming a published author:

> To my knowledge, there are no literary agencies in my country and only a handful of local presses, and making a living exclusively from the arts is very, very difficult here. Fulfilling my dream to become an author was not in the cards for me until I had fandom reach and support, and I'll always be grateful for that and proud of my origins. (qtd. in Milas)

Guanzon's example demonstrates the potential for authors who engage in fanfic or who post their writing online to build a following and attract the attention of mainstream publishers. While Harper Voyager's online advertising strategy does show that large publishers are acquiring and marketing more fantasy by authors of color, especially romantic and YA fantasy, it is worth pointing out that *Facebook* ads are only shown to targeted individuals based on their age, location, and current interests.[9] This fact means that only *Facebook* users within a specific demographic will be exposed to these ads. Online advertising and events are also much less costly than paying for authors to travel and promote their books, although the authors whom Harper Voyager promotes seem to be going on physical book tours as well.

---

7. For one example of such statements, see Lodge.

8. In 2022 there was an online controversy when authors discovered that Barnes & Noble had decided to stock hardcover books only by authors with proven sales records, essentially shutting the door for debut authors. For more information, see Northington.

9. See "How Facebook Ads Work."

Harper Voyager's online marketing strategies reflect an interesting trend for fantasy publishers; since online marketing posts are cheaper than print magazine ads, publishers can afford to take more chances on fantasy authors like Guanzon, who has skillfully used online writing platforms to build a fanbase and demonstrate her marketability. The fact that *The Hurricane Wars* achieved a number-one status in *Amazon* rankings in the Fantasy Romance and Epic Fantasy categories may indicate that an online marketing strategy works well for authors like Guanzon who already have a strong online fanbase. Whether Harper Voyager's online marketing will reach online users who are not currently fantasy readers is more difficult to judge.

Another way that mainstream publishers are marketing fantasy authors of color is through special editions of books designed either for a specific bookstore (such as Barnes & Noble or Waterstones) or for book subscription services such as *Fox and Wit*, *The Broken Binding*, *Illumicrate*, and *Fairyloot*. R. F. Kuang's *Babel* received a staggering eight editions, featuring two different options of cover art, with special extras such as different colors for the covers or edges of the book, signed editions, and special bookmarks or other extras. It is important to note that Kuang's first fantasy series, The Poppy Wars, was also published in a few limited editions with different cover art and in an *Illumicrate* special-edition subscription box, so the series overall garnered a fair amount of attention. But the marketing of *Babel* was a viral sensation with fans posting online about buying multiple hardcopies of Kuang's novel.[10] The marketing of *Babel* is not that surprising because Kuang's initial series helped her to build a fanbase among fantasy readers. But the fact that readers were willing to invest money in buying multiple hardcover editions of this book, and the fact that some of the special editions are currently selling online for more than their original price,[11] seems to indicate that mainstream publishers have found a way to sell more hardcover fantasy books through online social media campaigns. However, like the example of Guanzon, the examples discussed highlight how many fantasy authors of color must first prove that they can build a fanbase before a mainstream publisher is willing to invest time and money in publishing and marketing their writing. This fact means that the average fantasy author might need to invest time and resources in building an online presence to attract the interest of mainstream publishers. While engaging in online promotional work is better than being turned down by publishers who frequently claimed that a fanbase for diverse fantasy literature didn't exist, it still puts

---

10. For an article on *Babel* and the trend of special editions, see Franzen.

11. On 19 Jan. 2024, multiple special-edition copies of *Babel* were listed on online bookselling sites for $80–$400.

the onus on the author to spend time figuring out how to market their writing online and crowdfund for resources to buy time to create, a hurdle that a white debut author may not have to jump through. And the example of Brandon Sanderson, a popular white fantasy author who raised over $41 million on *Kickstarter* for his four-novel surprise collection, demonstrates that when white mainstream authors do go online, they have the potential to amass great wealth and circumvent publishing barriers altogether.[12]

Overall, online marketing and publishing seems to be helping some fantasy authors of color become more visible to fans. But the fact that only a small percentage of these fantasy authors are receiving such specialized assistance shows that there is still a need for more publishers and other avenues for fantasy authors of color to showcase their work, crowdfund for resources, and build their fanbase.

Independent Publishers

Another avenue for fantasy authors of color is small speculative presses that support diverse fantasy work. Milton Davis, owner of the publishing company MVmedia, frequently comments on his *Facebook* page about barriers and gatekeeping of Black authors in the publishing industry. On January 18, 2024, he stated, "Understanding how gatekeepers worked in the publishing industry back in the day and now, I wonder sometimes about Black and other marginalized authors that wrote the stories like the ones we write now that gave up writing because they couldn't get published." Davis notes that one of the reasons he started MVmedia was to give publishing opportunities to other speculative authors after he struggled to find publishers for his sword and soul writing. Other authors who have created publishing platforms after having difficulty publishing in traditional venues include Nicole Givens Kurtz and her company Mocha Memoirs Press and Oghenechovwe Donald Ekpeki, who has edited multiple speculative literary anthologies with authors like Davis and Sheree Renée Thomas and founded the press OD Ekpeki Presents.

Somos en Escrito is another publisher supporting Chicanx and Latinx speculative fiction writing. The press runs a literary magazine and press that, according to its website, seek to "express the narratives and needs of our communities, which typically get overlooked by the mainstream

---

12. For more information on Sanderson's crowdfunding success, see Holt.

presses" ("About"). Somos en Escrito also runs the Palabras del Pueblo Writing Workshop, an affordable online writing workshop where Chicanx and Latinx speculative writers can work with established Chicanx and Latinx speculative authors to expand their knowledge about speculative fiction within these cultures and to workshop their writing and develop relationships with other authors. The magazine and press depend on donations from individuals and cultural organizations, and they have run several *Kickstarter* campaigns to try to crowdsource funds for projects like the first Chicanx speculative anthology *El Porvenir ¡Ya!* (2022). While the *Kickstarter* campaign was unsuccessful, editors Scott Russell Duncan, Jenny Irizary, and Armando Rendón were still able to get the collection published through Somos en Escrito press likely by working with local arts organizations.

The advantage of publishing with one of these independent presses is that fantasy authors of color don't have to spend time trying to convince a publisher that their fantasy writing has merit and an audience. However, Davis has commented in his social media posts about his difficulties running MVmedia while also working a full-time job. Davis's press is well-known and publishes a range of speculative fiction, anthologies, graphic novels, artwork, and merchandise. But Davis has to travel to science fiction conventions to sell his stock or convince another author to do so for him. He is also currently running multiple *Facebook* pages related to Black speculative fiction and attempting to draw in more readers with targeted *Facebook* advertising. The fact that Davis is unable to fully support himself through his writing and publishing efforts highlights the difficulties that even established authors encounter when they decide to work outside of mainstream publishing franchises.

Small speculative presses that publish diverse fantasy authors are an important means of support, but these presses need more public funding to be profitable enough to succeed. It is up to fantasy fans to support these efforts by purchasing books and merchandise directly from the press websites or at conventions. Because small presses don't have a large staff and abundant funding to market their authors, word-of-mouth recommendations and online fan support are critical for these presses to continue to support diverse fantasy writing. It is also important to consider the impact of small-press books not always being available in chain bookstores and libraries, which makes them less accessible to fans and scholars.[13]

---

13. I would like to acknowledge scholar Kate Heffner for reminding me that libraries play a critical role in the sales and availability of fantasy literature.

Online Fantasy Resources

When I began researching science fiction and fantasy literature by authors of color in 2012, the only way I could find reading recommendations was through internet fan forums. I combed posts on websites like *Reddit* and eventually joined websites like *Black Girl Nerds* and *Black Science Fiction Society* to find the authors and texts I was looking for. One of the positives of science fiction and fantasy writing by authors of color is that these authors are much less likely to hold to strict boundaries between speculative genres, which means that I am often able to get recommendations for fantasy writing or science fiction–fantasy hybrid writing through online science fiction resources. These are currently more plentiful than online resources specifically for diverse fantasy writing, although *Facebook* pages like "Diverse Books with Magic" (5.7K members) are actively working to promote diverse fantasy works. What over a decade of engaging with this research has taught me is that online forums, review websites, and reading recommendation lists are critical for fans who want to diversify their fantasy reading.

Fans and authors interested in diverse fantasy currently have some venues they can look to for recommendations. In 2020 author and editor Sheree Renée Thomas took the helm of one of the longest-running speculative publications, *The Magazine of Fantasy & Science Fiction*. While her presence at the magazine alone would likely have encouraged fantasy authors of color to take a chance on submitting, Thomas has also actively worked to diversify the magazine's featured authors. Other online publications like *Tor.com*, *Fantasy Magazine*, *Lightspeed Magazine*, and *Apex* have also worked to be more inclusive in their story and essay selections. One of the most exciting developments related to diverse fantasy has been the founding of *FIYAH: A Magazine of Speculative Black Fiction*, an award-winning semiprozine devoted to publishing stories by Black speculative authors. The magazine was founded in 2016 after the magazine *Fireside Fiction* released a report on the current state of Black-author acceptance in speculative venues. The *FIYAH* website explains the magazine's origins, noting that "out of 2,039 stories published in 2015, only 38 were written by Black authors. More than half of all speculative fiction publications did not publish a single original story by a Black author over the span of the previous year. The report spurred debate, discussion and more than a few write-ups." Volunteer-run magazines like *FIYAH* have been labors of love provided by fans and creators working to offer a space that is "as intersectional as it is interdimensional." These volunteers held the first FIYAHCON convention in 2020, which included the inaugural IGNYTE awards. Organized by L. D. Lewis and Suzan Palumbo, these speculative fiction awards specifically acknowledge the contributions of BIPOC authors and scholars to speculative genres. Publications like *FIYAH* help to fill the gaps that traditional speculative publications don't always acknowledge. They are also a way for speculative authors of color to be acknowledged by their peers, and for fans to discover new diverse speculative works.

Fantasy reading recommendations lists can be a useful resource for readers looking to diversify their interests depending on the list and the author compiling it. While there are still plenty of "best of" fantasy lists that are all or predominantly white, in 2016 speculative author Nisi Shawl published a list of forty science fiction and fantasy texts that she titled "A Crash Course in the History of Black Science Fiction." Other recommendation lists by authors like Charlie Jane Anders and online book bloggers such as Anxious Nachos are helping readers discover alternatives to Eurocentric fantasy texts.

Overall, a recommendation list is only as diverse as the knowledge of the author who writes it, so fantasy fans who want more diverse reading should make a point of following the online accounts of fantasy authors of color, who often support and recommend other fantasy authors of color. The practice of review-bombing speculative authors of color is now, unfortunately, all too frequent, which can have a negative effect on sales and put authors in the path of internet trolls. In 2023 speculative author Cait Corrain was outed by other authors for review-bombing forthcoming books by debut speculative authors of color on *Goodreads* using fake accounts. Corrain was released by Del Ray Books and her agent after author Xiran Jay Zhao posted a *TikTok* video detailing evidence that Corrain was leaving one-star reviews for debut authors of color through fake accounts while boosting her own reviews using the same accounts (Zornosa). The authors affected have spoken out about experiencing online harassment, and popular fantasy author Kalynn Bayron revealed that their books were also review-bombed, and that *Goodreads* took no action at the time (Stewart). Nigerian speculative author Oghenechovwe Donald Ekpeki has discussed receiving death threats via social media and was detained and deported when attempting to travel to the United States for an awards ceremony ("Ekpeki"). These authors' experiences demonstrate the double-edged sword of online promotion: authors of color need to be visible to be published and sell their writing, but this visibility also exposes them to the possibility of online trolling and threats.

Online fan communities are the lifeblood of diverse fantasy awareness. Two of the most active communities to date are the *TikTok* pages "Fantasy Books with Diversity" and "Diverse Na Fantasy Books" and several *Facebook* pages devoted to BIPOC science fiction and fantasy visibility: "Sword and Soul Adventures" (336 members), "Asian Science Fiction and Fantasy" (1.3K members), "Imagining Indigenous Futurisms" (6.3K members), "The State of Black Science Fiction" (20.2K members), and "Black Science Fiction Society" (10.7K members). Speculative bookstores with online presence such as Sistah Scifi are also helping Black and Indigenous fantasy authors by creating space for online author talks, book clubs, and special signed copies of speculative fiction by authors from these groups. Through these and other online resources, fans can share reading recommendations and help fantasy authors of color promote their works while these authors are simultaneously sharing their fantasy works and announcements for crowdfunding efforts. These efforts are important for building a diverse community of fantasy fans, authors, and scholars who can share resources and help fantasy authors of color gain more visibility. It should be noted, however, that such efforts cannot make up for the lack of monetary resources that many aspiring fantasy authors face. On January 19, 2024, Bayron, author of several popular YA fantasy fairy-tale retellings featuring Black, queer protagonists, noted on her *Twitter/X* page: "It's wild how BookTok buzz translates to huge sales and popularity for white authors. Even when BIPOC books are successful over there, it doesn't translate to the same benefits for us." While online efforts can increase visibility for diverse fantasy authors, visibility doesn't always lead to book deals or high sales. Authors also risk fan exhaustion from too many crowdfunding requests for income that should be coming from publishers and book sales.

What Is Still Needed

When I think about the current landscape of fantasy literature and the ways that it incorporates diverse identities, I am both excited by new opportunities available to fantasy authors of color and saddened by the continued dominance of white supremacy in fantasy publishing and academia. Until the people making decisions about which authors to invest in and study are as diverse as the authors writing fantasy literature, fantasy authors and scholars of color will continue to struggle in their quest for tangible support. The truth is that like often attracts like; Western publishers, the dominant force in publishing, may feel more connected to Western-style fantasy works. And white scholars dominate the study of fantasy literature because a PhD is a costly endeavor that many scholars of color cannot afford. Even when the odds seem even and fantasy authors of color appear to have more opportunities than they did a decade ago, there are systemic structures that need to be addressed before fantasy authors and scholars of color will truly have an even playing field with their white counterparts.

There is also a critical need for more open and welcoming publishing environments for fantasy authors of color. Often, authors must obtain an agent before they can approach publishers, creating additional barriers for newer authors. But specific, open calls for diverse fantasy stories from presses can help overcome such barriers. One example is the open call for diverse fantasy works sent out by Stelliform Press, an independent, climate-focused press. In January 2024 it ran online ads with large lettering in black and white stating, "We want diverse stories" and explained the reasoning for this ad in an *Instagram* post:

> Traditionally, the "climate fiction" space is perceived as very white. This is because the stories that get called "cli-fi" are often focused on white, male, cis, hetero Western experiences, highlighting technology and "progress." But marginalized people around the world have always told environmental stories and we want to publish them. We want to see stories that contend with the way climate impacts marginalized communities and the ingenious, creative, and holistic ways these communities contend with the challenges of the future. (@stelliformpress)

Stelliform is using clear online advertising to attract a diverse group of speculative authors to their open call. The lack of barriers for submitting means that newer authors may feel more welcome to do so. It would be helpful if larger, mainstream publishers would also engage in such diversifying efforts.

It is important to acknowledge that opportunities for fantasy authors and scholars of color are better if they involve monetary resources; paid internships, scholarships, money for author appearances, and living wages for workers in the publishing industry and in academia are necessary to ensure that BIPOC authors and scholars are not excluded from these fields due to a lack of resources. The recent theft of authors' writing to train generative AI[14] programs coupled with the fact that the median income for fiction writers and non–tenure track faculty is often still below the poverty line shows that it is exceedingly difficult for even established authors and scholars to make money from their work.[15] I often wonder how much more writing I would see from some of my favorite authors if they didn't need to devote extra time to side-gigs to make a living.

---

14. For more information on this case, see Alter and Harris.

15. A 2022 article in *Publishers Weekly* titled "Writing Books Remains a Tough Way to Make a Living" states that "a new Authors Guild survey finds that median book and writing-related income for authors in 2022 was below the poverty level."

It is more important than ever to support fantasy authors of color because diverse literature in general is currently under attack. Recent book bans in the United States have demonstrated that there is an organized movement of Christofascists who don't want young readers exposed to books that would diversify their imaginations.[16] These groups aren't looking for new or different worlds, especially if those worlds contradict the racialized and gendered fantasies, historically justified using Christian rhetorics of salvation, they have grown up believing. The world that such groups are so invested in is one where whiteness and heteronormativity are set as the default norm, and other racial and gender groups are tolerated if they don't threaten ideals of white supremacy and the patriarchy. But the imagination belongs to us all, and some of the fantasy stories discussed in this project are very real depictions of colonial oppression and the erasure of Indigenous ways of knowing. They are stories about what it means to defy boundaries and create spaces where characters get to live outside of racial and gendered binaries. Fantasy literature by authors of color includes some of the most "dangerous" of these stories because they get to the heart of the truth that peoples of color everywhere need to hear: that we were never inferior peoples, and we never needed saving. I hope that this project helps in some small way to document the efforts of authors who are helping to express this message.

---

16. For more information on US book bans, see the Teachers College at Columbia University's website "What You Need to Know About the Book Bans Sweeping the US" (2023).

ACKNOWLEDGMENTS

It takes a great deal of time and support to write a book, and although I am the author of this project, it would not have been possible without the following people and support systems. First, to my wonderful husband and family—Sam Taylor, Theresa Sanchez, Raymond Sanchez, and Amanda Phillips—who supported me and listened as I droned on and on about fantasy literature for the last two years. To the Mellon Foundation and the American Council of Learned Societies (ACLS); the jointly funded Mellon/ACLS Community College Faculty Fellowship I was awarded in 2022 gave me the resources and time I needed to complete this research. To LaGuardia Community College, for awarding me a sabbatical that allowed me to complete the manuscript for this project. To my editor, Ana Maria Jimenez-Moreno, and the staff at The Ohio State University Press for all their support. To Palabras del Pueblo and author E. G. Condé, who graciously allowed me to sit in on Condé's fall 2023 Speculative Fiction workshop. To my academic friends who helped me troubleshoot ideas through rich and rewarding conversations and emails: Farah Mendlesohn, Rachel Haywood, Taryne Taylor, Chuckie Palmer-Patel, and T. S. Miller. And to my family and friends who helped me crowdsource the title: Suzanne Dickenson, Nancy Cruz, Liza Baez Kemp, Farah Mendlesohn, Joan Gordon, Jacob Steward, Sean Guynes, Anastasia Klimchynskaya, Paul Quigley, Katherine McGee, Carlos Hernandez,

Marleen Barr, Jessica FitzPatrick, Avery Delany, and Jennie Fahn. I may not have listened to most of you, but my title is much better because of all of you. Finally, any typos in this book are entirely due to my cat, James Tiberius Cat, and his unbreakable habit of putting his paw on my keyboard as I am typing.

And finally, to all of the academics out there who feel undervalued or unrecognized because of the horrible nature of today's job market: I see you. Creating full-time, tenure-track jobs in literature and employing more underrepresented scholars in these jobs must become a reality.

WORKS CITED

Abiodun, Rowland. "Àse: Verbalizing and Visualizing Creative Power through Art." *Journal of Religion in Africa*, vol. 24, no. 4, 1994, pp. 309–22, https://doi.org/10.2307/1581339.

"About." *Somos en Escrito*, Somos En Escrito Literary Foundation, 2022, https://www.somosenescrito.com/about.html.

Adichie, Chimamanda Ngozi. "The Danger of a Single Story." *TED*, July 2009, https://www.ted.com/talks/chimamanda_ngozi_adichie_the_danger_of_a_single_story?subtitle=en.

Ahmed, Sara. *Queer Phenomenology: Orientations, Objects, Others*. eBook, Duke UP, 2006.

Allison, Sophia Nahli. "Revisiting the Legend of Flying Africans." *New Yorker*, 7 Mar. 2019, https://www.newyorker.com/culture/culture-desk/revisiting-the-legend-of-flying-africans.

Alonso, Paola. "Autonomy Revoked: The Forced Sterilization of Women of Color in 20th Century America." *Texas Women's University*, Department of History-Government, https://twu.edu/media/documents/history-government/Autonomy-Revoked--The-Forced-Sterilization-of-Women-of-Color-in-20th-Century-America.pdf, accessed 15 Dec. 2024.

Alter, Alexandra, and Elizabeth A. Harris. "Franzen, Grisham and Other Prominent Authors Sue OpenAI." *New York Times*, 20 Sept. 2023, https://www.nytimes.com/2023/09/20/books/authors-openai-lawsuit-chatgpt-copyright.html.

Althaus-Reid, Marcella. *Indecent Theology: Theological Perversions in Sex, Gender and Politics*. 1st ed., Routledge, 2000, https://doi.org/10.4324/9780203468951.

Amberstone, Celu. *Refugees and Other Stories*. Kashallan Press, 2022.

The Analects of Confucius. Translated by Burton Watson, Columbia UP, 2009.

Ansell, Amy Elizabeth. *Race and Ethnicity: The Key Concepts.* Routledge, 2013, https://doi.org/10.4324/9780203448236.

Aoki, Ryka. *Light from Uncommon Stars.* eBook, Tor Books, 2021.

Apollonius Rhodius. *The Project Gutenberg EBook of The Argonautica, by Apollonius Rhodius.* Produced by Douglas B. Killings and David Widger, 21 July 2008, https://www.gutenberg.org/files/830/830-h/830-h.htm#chap02.

Archibald, Elizabeth, and Ad Putter, editors. *The Cambridge Companion to the Arthurian Legend.* Cambridge UP, 2009.

Attebery, Brian. *Strategies of Fantasy.* Indiana UP, 1992.

Ayorinde, Christine. "Yoruba Religion and Culture in the Americas." *Encyclopedia of African-American Culture and History,* vol. 5, 2006, pp. 2343–47.

Bacon, Eugen, and Milton Davis. *Hadithi & The State of Black Speculative Fiction.* Luna Press, 2020.

Badejo, Diedre. "Olokun." *Encyclopedia of African Religion,* vol. 2, 2008, pp. 489–91.

Barnett, David. "George RR Martin defends Game of Thrones rape as portraying reality of war." *The Guardian,* 4 June 2015, https://www.theguardian.com/books/2015/jun/04/george-rr-martin-game-of-thrones-rape-reality-of-war.

Barraclough, Leo. "'Rings of Power' Cast Slams Racist Backlash at Monte-Carlo Television Festival, Teases 'Action-Packed' Season 2." *Variety,* 18 June 2023, https://variety.com/2023/scene/global/rings-of-power-lord-of-the-rings-monte-carlo-television-festival-1235648051/.

Bayron, Kalynn. "It's wild how BookTok buzz . . ." X, 19 Jan. 2024, https://twitter.com/KalynnBayron/status/1748511019951960462.

Behr, Charlotte. "The Symbolic Nature of Gold in Magical and Religious Contexts." *The Portable Antiquities Scheme,* The British Museum, mmiii–mmxxiii, https://finds.org.uk/staffshoardsymposium/papers/charlottebehr.

Ben-Amos, Dan. "Straparola: The Revolution That Was Not." *Journal of American Folklore,* vol. 123, no. 490, 2010, pp. 426–46, https://doi.org/10.1353/jaf.2010.0000.

"The Benefits of Prescribed Fire on Natural Areas." *Minnesota Department of Natural Resources,* Minnesota Department of Natural Resources, 2024, https://www.dnr.state.mn.us/snap/prescribed-fire-natural-areas.html.

Berens, E. M. *The Project Gutenberg EBook of Myths and Legends of Ancient Greece and Rome, by E. M. Berens.* Produced by Alicia Williams, Keith Edkins, and the Online Distributed Proofreading Team at http://www.pgdp.net, 23 Aug. 2007, https://www.gutenberg.org/files/22381/22381-h/22381-h.htm.

Betancourt, Theresa S., et al. "Research Review: Psychosocial adjustment and mental health in former child soldiers—a systematic review of the literature and recommendations for future research." *Journal of Child Psychology and Psychiatry,* 12 Oct. 2012, https://doi-org.laguardia.ezproxy.cuny.edu/10.1111/j.1469-7610.2012.02620.x.

Blackgoose, Moniquill. *To Shape a Dragon's Breath.* eBook, Del Rey, 2023.

Blake, John. "When 'Wokeness' Comes to Middle-Earth: Why Some Say Diverse Casting Ruins the New 'Lord of the Rings' Series." *CNN,* 5 Sept. 2022, https://www.cnn.com/2022/09/03/entertainment/lord-of-the-rings-amazon-controversy-blake-cec/index.html.

Blankmarks. "How to Write Magic Types: Blood (Creative Writing)." *Medium*, 5 Mar. 2021, https://blankmarks.medium.com/magic-types-blood-magic-19e82e44c4a8.

Bond, Sarah E., and Joel Christensen. "The Man behind the Myth: Should We Question the Hero's Journey?" *Los Angeles Review of Books*, 12 Aug. 2021, https://lareviewofbooks.org/article/the-man-behind-the-myth-should-we-question-the-heros-journey/.

Borowska-Szerszun, Sylwia. "Representation of Rape in George R. R. Martin's A Song of Ice and Fire and Robin Hobb's Liveship Traders." *Extrapolation*, vol. 60, no. 1, 2019, pp. 1–22, https://doi.org/10.3828/extr.2019.2.

Bould, Mark. "The Ships Landed Long Ago: Afrofuturism and Black SF." *Science Fiction Studies*, vol. 34, no. 2, 2007, pp. 177–86, https://www.jstor.org/stable/4241520.

Brown, Alex. "Alex Brown Reviews *Black Sun* by Rebecca Roanhorse." *Locus*, 12 Feb. 2021, Locus Publications, https://locusmag.com/2021/02/alex-brown-reviews-black-sun-by-rebecca-roanhorse/.

Brown, Stephen F. *Christianity*. Facts on File, 1991.

Brown, Tracy. "It turns out 'House of the Dragon' is as homophobic as 'Game of Thrones.'" *Los Angeles Times*, 18 Sept. 2022, https://www.latimes.com/entertainment-arts/tv/story/2022-09-18/house-of-the-dragon-game-of-thrones-lgbtq-representation.

Brown Spiers, Miriam C. *Encountering the Sovereign Other: Indigenous Science Fiction*. Michigan State UP, 2021.

Bruney, Gabrielle. "Game of Thrones's Treatment of Women Will Tarnish Its Legacy." *Esquire*, 11 Apr. 2019, https://www.esquire.com/entertainment/tv/a27099255/game-of-thrones-treatment-of-women-controversy-legacy/.

Bukowick, Karen Elizabeth. *Truth and Symbolism: Mythological Perspectives of the Wolf and Crow*. 2004, Boston College, BA, online repository, https://dlib.bc.edu/islandora/object/bc-ir:102331.

Burnett, Joshua Yu. "The Collar and the Sword: Queer Resistance in Samuel R. Delany's 'Tales of Nevèrÿon.'" *African American Review*, vol. 48, no. 3, 2015, pp. 257–69, https://doi.org/10.1353/afa.2015.0036.

Callender, Kacen. *Queen of the Conquered*. Orbit, 2019.

Carr, Bryan J., and Meta G. Carstarphen, editors. *Gendered Defenders: Marvel's Heroines in Transmedia Spaces*. The Ohio State UP, 2022.

Chan, Eliza. "The Tails That Make You." *Fantasy Magazine*, Aug. 2022, issue 82, https://www.fantasy-magazine.com/fm/fiction/the-tails-that-make-you/.

Chaosattractor. "The World of Children of Blood and Bone: A Nigerian's Review." *Reddit*, 2019, https://www.reddit.com/r/Fantasy/comments/clrhhf/the_world_of_children_of_blood_and_bone_a/.

Cheek, Sheldon. "How the Concepts of Evil and Darkness Became Linked to African People." *The Root*, 10 Feb. 2015, https://www.theroot.com/how-the-concepts-of-evil-and-darkness-became-linked-to-1790858757.

Chen, Stella. "The Manananggal—Filipino Myth." *USC Digital Folklore Archives*, University of Southern California, 6 Apr. 2023, https://folklore.usc.edu/the-manananggal-filipino-myth/.

Chesterton, G. K. *The Ballad of the White Horse*. Project Gutenberg, Apr. 1999, https://www.gutenberg.org/files/1719/1719-h/1719-h.htm.

"China and Europe: 1780–1937." *Asia for Educators: Weatherhead East Asian Institute Columbia University,* Columbia University Asia for Educators, 2023, http://afe.easia.columbia.edu/chinawh/web/s6/s6_3.html.

"Church of the Lukumi Babalu Aye v. City of Hialeah (91-948), 508 U.S. 520 (1993)." *Legal Information Institute,* Cornell Law School, https://www.law.cornell.edu/supct/html/91-948.ZO.html.

Chuwa, Leonard Tumaini. *African Indigenous Ethics in Global Bioethics: Interpreting Ubuntu.* Springer Netherlands, 2014. ProQuest Ebook Central, http://ebookcentral.proquest.com/lib/lagcc-ebooks/detail.action?docID=1783751.

Clair, Matthew. "Black Intellectuals and White Audiences." *Public Books,* 1 May 2016, https://www.publicbooks.org/black-intellectuals-and-white-audiences/.

Claybourne, ZZ. "The Air in My House Tastes like Sugar." *Giganotosaurus,* 1 Mar. 2020, https://giganotosaurus.org/2020/03/01/the-air-in-my-house-tastes-like-sugar/.

Clark, C. L. *The Faithless.* Orbit, 2023.

Clark, C. L. *The Unbroken.* Orbit, 2021.

Clute, John and John Grant, editors. *The Encyclopedia of Fantasy.* Orbit, 1997, https://sf-encyclopedia.com/fe/.

Cohen, Jeffrey Jerome, ed. *Monster Theory: Reading Culture.* U of Minnesota P, 1996.

Cohen-Perez, Stephanie. "Kacen Callender." *BookPage,* 12 Nov. 2019, https://www.bookpage.com/interviews/24598-kacen-callender-science-fiction-fantasy/.

Compton, Julie. "Lia Thomas and the Long Tradition of 'Gender Policing' Female Athletes." *NBC News,* 16 Mar. 2022, https://www.nbcnews.com/nbc-out/out-news/lia-thomas-long-tradition-gender-policing-female-athletes-rcna20091.

Condé, E. G. "Multilingual Magia, Genre-Bending Chupacabras, & Indígena Poetics in Our Speculative Tradiciónes." *Palabras del Pueblo,* 2023.

Coogan, Michael D., editor. *The New Oxford Annotated Bible: New Revised Standard Version: With the Apocrypha: An Ecumenical Study Bible.* Fully revised 4th ed., Oxford UP, 2010.

Córdova, Zoraida. *Labyrinth Lost.* Sourcebooks, 2017.

Cornog, Bridget. "The Story of Hun Hunahpu, the Mayan Maize God." *Delaware Valley University,* Delaware Valley University, 6 Dec. 2021, https://delval.edu/blog/hun-hunahpu-mayan-maize-god.

"Cozy Fantasy Books." *Goodreads,* Goodreads, 2024.

Crenshaw, Kimberle. "Mapping the Margins: Intersectionality, Identity Politics, and Violence against Women of Color." *Stanford Law Review,* vol. 43, no. 6, 1991, pp. 1241–99, https://doi.org/10.2307/1229039.

"Crows." *Encyclopedia of the Great Plains.* Edited by David J. Wishart, *Center for Great Plains Studies,* U of Nebraska–Lincoln, 2011, http://plainshumanities.unl.edu/encyclopedia/doc/egp.na.024.

Cruz, Vida. "We Are the Mountain: A Look at the Inactive Protagonist." *Fantasy Magazine,* issue 70, Aug. 2021, https://www.fantasy-magazine.com/fm/non-fiction/we-are-the-mountain-a-look-at-the-inactive-protagonist/.

Cusmano, Danielle. "Rape Culture Rooted in Patriarchy, Media Portrayal, and Victim Blaming." *Writing Across the Curriculum,* 2018, https://digitalcommons.sacredheart.edu/wac_prize/30.

Cutter, Martha J. "Malinche's Legacy: Translation, Betrayal, and Interlingualism in Chicano/a Literature." *Arizona Quarterly: A Journal of American Literature, Culture, and Theory*, vol. 66, no. 1, 2010, pp. 1–33. Project MUSE, https://doi.org/10.1353/arq.0.0058.

Davenport, N. E. *The Blood Trials*. Harper Voyager, 2022.

Davis, Milton. *Changa's Safari*. eBook, Mvmedia, LLC, 2011.

Davis, Milton. "Milton Davis." *Facebook*, 19 Jan. 2024, https://www.facebook.com/milton.davis.52/posts/pfbidoyrzbCwBtakzE8XXhjjvJfe9onRTLfXnUbNPvnTwQA-PcVcXiPM5csAycSa6PChWNl?comment_id=2203062678151113&reply_comment_id=744793297225804&notif_id=1705623571770447&notif_t=feed_comment_reply&ref=notif.

Davis, Milton. *MVMedia, LLC*, https://www.mvmediaatl.com/.

Davis, Milton, and Charles R. Saunders, editors. *Griots: A Sword and Soul Anthology*. Mvmedia, 2012.

Delgado, Maggi. *Brujas of Yesterday, Their Legacy Today*. CUNY Academic Works, https://brujasofyesterday.com/.

Díaz, Junot. *The Brief Wondrous Life of Oscar Wao*. Riverhead Books, 2007.

Dickson-Hoyle, Sarah, et al. "Walking on Two Legs: A Pathway of Indigenous Restoration and Reconciliation in Fire-Adapted Landscapes." *Restoration Ecology*, vol. 30, no. 4, 2022, https://doi.org/10.1111/rec.13566.

Dokras, Uday. "Women in and around Hinduism." *INAC*, 2022, pp. 1–115, https://www.academia.edu/74536848/Women_in_Hinduism.

Dokras, Uday, and Anh Nguyen Thi Tam. "Origin of the Yakshas." Indo Nordic Author's Collective, *Academia*, 2022, https://www.academia.edu/78928997/Origin_of_the_Yakshas.

"Domestic Violence in Communities of Color." *Jersey Battered Women's Service* (JBWS), Women of Color Network (WOCN), 2021, https://jbws.org/wp-content/uploads/2021/07/Domestic-Violence-in-Communities-of-Color-compressed.pdf.

Domonoske, Camila. "'Father of Gynecology,' Who Experimented on Slaves, No Longer on Pedestal in NYC." NPR, 17 Apr. 2018, https://www.npr.org/sections/thetwo-way/2018/04/17/603163394/-father-of-gynecology-who-experimented-on-slaves-no-longer-on-pedestal-in-nyc.

Dong, Lan. *Mulan's Legend and Legacy in China and the United States*. Temple UP, 2010. ProQuest Ebook Central, http://ebookcentral.proquest.com/lib/lagcc-ebooks/detail.action?docID=686235.

Doniger, Wendy. *Redeeming the Kamasutra*. Oxford UP, 2016.

Downs, Kristina. "Mirrored Archetypes: The Contrasting Cultural Roles of La Malinche and Pocahontas." *Western Folklore*, vol. 67, no. 4, 2008, pp. 397–414, http://www.jstor.org/stable/25474939.

Driggers, Taylor. *Queering Faith in Fantasy Literature: Fantastic Incarnations and the Deconstruction of Theology*. eBook, Bloomsbury Academic, 2022.

Drumright, Kelly J. "The Library Coven: Labyrinth Lost by Zoraida Córdova." *Ancillary Review of Books*, 3 Dec. 2019, https://ancillaryreviewofbooks.org/2020/11/30/the-library-coven-labyrinth-lost-by-zoraida-cordova/.

Du Bois, W. E. B. *The Souls of Black Folk*. Myers Education Press, 2018.

Egner, Justine, and Patricia Maloney. "'It Has No Color, It Has No Gender, It's Gender Bending': Gender and Sexuality Fluidity and Subversiveness in Drag Performance." *Journal of Homosexuality*, vol. 63, no. 7, 2016, pp. 875–903, https://doi.org/10.1080/00918369.2015.1116345.

Ekman, Stefan. *Here Be Dragons: Exploring Fantasy Maps and Settings*. Wesleyan UP, 2013.

Ekpeki, Oghenechovwe Donald. "OD Ekpeki Presents/The Pantheologist." *Oghenechovwe Donald Ekpeki: The Place of the Pen*, 2023, https://odekpeki.com/od-ekpeki-presents-the-pantheologist/.

Ekpeki, Oghenechovwe Donald. "Too Dystopian for Whom? A Continental Nigerian Writer's Perspective." *Uncanny Magazine*, issue 48, Sept./Oct. 2022, https://www.uncannymagazine.com/article/too-dystopian-for-whom-a-continental-nigerian-writers-perspective/.

Ekpeki, Oghenechovwe Donald, and Joshua Uchenna Omenga, editors. *Between Dystopias: The Road to Afropantheology*. Jembefola Press, Caezik SF and Fantasy, 2023.

"Ekpeki Denied US Entry." *Locus*, 27 Feb. 2023, https://locusmag.com/2023/02/ekpeki-denied-us-entry/.

Elison, Meg. "Author Kamilah Cole on 'So Let Them Burn' and Debuting with Dragons." *Black Girl Nerds*, accessed 20 Jan. 2024.

Elswit, Sharon. *The Caribbean Story Finder: A Guide to 438 Tales from 24 Nations and Territories, Listing Subjects and Sources*. McFarland, 2017.

"Ep. 1: Joseph Campbell and the Power of Myth—'The Hero's Adventure.'" *Moyers*, 21 June 1988, https://billmoyers.com/content/ep-1-joseph-campbell-and-the-power-of-myth-the-hero%E2%80%99s-adventure-audio/.

"Epic Fantasy." *The Encyclopedia of Fantasy*. Edited by John Clute and John Grant, Orbit, 1997.

"Eucatastrophe." *Oxford English Dictionary*, Oxford UP, 2023, https://www.oed.com/dictionary/eucatastrophe_n.

"Eugenics and Reproductive Coercion in Puerto Rico." *College of Letters and Science: Center for Latin American & Caribbean Studies*, University of Wisconsin Milwaukee, 28 Apr. 2022, https://uwm.edu/clacs/eugenics-and-reproductive-coercion-in-puerto-rico/.

Evans, Tobi. *Reimagining Masculinity and Violence in "Game of Thrones" and "A Song of Ice and Fire."* Liverpool UP, 2022.

Farrar, Tarikhu. "The Queenmother, Matriarchy, and the Question of Female Political Authority in Precolonial West African Monarchy." *Journal of Black Studies*, vol. 27, no. 5, 1997, pp. 579–97, https://doi.org/10.1177/002193479702700501.

"Feminism." *The Encyclopedia of Fantasy*. Edited by John Clute and John Grant, Orbit, 1997.

Figueroa-Vásquez, Yomaira, and Kyle Powys Whyte. "Bridging the Divides: Yomaira Figueroa-Vásquez & Kyle Powys Whyte on Apocalypse and Indigenizing Futures." *Eventbrite*, 31 Jan. 2024, https://www.eventbrite.com/x/793568764537/?keep_tld=1.

Flo, Lysz. "The Magic Is in the Roots: Cultural Reconnection through Magical Realism." *FIYAH Magazine of Black Speculative Fiction*, issue 25, winter 2023.

Forna, Namina. *The Eternal Ones*. eBook, Delacorte Press, 2024.

Forna, Namina. *The Gilded Ones*. eBook, Delacorte Press, 2021.

Forna, Namina. *The Merciless Ones*. eBook, Delacorte Press, 2022.

Franzen, Mara. "What's Up with Special Edition Hardcovers?" *Book Riot*, 23 Jan. 2023, https://bookriot.com/whats-up-with-special-edition-hardcovers/.

Fredrick, Candice, and Sam McBride. *Women among the Inklings: Gender, C. S. Lewis, J. R. R. Tolkien, and Charles Williams*. Praeger, 2001.

Fries, Maureen, et al. *On Arthurian Women: Essays in Memory of Maureen Fries*. Scriptorium Press, 2001.

Gates, Henry Louis. *The Black Church: This Is Our Story, This Is Our Song*. PBS, 2021, https://www.pbs.org/weta/black-church/.

Gaudet, Marcia. "Bouki, the Hyena, in Louisiana and African Tales." *Journal of American Folklore*, vol. 105, no. 415, 1992, pp. 66–72, https://doi.org/10.2307/542000.

"Gender Bender." *Cambridge Dictionary*. Cambridge UP and Assessment, 2024, https://dictionary.cambridge.org/us/dictionary/english/gender-bender.

Ghoshal, Neela. "Human Rights Body Calls for Repeal of Jamaica's Anti-LGBT Laws." *Human Rights Watch*, 17 Feb. 2021, https://www.hrw.org/news/2021/02/17/human-rights-body-calls-repeal-jamaicas-anti-lgbt-laws.

Giesecke, Annette. *Classical Mythology A to Z: An Encyclopedia of Gods & Goddesses, Heroes & Heroines, Nymphs, Spirits, Monsters, and Places*. Black Dog and Leventhal, 2020.

Gilbert, Sophie. "What the Sexual Violence of Game of Thrones Begot." *The Atlantic*, 2021, https://www.theatlantic.com/culture/archive/2021/05/game-of-thrones-the-handmaids-tale-them-tv-sexual-violence/618782/.

Godoy, Emilio. "Agave Sweetens Livelihoods for Indigenous Women." *Our World: Brought to You by United Nations University*. 14 Feb. 2011, https://ourworld.unu.edu/en/agave-sweetens-livelihoods-indigenous-women.

Goldenberg, David M. *Black and Slave: The Origins and History of the Curse of Ham*. Walter de Gruyter GmbH, 2017. ProQuest Ebook Central, http://ebookcentral.proquest.com/lib/lagcc-ebooks/detail.action?docID=4866632.

Grady, Constance. "Tomi Adeyemi on writing YA about black girls: 'I didn't think black people could be in stories.'" *Vox*, 5 June 2018, https://www.vox.com/culture/2018/6/5/17417604/tomi-adeyemi-interview-children-of-blood-and-bone.

Green, David. "The best cosy [sic] fantasy books to curl up with right now." *Pan Macmillan*, 20 Nov. 2023, https://www.panmacmillan.com/blogs/science-fiction-and-fantasy/the-best-cosy-fantasy-books.

Grossman, Paul. "Why Were Colonial Powers Interested in Sexuality?" *MHR*, The Midlands Historical Review, http://www.midlandshistoricalreview.com/why-were-colonial-powers-interested-in-sexuality/, accessed 16 Dec. 2024.

Guanzon, Thea. *The Hurricane Wars*. Harper Voyager, 2023.

Hansen, Christopher. "The Monstrous Feminine: Ungoliant, Shelob, and Women in Tolkien's Middle-Earth." *CrossRoads*, no. 34, 2021, pp. 4–15, https://doi.org/10.15290/10.15290/CR.2021.34.3.01.

Hawkins, Amy. "Science fiction awards held in China under fire for excluding authors." *The Guardian*, 24 Jan. 2024, https://www.theguardian.com/books/2024/jan/24/science-fiction-awards-held-in-china-under-fire-for-excluding-authors.

Henao, Luis Andres. "At a Glance: Laws in the Caribbean Region That Criminalize Gay Sex." *AP News*, 11 June 2023, https://apnews.com/article/lgbtq-caribbean-religion-antigay-law-christians-21b3bcf6fe6e8976109f0c8e70050fd2.

Herne, Jed. "How Much Money I Made as a Fantasy Author in 2022." *YouTube*, 9 Jan. 2023, https://www.youtube.com/watch?v=Xjh2I8-gJS0.

Hey-Colón, Rebeca L. *Channeling Knowledges: Water and Afro-Diasporic Spirits in Latinx and Caribbean Worlds.* U of Texas P, 2023.

"Hinduism." *California State University Long Beach,* 9 Sept. 2010, https://home.csulb.edu/~cwallis/100/worldreligions/hinduism.html.

"Historical Worldbuilding: A Conversation with Kameron Hurley and Ken Liu." *Tor.com,* 14 Apr. 2015, https://www.tor.com/2015/04/14/historical-worldbuilding-an-interview-with-kameron-hurley-and-ken-liu/.

"A History of FIYAH." *FIYAH: Magazine of Black Speculative Fiction,* 2022, https://fiyahlitmag.com/2016/09/01/a-history/.

Holland, Todd. "The Symbolic Power of Gold." *SAIS Review of International Affairs,* vol. 25, no. 2, 2005, pp. 139–40. *Project MUSE,* https://doi.org/10.1353/sais.2005.0036.

Holt, Kris. "Brandon Sanderson's record-breaking Kickstarter campaign ends with $41.7 million." *Engadget,* 1 Apr. 2022, https://www.engadget.com/brandon-sanderson-kickstarter-campaign-record-most-funded-091530765.html.

Hopkinson, Nalo. Introduction. *So Long Been Dreaming: Postcolonial Science Fiction & Fantasy,* edited by Nalo Hopkinson and Uppinder Mehan, Arsenal Pulp Press, 2004, pp. 7–9.

"How Facebook Ads Work." *Meta,* 2024, https://www.facebook.com/business/news/How-Facebook-Ads-Work.

Hucks, Tracey E. *Obeah, Orisa, and Religious Identity in Trinidad,* vol. 1, *Obeah: Africans in the White Colonial Imagination.* Duke UP, 2022, https://doi.org/10.1215/9781478022145.

Hyde, Lewis. *Trickster Makes This World: Mischief, Myth, and Art.* New York: Farrar, Straus and Giroux, 1998.

"Intersectionality." *Oxford Languages.* Oxford UP, 2024.

"Interview: Ken Liu." Interviewed by The Geek's Guide to the Galaxy, issue 64, Sept. 2015, *Lightspeed Magazine,* https://www.lightspeedmagazine.com/nonfiction/interview-ken-liu/.

Jager, Rebecca K. *Malinche, Pocahontas, and Sacagawea: Indian Women as Cultural Intermediaries and National Symbols.* U of Oklahoma P, 2015.

James, Edward, and Farah Mendlesohn, editors. *The Cambridge Companion to Fantasy Literature.* Cambridge UP, 2012.

James, Marlon. *Black Leopard Red Wolf.* Riverhead Books, 2019.

James, Marlon. *Moon Witch Spider King.* Riverhead Books, 2022.

Janca, Aleksandar, and Clothilde Bullen. "The Aboriginal Concept of Time and Its Mental Health Implications." *Australasian Psychiatry: Bulletin of the Royal Australian and New Zealand College of Psychiatrists,* vol. 11, no. 1_suppl, 2003, pp. S40–S44, https://doi.org/10.1046/j.1038-5282.2003.02009.x.

Jemisin, N. K. *The Broken Kingdoms.* Orbit, 2011.

Jemisin, N. K. *The Hundred Thousand Kingdoms.* Orbit, 2010.

Jennings, Willie James. *The Christian Imagination: Theology and the Origins of Race.* Yale UP, 2010, https://doi.org/10.12987/9780300163087.

Jourian, T. J. "What Are the Connections between Transphobia, Racism and Sexual Violence?" *National Sexual Violence Resource Center,* 8 Mar. 2023, https://www.nsvrc.org/blogs/saam/what-are-connections-between-transphobia-racism-and-sexual-violence.

Joyce, Rosemary A. "Gender in the Ancient Americas." *A Companion to Global Gender History*, John Wiley and Sons, 2020, pp. 269–84, https://doi.org/10.1002/9781119535812.ch16.

"Junot Díaz Aims to Fulfill His Dream of Publishing Sci-Fi Novel with Monstro." *Wired*, 3 Oct. 2012, https://www.wired.com/2012/10/geeks-guide-junot-diaz/.

Kang, Xiaofei. *The Cult of the Fox: Power, Gender, and Popular Religion in Late Imperial and Modern China*. Columbia UP, 2005, https://doi.org/10.7312/kang13338.

Karras, Ruth Mazo. *Unmarriages: Women, Men, and Sexual Unions in the Middle Ages*. 1st ed., U of Pennsylvania P, 2012, https://doi.org/10.9783/9780812206418.

Keene, Adrienne. "'Magic in North America': The Harry Potter franchise veers too close to home." *Native Appropriations*, 7 Mar. 2016, https://nativeappropriations.com/2016/03/magic-in-north-america-the-harry-potter-franchise-veers-too-close-to-home.html.

Keown, Damien. "Karma, Character, and Consequentialism." *Journal of Religious Ethics*, vol. 24, 1996, pp. 329–50, https://blogs.dickinson.edu/buddhistethics/files/2011/01/keown01.pdf.

Kuang, R. F. *Babel: or, The Necessity of Violence: An Arcane History of the Oxford Translators' Revolution*. Harper Voyager, 2022.

Languzzi, Ezzy G. "Soledad." *Speculative Fiction for Dreamers: A Latinx Anthology*, edited by Alex Hernandez, Matthew David Goodwin, and Sarah Rafael García, Mad Creek Books, 2021.

Lara, Irene. "Bruja Positionalities: Toward a Chicana/Latina Spiritual Activism." *Chicana/Latina Studies*, vol. 4, no. 2, spring 2005, pp. 10–45.

Lee, Fonda. *Jade City*. Orbit Books, 2017.

Lee, Keekok. *The Philosophical Foundations of Classical Chinese Medicine: Philosophy, Methodology, Science*. Lexington Books, 2017.

"Left-Justified Fantasy Map." *TV Tropes*, accessed 16 Nov. 2023, https://tvtropes.org/pmwiki/pmwiki.php/Main/LeftJustifiedFantasyMap.

Leith, Mary Joan Winn. *The Virgin Mary: A Very Short Introduction*. Oxford UP, 2021.

Littlejohn, Ronnie. *Daoism: An Introduction*. 1st ed., I. B. Tauris, 2009, https://doi.org/10.5040/9780755692583.

Littleton, Cynthia. "'Game of Thrones' Rape Scene Stirs Backlash." *Variety*, 19 May 2015, https://variety.com/2015/tv/news/game-of-thrones-rape-scenes-controversy-hbo-1201500961/.

Liu, Jingyu. "The Unimpeded Passage: The Making of Universal Salvation Rites and Buddho-Daoist Interactions in Medieval China." Doctoral dissertation, Harvard University, Graduate School of Arts and Sciences, 2020.

Liu, Ken. *The Grace of Kings*. Saga Press, 2015.

Liu, Ken. *Speaking Bones*. Saga Press, 2022.

Liu, Ken. *The Veiled Throne*. Saga Press, 2021.

Liu, Ken. *The Wall of Storms*. Saga Press, 2016.

Lodge, Sally. "BookExpo 2019: Tomi Adeyemi Keeps Fantasy Real." *Publishers Weekly*, 31 May 2019, https://www.publishersweekly.com/pw/by-topic/industry-news/bea/article/80273-bookexpo-2019-tomi-adeyemi-keeps-fantasy-real.html.

Lord, Karen. *Redemption in Indigo: A Novel*. Small Beer Press, 2010.

Luxon, Thomas H., editor. *The John Milton Reading Room*. Dartmouth College, 1997–2023, https://milton.host.dartmouth.edu/reading_room/pl/book_10/text.shtml.

Mandela, Nelson. *Nelson Mandela's Favorite African Folktales*. Hachette Book Group, 2009.

Mason, Phillip L. "Soul in the Culture of African Americans: Phillip L. Mason Explores the Research and Ideas Surrounding the Traces of African Culture That Have Been Integrated into African-American Life." *Music Educators Journal*, vol. 79, no. 3, 1992, pp. 49–52, https://doi.org/10.2307/3398484.

Matyushina, Inna. "Treacherous Women at King Arthur's Court: Punishment and Shame." *Treason*, BRILL, 2019, p. 288–319, https://doi.org/10.1163/j.ctv2gjwz1j.19.

McLemore, Anna-Marie. "Reign of Diamonds." *Reclaim the Stars: 17 Tales across Realms of Space*, eBook, edited by Zoraida Córdova, Wednesday Books, 2022.

MedievalPOC. "People of Color in European Art History." *Tumblr*, 2020, https://medievalpoc.tumblr.com/.

Mendlesohn, Farah. "Peake and the Fuzzy Set of Fantasy: Some Informal Thoughts." *Miracle Enough: Papers on the Works of Mervyn Peake*, edited by G. Peter Winnington, Cambridge Scholars, 2013, pp. 61–74.

Mendlesohn, Farah. *Rhetorics of Fantasy*. Wesleyan UP, 2008.

Mercuri, Monica. "Taylor Swift Didn't Need Lucrative Side Hustles to Become a Billionaire." *Forbes*, 30 Oct. 2023, https://www.forbes.com/sites/monicamercuri/2023/10/30/taylor-swift-didnt-need-lucrative-side-hustles-to-become-a-billionaire.

Middleton, John F. M., et al. "History of magic in Western worldviews." *Britannica*, 27 Nov. 2023, https://www.britannica.com/topic/magic-supernatural-phenomenon/History-of-magic-in-Western-worldviews.

Milas, Lacy Baugher. "Thea Guanzon on How *The Hurricane Wars* Reflects Her Family's Heritage and Her Own Roots in Fanfiction." *Paste*, 13 Oct. 2023, https://www.pastemagazine.com/books/thea-guanzon/the-hurricane-wars-interview-fantasy-fiction-sequel.

Milliot, Jim. "Romance Books Were Hot in 2022." *Publishers Weekly*, 13 Jan. 2023, https://www.publishersweekly.com/pw/by-topic/industry-news/bookselling/article/91298-romance-books-were-hot-in-2022.html.

Milliot, Jim. "Writing Books Remains a Tough Way to Make a Living." *Publishers Weekly*, 29 Sept. 2023, https://www.publishersweekly.com/pw/by-topic/industry-news/publisher-news/article/93301-author-incomes-post-small-gains.html.

Mills, Charles W. "The Wretched of Middle-Earth: An Orkish Manifesto." *Southern Journal of Philosophy*, vol. 60, no. S1, 2022, pp. 105–35, https://doi.org/10.1111/sjp.12477.

"The Mission." *FIYAH: Magazine of Black Speculative Fiction*, 2022, https://fiyahlitmag.com/the-mission/.

Mitchell, Betsy. "Truth Is Change: The Evolution of Octavia Butler's Cover Art." *Portalist*, 22 Aug. 2022, https://theportalist.com/octavia-butler-cover-art.

Mitsein, Rebekah. *African Impressions: How African Worldviews Shaped the British Geographical Imagination across the Early Enlightenment*. U of Virginia P, 2022.

Moreno-Garcia, Silvia. *Mexican Gothic*. eBook, Del Rey, 2020.

Moreno-Garcia, Silvia. "Silvia Moreno-Garcia ignored the experts and trusted her instincts. Now she's a bestseller." *Los Angeles Times*, 19 Sept. 2022, https://www.latimes.com/entertainment-arts/books/story/2022-09-19/silvia-moreno-garcia-genres-daughter-of-doctor-moreau.

Morris, Jan. *Oxford*. 3rd ed., Oxford UP, 1987.

Morrison, Susan Signe. *A Medieval Woman's Companion: Women's Lives in the European Middle Ages*. Oxbow Books, 2016. *EBSCOhost*, search.ebscohost.com/login.aspx?direct=true&db=nlebk&AN=1243061&site=ehost-live.

Motayne, Maya. *Nocturna*. eBook, Balzer and Bray, 2019.

Muñoz, José Esteban. *Cruising Utopia: The Then and There of Queer Futurity*. 10th anniversary ed., New York UP, 2019.

Murrell, Nathaniel Samuel. *Afro-Caribbean Religions: An Introduction to Their Historical, Cultural, and Sacred Traditions*. Temple UP, 2010.

Newkirk, Vann R., II. "N. K. Jemisin and the Politics of Prose." *The Atlantic*, 2 Sept. 2016, https://www.theatlantic.com/entertainment/archive/2016/09/nk-jemisin-hugo-award-conversation/498497/.

Nielsen, Leon. *Robert E. Howard: A Collector's Descriptive Bibliography, with Biography*. MacFarland, reprint, 2007.

Nielsen, Leon. *Robert E. Howard: A Collector's Descriptive Bibliography of American and British Hardcover, Paperback, Magazine, Special and Amateur Editions, with a Biography*. McFarland, 2010. ProQuest Ebook Central, http://ebookcentral.proquest.com/lib/lagcc-ebooks/detail.action?docID=2066549.

"19th Century: European Encroachment & the Assault on Traditional Chinese Thought." *Asia for Educators*, Columbia U, 2024, http://afe.easia.columbia.edu/cosmos/bgov/19th.htm.

Northington, Jenn. "What Is Going on with Barnes & Noble?" *Book Riot*, 19 Aug. 2022, https://bookriot.com/barnes-noble-hardcover-stock-change/.

Nuñez, Alicia, et al. "Machismo, Marianismo, and Negative Cognitive-Emotional Factors: Findings from the Hispanic Community Health Study/Study of Latinos Sociocultural Ancillary Study." *Journal of Latina/o Psychology*, vol. 4, no. 4, 2016, pp. 202–17, https://doi.org/10.1037/lat0000050.

Okolo, Edwin, et al. "The Native Exclusive: Nnedi Okorafor on Africanfuturism and the Challenges of Pioneering." *Native*, 2018, https://thenativemag.com/native-exclusive-nnedi-okorafor-africanfuturism-challenges-pioneering/.

Okorafor, Nnedi. *Akata Witch*. eBook, Speak, 2011.

Okorafor, Nnedi. *Nnedi's Wahala Zone Blog*. 19 Oct. 2019, http://nnedi.blogspot.com/2019/10/africanfuturism-defined.html.

Older, Daniel José. *Ballad and Dagger*. eBook, Rick Riordan Presents, 2022.

Ovadje, Pamela, et al. "Dandelion Root Extract Affects Colorectal Cancer Proliferation and Survival through the Activation of Multiple Death Signalling Pathways." *Oncotarget*, vol. 7, no. 45, 8 Nov. 2016, pp. 73080–100, https://doi.org/10.18632/oncotarget.11485.

Pallapothu, Vaishnavi. "The Role of Patriarchy in Hinduism." *Medium*, 24 Sept. 2017, https://medium.com/the-red-elephant-foundation/the-role-of-patriarchy-in-hinduism-414424eed59a.

Palmer-Patel, C. *The Shape of Fantasy: Investigating the Structure of American Heroic Epic Fantasy*. eBook, Routledge, 2019.

Palumbo, Suzan. *Skin Thief: Stories*. Neon Hemlock Press, 2023.

Pané, Fray Ramón, et al. *An Account of the Antiquities of the Indians: A New Edition, with an Introductory Study, Notes, and Appendices by José Juan Arrom*. Duke UP, 1999. https://doi.org/10.2307/j.ctv11g96dw.

Paravisini-Gebert, Lizabeth, and Lizabeth Fernández Olmos. *Creole Religions of the Caribbean: An Introduction from Vodou and Santeria to Obeah and* Espiritismo. 2nd ed., New York UP, 2011, https://doi.org/10.18574/9780814728253.

Parker-Chan, Shelley. *He Who Drowned the World*. eBook, Tor Books, 2023.

Parker-Chan, Shelley. *She Who Became the Sun*. Tor Books, 2021.

Patel, Vaishnavi. "Kaikeyi." *Goodreads*, 10 Mar. 2022, https://www.goodreads.com/review/show/3852193413.

Patel, Vaishnavi. *Kaikeyi: A Novel*. eBook, Redhook, 2022.

Paton, Diana. "Obeah Acts: Producing and Policing the Boundaries of Religion in the Caribbean." *Small Axe: A Journal of Criticism*, vol. 13, no. 1, 2009, pp. 1–18, https://doi.org/10.1215/07990537-2008-002.

Perkins, Franklin. *Heaven and Earth Are Not Humane: The Problem of Evil in Classical Chinese Philosophy*. Indiana UP, 2014.

Perry, David M. "Yes, There Were People of Color in Pre-Modern Europe." *Pacific Standard*, 2017, https://psmag.com/education/yes-there-were-poc-in-medieval-europe.

Poniewozik, James. "GRRM Interview Part 2: Fantasy and History." *Time*, 18 Apr. 2011, https://entertainment.time.com/2011/04/18/grrm-interview-part-2-fantasy-and-history/.

Prater, Lenise. "Monstrous Fantasies: Reinforcing Rape Culture in Fiona McIntosh's Fantasy Novels." *Hecate*, vol. 39, no. 1/2, 2014, pp. 148–67.

Pratten, David. *The Man-Leopard Murders: History and Society in Colonial Nigeria*. Edinburgh UP, 2007, https://doi.org/10.1515/9780748631001.

Prida, Jonas. *Conan Meets the Academy: Multidisciplinary Essays on the Enduring Barbarian*. McFarland, 2013.

The Rámáyan of Válmíki. Translated by Ralph T. H. Griffith, Trübner, 1870–74, *Project Gutenberg*, eBook, 18 Mar. 2018, https://www.gutenberg.org/files/24869/24869-pdf.

Rearick, Anderson. "Why Is the Only Good Orc a Dead Orc? The Dark Face of Racism Examined in Tolkien's World." *Modern Fiction Studies*, vol. 50, no. 4, 2004, pp. 861–74, https://doi.org/10.1353/mfs.2005.0008.

Reid, Robin Anne, et al. "Nine Tolkien Scholars Respond to Charles W. Mills's 'The Wretched of Middle-Earth: An Orkish Manifesto.'" *Mythlore*, vol. 42, no. 1, 2023, pp. 183–97.

Reid-Henry, Simon. "Do resource extraction and the legacy of colonialism keep poor countries poor?" *The Guardian*, 22 Oct. 2022: https://www.theguardian.com/global-development/2012/oct/22/resource-extraction-colonialism-legacy-poor-countries.

Rhude, Kristofer. "The Third Gender and Hijras." Edited by Diane L. Moore, *Harvard Divinity School: Religious Literacy Project*, 2018, https://rpl.hds.harvard.edu/religion-context/case-studies/gender/third-gender-and-hijras.

Roanhorse, Rebecca. *Black Sun*. eBook, Saga Press, 2020.

Rodriguez, Karlo Yeager. "Up in the Hills, She Dreams of Her Daughter in the Ground." *Strange Horizons*, 31 July 2023, http://strangehorizons.com/fiction/up-in-the-hills-she-dreams-of-her-daughter-deep-in-the-ground/.

Rodriguez-Morales, Maria. "Brujas: A Conversation in Reclamation and Commodification." *BKWRITA: All Switchblade Tongue*, WordPress, 2018, https://bkwrita.wordpress.com/2018/01/09/brujas-a-conversation-in-reclamation-and-commodification/.

Roman, Daniel. "Exclusive: Tasha Suri tells us about writing The Oleander Sword." *Fansided*, 2022, https://winteriscoming.net/2022/08/18/tasha-suri-talks-us-through-the-oleander-sword-exclusive/.

Roos, Dave. "6 Ancient Resurrection Stories." *History*, 2023, https://www.history.com/news/resurrection-stories-ancient-cultures.

Rosebury, Brian. "Revenge and Moral Judgement in Tolkien." *Tolkien Studies*, vol. 5, no. 1, 2008, pp. 1–20, https://doi.org/10.1353/tks.0.0004.

Rutherdale, Myra, and Katie Pickles. *Contact Zones: Aboriginal and Settler Women in Canada's Colonial Past*. UBC Press, 2005.

Sachiko Cecire, Maria. "Empire of Fantasy." 30 Nov. 2020, https://aeon.co/essays/the-rise-and-fall-of-the-oxford-school-of-fantasy-literature.

Salmón, Enrique. "Grandma's 'Bawena': On the Kinship of Plants and People." *The MIT Press Reader*, 14 Nov. 2022, https://thereader.mitpress.mit.edu/grandmas-bawena-on-the-kinship-of-plants-and-people/.

Salmón, Enrique. "Kincentric Ecology: Indigenous Perceptions of the Human-Nature Relationship." *Ecological Applications*, vol. 10, no. 5, 2000, pp. 1327–32, https://doi.org/10.1890/10510761.

Sangster, Matthew. *An Introduction to Fantasy*. eBook, Cambridge UP, 2023.

Saunders, Charles R. "The Soul in the Sword by Charles R. Saunders." *Griots: A Sword and Soul Anthology*, edited by Charles R. Saunders and Milton Davis, MV Media, 2012.

Senior, W. A. "Quest Fantasies." *The Cambridge Companion to Fantasy Literature*, edited by Edward James and Farah Mendlesohn, Cambridge UP, 2012.

Schiff, Stacy. "Unraveling the Many Mysteries of Tituba, the Star Witness of the Salem Witch Trials." *Smithsonian Magazine*, Nov. 2015, https://www.smithsonianmag.com/history/unraveling-mysteries-tituba-salem-witch-trials-180956960/.

Scull, Andrew T. *Hysteria: The Biography*. Oxford UP, 2009.

Shaffi, Sarah. "JK Rowling says she knew her views on transgender issues would make 'many folks deeply unhappy.'" *The Guardian*, 15 Mar. 2023, https://www.theguardian.com/books/2023/mar/15/jk-rowling-views-transgender-issues-many-folks-deeply-unhappy.

Shanfeld, Ethan. "'House of the Dragon' Star Steve Toussaint Slams Racist Viewers: 'They're Happy with a Dragon Flying' but Not a 'Rich Black Guy.'" *Variety*, 22 Aug. 2022, https://variety.com/2022/tv/news/house-of-the-dragon-steve-toussaint-racist-trolls-1235347554/.

Shawl, Nisi. "A Crash Course in the History of Black Science Fiction." *Nisishawl.com*, 2016, http://www.nisishawl.com/CCHBSF.html.

Shawl, Nisi. "Ifa: Reverence, Science, and Social Technology." *Extrapolation*, vol. 57, no. 1/2, 2016, pp. 221–28, https://doi.org/10.3828/extr.2016.12.

Shawl, Nisi. "Modern Middle Ages: *Changa's Safari* by Milton J. Davis." *Tor.com*, 25 Feb. 2020, https://www.tor.com/2020/02/25/modern-middle-ages-changas-safari-by-milton-j-davis/.

Shen, Vincent. "Confucian Spirituality: Desire, Self-Cultivation, and Religiosity." *Journal of Korean Religions*, vol. 9, no. 2, 2018, pp. 33–54, https://doi.org/10.1353/jkr.2018.0011.

Shrodes, Addie. "Humor and Oppression: The Queer Work of Radical Joy in Critical Literacy Education." *Literacy Today*, vol. 39, no. 1, International Literacy Association, 2021, pp. 22–24.

Shunyata, Kaiya. "Game of Thrones Has Always Had a Gay Problem." *Queer Atmospheres*, 25 Sept. 2022, https://kaiyashunyata.substack.com/p/game-of-thrones-has-always-had-a.

Slingerland, Ted. "The Conception of Ming in Early Confucian Thought." *Philosophy East and West*, vol. 46, no. 4, Oct. 1996, pp. 567–81.

Smart, Ciannon. *Witches Steeped in Gold*. eBook, HarperTeen, 2021.

Smithers, Gregory. *Reclaiming Two-Spirits: Sexuality, Spiritual Renewal & Sovereignty in Native America*. eBook, Beacon Press, 2022.

Snyder, Lucy A. "An Exploration of Racism in Heart of Darkness." *Apex Magazine*, 14 Jan. 2016, https://apex-magazine.com/nonfiction/an-exploration-of-racism-in-heart-of-darkness/.

"Solomon Kane." Mythic Games, 12 June 2018, *Kickstarter*, https://www.kickstarter.com/projects/1162110258/solomon-kane.

Sorg, Arley. "Interview: N. K. Jemisin." *Fantasy Magazine*, issue 63, Jan. 2021, https://www.fantasy-magazine.com/fm/non-fiction/interview-n-k-jemisin/.

"Spiritual Conquest." *University of Texas at Austin Exhibits*, accessed 1 Mar. 2024, https://exhibits.lib.utexas.edu/spotlight/a-new-spain/feature/spiritual-conquest.

Staloff, Darren. "Deism and the Founding of the United States." *National Humanities Center: TeacherServe*, National Humanities Center, 2008, https://nationalhumanitiescenter.org/tserve/eighteen/ekeyinfo/deism.htm.

Steady, F. "The Legacy and Importance of Female Leadership in Africa." *Women and Leadership in West Africa*, Palgrave Macmillan, 2011, pp. 13–20, https://doi.org/10.1057/9781137010391_2.

Steinwert, T. L. "Karma." *Office for Religious & Spiritual Life*, Stanford University, accessed 20 Sept. 2023, https://orsl.stanford.edu/news/karma.

@stelliformpress. "We Want Diverse Stories." *Instagram*, 24 Jan. 2024, https://www.instagram.com/p/C2fQiq9xlTT/.

Stephanou, Aspasia. "Helen Oyeyemi's 'White Is for Witching' and the Discourse of Consumption." *Callaloo*, vol. 37, no. 5, 2014, pp. 1245–59, https://doi.org/10.1353/cal.2014.0209.

Stern, Alexandra Minna. "Sterilized in the name of public health: race, immigration, and reproductive control in modern California." *Am J Public Health*, vol. 95, no. 7, July 2005, pp. 1128–38, https://doi.org/10.2105/AJPH.2004.041608.

Stewart, Ky. "Babe Wake Up, There's New Goodreads Drama." *Junkee*, 14 Dec. 2023, https://junkee.com/goodreads-debut-author-review-bombing-drama-explained/356026.

"Strange Jamaica." *Fortean Times*, no. 406, Diamond Publishing, 2021, pp. 17.

Strickland, Galen. "The Dandelion Dynasty." *Templetongate.net*, 10 Oct. 2022, http://templetongate.net/dandelion-dynasty.htm.

Su, Ping, and Adam Grydehøj. "Caribbean legacies and interspecies community: Nalo Hopkinson's decolonial strategies in Midnight Robber." *Neohelicon*, vol. 49, 2022, pp. 685–703.

Suri, Tasha. *The Jasmine Throne*. Orbit, 2021.

Suri, Tasha. *The Lotus Empire*. Orbit, 2024.

Suri, Tasha. *The Oleander Sword*. Orbit, 2022.

Suvin, Darko. *Metamorphoses of Science Fiction: On the Poetics and History of a Literary Genre*. Yale UP, 1979.

Swinson, Brock. "'Overwhelming in the Best Possible Way' Tananarive Due & Steven Barnes on 'Marvel's Black Panther: Sins of the King.'" *Creative Screenwriting*, 1 Apr. 2021, https://www.creativescreenwriting.com/overwhelming-in-the-best-possible-way-tananarive-due-steven-barnes-on-marvels-black-panther-sins-of-the-king/.

Temblador, Alex. "Curanderas on the Ceiling." *Speculative Fiction for Dreamers*, edited by Alex Hernandez et al., The Ohio State UP, 2021.

Thomas, Aiden. *The Sunbearer Trials*. eBook, Feiwel and Friends, 2022.

Thomas, Ebony Elizabeth. *The Dark Fantastic: Race and the Imagination from Harry Potter to the Hunger Games*. eBook, New York UP, 2019.

Thornton, John K. "Afro-Christian Syncretism in the Kingdom of Kongo." *Journal of African History*, vol. 54, no. 1, 2013, pp. 53–77, https://doi.org/10.1017/S0021853713000224.

Tolentino, Jia. "Why Marlon James Decided to Write an African 'Game of Thrones.'" *New Yorker*, 21 Jan. 2019, https://www.newyorker.com/magazine/2019/01/28/why-marlon-james-decided-to-write-an-african-game-of-thrones.

Toliver, S. R. "Review of The Dark Fantastic: Race and the Imagination from Harry Potter to the Hunger Games." *Research on Diversity in Youth Literature*, 2019, https://www.academia.edu/39611557/Review_of_The_Dark_Fantastic_Race_and_the_Imagination_from_Harry_Potter_to_the_Hunger_Games.

Tolkien, J. R. R. *Tree and Leaf*. International ed., HarperCollins, 2001.

"Tricksters." *World Mythology*. Michael Webster, Grand Valley State University, https://faculty.gvsu.edu/websterm/Tricksters.htm.

Tschurenev, Jana. "Women and Education Reform in Colonial India." *New Perspectives on the History of Gender and Empire: Comparative and Global Approaches*, edited by Ulrike Lindner and Dörte Lerp, 1st ed., Bloomsbury Academic, 2018, https://doi.org/10.5040/9781350056343.

Tu, Maylin. "We Do What We Can: A Conversation with Ryka Aoki." *The Rumpus*, 13 Dec. 2021, https://therumpus.net/2021/12/13/the-rumpus-interview-with-ryka-aoki/.

Turner, Tina. "We Don't Need Another Hero." *Mad Max Beyond Thunderdome*, Universal Music Group, 1985.

"12 Cozy Fantasy Books with Cottagecore Vibes." *Epic Reads*, HarperCollins, 2024, https://www.epicreads.com/blog/cozy-fantasy-books/.

"Understanding Asexuality." *Trevor Project*, 20 Aug. 2021, https://www.thetrevorproject.org/resources/article/understanding-asexuality/.

Utomi, Moses Ose. *The Lies of the Ajungo*. eBook, Tor.com, 2023.

Van Beurden, Sarah. "LOOT: Colonial Collections and African Restitution Debates." *Origins: Current Events in Historical Perspective*, 2024, *OSU.edu*, The Ohio State University, https://origins.osu.edu/read/loot-colonial-collections-and-african-restitution-debates?language_content_entity=en.

Van Mead, Nick. "China in Africa: Win-Win Development, or a New Colonization?" *The Guardian*, 31 July 2018, https://www.theguardian.com/cities/2018/jul/31/china-in-africa-win-win-development-or-a-new-colonialism.

Verplaetse, Jan, and Andy Brown. "Part One: Blood Magic." *Blood Rush: The Dark History of a Vital Fluid*, Reaktion Books, 2020.

"Virtuous." *Cambridge Dictionary*, Cambridge UP, 2023, https://dictionary.cambridge.org/us/dictionary/english/virtuous.

"Vishnu: Who Is Vishnu?" *BBC*, 24 Aug. 2009, https://www.bbc.co.uk/religion/religions/hinduism/deities/vishnu.shtml.

Vo, Nghi. *The Brides of High Hill*. eBook, Tordotcom, 2024.

Vo, Nghi. *The Empress of Salt and Fortune*. eBook, Tordotcom, 2020.

Vo, Nghi. *Into the Riverlands*. eBook, Tordotcom, 2022.

Vo, Nghi. *Mammoths at the Gates*. eBook, Tordotcom, 2023.

Vo, Nghi. *When the Tiger Came Down the Mountain*. eBook, Tordotcom, 2020.

Walton, Jo. "Mentioning Everything Twice: Samuel R. Delany's Tales of Nevèrÿon." *Reactor*, 16 Aug. 2022, https://reactormag.com/mentioning-everything-twice-samuel-r-delanys-tales-of-neveryon/.

Wander, Philip C. "Salvation through Separation: The Image of the Negro in the American Colonization Society." *Quarterly Journal of Speech*, vol. 57, no. 1, 1971, pp. 57–67, https://doi.org/10.1080/00335637109383042.

Warner, Marina. *From the Beast to the Blonde: On Fairy Tales and Their Tellers*. 1st American ed., Farrar, Straus and Giroux, 1995.

Washington, Harriet A. *Medical Apartheid: The Dark History of Medical Experimentation on Black Americans from Colonial Times to the Present*. Vintage, 2006.

West, Michelle. "State of the Author July 2021 Edition, Ending an Era." *Michellesagara.com*, 27 July 2021, https://michellesagara.com/state-of-the-author-july-2021-edition-ending-an-era/.

"What You Need to Know about the Book Bans Sweeping the U.S." *Teachers College: Columbia University*, 2023, https://www.tc.columbia.edu/articles/2023/september/what-you-need-to-know-about-the-book-bans-sweeping-the-us/.

Williams, Walter L. "The 'two-spirit' people of Indigenous North Americans." *The Guardian*, 11 Oct. 2010, https://www.theguardian.com/music/2010/oct/11/two-spirit-people-north-america.

"Winners." *World Fantasy Convention*, 2016, https://worldfantasy.org/awards/winners/.

Wright, Paul J., et al. "Pornography, Alcohol, and Male Sexual Dominance." *Communication Monographs*, vol. 82, no. 2, 2015, pp. 252–70, https://doi.org/10.1080/03637751.2014.981558.

Yap, Isabel. "Good Girls." *Never Have I Ever: Stories*. eBook, Small Beer Press, 2021.

Young, Helen. *Race and Popular Fantasy Literature: Habits of Whiteness*. Routledge, 2015.

Young, Helen. "Race in Online Fantasy Fandom: Whiteness on Westeros.Org." *Continuum*, vol. 28, no. 5, 2014, pp. 737–47, https://doi.org/10.1080/10304312.2014.941331.

Young, Maia, et al. "Deity and Destiny: Patterns of Fatalistic Thinking in Christian and Hindu Cultures." *Journal of Cross-Cultural Psychology*, vol. 42, no. 6, 2011, pp. 1030–53, https://doi.org/10.1177/0022022110381123.

Zaleski, Philip, and Carol Zaleski. *The Fellowship: The Literary Lives of the Inklings: J. R. R. Tolkien, C. S. Lewis, Owen Barfield, Charles Williams*. eBook, Farrar, Straus and Giroux, 2015.

Zamora, Lois Parkinson, and Wendy B. Faris, editors. *Magical Realism: Theory, History, Community*. Duke UP, 1995.

Zhao, Xiran Jay. *Iron Widow*. eBook, Penguin Teen Canada, 2021.

Zhao, Xiran Jay. "I've emphasized many times that my payment talk is not a dig at my publishing team; it's industry critique . . ." X, 7 Feb. 2024, https://twitter.com/XiranJayZhao/status/1755321435843621243.

Zornosa, Laura. "An Author Review Bombed Books on Goodreads. Then Her Debut Book Was Dropped." *Time*, 13 Dec. 2023, https://time.com/6397305/cait-corrain-goodreads-review-bomb-authors/.

INDEX

Abercrombie, Joe, 84
Adeyemi, Tomi, 14–15, 14n24, 31, 137, 139, 139n6
adventure fantasy, 45–49
Africa and Africans depicted as savage Others, 6, 15–16, 24, 45–50, 53, 67, 107, 107n22, 115–35
African American culture and spirituality, 46–49
African cultures, folklore, and spirituality, 9–12, 14–15, 14n24, 32–33, 45–50, 46n11, 61–63, 66–67, 69, 72, 122, 126, 129
African Indigenous Ethics in Global Bioethics (Chuwa), 29
Afro-Caribbean cultures and diasporic communities, 29, 55–56, 62, 66–67, 69, 75, 77, 99–100, 102, 102n19, 122, 126
Afrojujuism, 10–11, 46, 49, 49nn12–13. *See also* juju
Afropantheology, 9, 9n16, 49, 49nn12–13, 63–64, 126–29
agave, 97–98, 98n15

Ahmed, Sara, 87
"Air in My House Tastes like Sugar, The" (Claybourne), 65
Akata Witch (Okorafor), 66–68
Akata Witch series (Okorafor), 11–12, 65–66, 66n13
aliens, 103–4
Alonso, Paola, 95
alternate histories, 38, 88–94, 130–34
Althaus-Reid, Marcella, 81–82
Amberstone, Celu, 94, 99–100
Anders, Charlie Jane, 145
antipolygamy laws, 82–83, 82n1
Aoki, Ryka, 103–5
artifacts, magical, 9, 21, 30, 131
àse/ache/ashe, 29
asexuality, 43, 92–93
Aslan (character), 27, 122n4
assimilation, 13, 23–24, 30, 35, 63, 69, 132; resistance to, 24, 35–36, 102
Atreides, Paul (character), 27
Attebery, Brian, 2, 2n1, 23

Babel (Kuang), 8, 21, 31, 129–32, 132n8, 137–38, 140–42
Bacon, Eugen, 49–50
Ballad and Dagger (Older), 74–75
"Ballad of King Geraint, The" (Howard), 6
"Ballad of the White Horse, The" (Chesterton), 5–6
Barnes, Steven, 17
Bayron, Kaylnn, 137, 145–46
Beloved (Morrison), 16, 76
Between Dystopias (Ekpeki and Omenga), 10n21, 50, 129
Between Earth and Sky trilogy (Roanhorse), 11
binary thinking, disruption of, 8, 23–25, 35–36, 78, 83, 94, 99–104, 121
BIPOC authors, 136–45; difficulty getting published, 138–40, 139n5; harassment of, 138, 138nn3–4
BIPOC publishers and publications, 142–46
Black and Slave (Goldenberg), 53
Black Church, the, 46, 46n11
Black Leopard Red Wolf (James), 31–33, 32n5, 36
black magic, 10, 22, 61–78, 63n11. *See also* blood magic; magic
black magicians. *See* sorcery/sorcerers
Black No More (Schuyler), 57
Blackgoose, Moniquill, 36, 38–39
Blackness, depictions of, 45–50, 53–54, 54n3, 56–61, 94–95, 108, 116
blood, 23, 34, 127; Black and brown blood as contaminant, 23, 55–61, 56n7, 94, 94n13; nonred, 57–59, 58n10; and race, 57–61. *See also* blood magic; "one-drop" rule
Blood Gift duology (Davenport), 59–61
blood magic, 23, 55–78, 55n6. *See also* black magic; magic
bloodlines, 57–61, 67–68, 76–77, 94, 97
Bond, Sarah E., 27–28
book bans, 148, 148n16
Borowska-Szerszun, Sylwia, 83–85
Brides of High Hill, The (Vo), 41–42
Brief Wondrous Life of Oscar Wao, The (Diaz), 12

Britten, Terry, 134
Broken Earth trilogy (Jemisin), 15, 18
Broken Kingdoms, The (Jemisin), 121, 123–27
Brontë, Emily, 110
Brooklyn Brujas series (Córdova), 24, 73, 76
Brooks, Kinitra, 17
Brooks, Terry, 3
Brown Spiers, Miriam C., 10
Bruising of Qilwa (Jamnia), 31
brujas/brujeria, 23, 55–56, 64–78, 78n22, 80–114
Buddhism, 28–29, 34
Burning Kingdoms series (Suri), 31–36
Butler, Octavia, 137

Callender, Kacen, 65–70
Cambridge Companion to Fantasy Literature, The (James and Mendlesohn), 1
Campbell, Joseph, 2, 27–28, 50–51
Carpentier, Alejo, 11
Catholicism, 78n22, 83
Cave of Treasures, 53
Chan, Eliza, 24, 90
Changa's Safari (Davis), 47–49
Changa's Safari (Davis), 47
Channeling Knowledges (Hey-Colón), 55–56
chaste idealized woman trope, 82–114. *See also* purity
Cheek, Sheldon, 53
Chesterton, G. K., 5–6
Chicanx cultures, 30, 64, 73–75, 78, 94, 97, 111, 122, 124–25; indigenous, 95–96, 98n15
Children of Blood and Bone (Adeyemi), 14–15, 139
Chinese culture, mythology, and spirituality, 24, 28–29, 37, 37n9, 71–72, 88–89, 106
Chosen One figure, 7, 120
Chronicles of Thomas Covenant, The (Donaldson), 83–84
Christ. *See* Jesus Christ
Christensen, Joel, 27–28
Christian Imagination, The (Jennings), 115

Christian missionary practices, 4–5, 29–30, 34, 49–50, 59, 63, 81–82
Christianity, 1–8, 26–29, 26n1, 27n2, 46–49, 46nn10–11, 52–57, 54n3, 56n7, 61–62, 67–72, 78n22, 80–83, 101, 115, 122; forced conversion to, 47–50, 63, 67–73, 115–16, 127; gender norms of, 80–83, 86, 88; influence on fantasy genre, 80–114; rhetoric of, 115–16; and white supremacy, 3–7, 81, 116. *See also* Catholicism
Chronicles of Narnia series (Lewis), 27, 122n4
Church of Lukumi Babalu Aye v. City of Hialeah (1993), 62
Chuwa, Leonard Tumaini, 29
"civilized" slave trope, 116–21
civilized/primitive binary, 4, 6, 9, 39, 44–45, 47–48, 62–66, 82, 94, 100–104, 115–35
Clark, C. L., 116–21, 131–32
Claybourne, Zig Zag, 65
club story, 40–42
Clute, John, 2, 7, 27, 52, 55, 80
Cohen, Jeffrey Jerome, 15–16, 23, 35
Cohen-Perez, Stephanie, 66
Cole, Kamilah, 139–40
Collins, Suzanne, 13–14, 21, 106
colonialism, 3–4, 8, 10, 14, 19, 21, 29–30, 37, 49–50, 61–78, 71n15, 72n16, 81–82, 82n1, 85–86, 86n7, 94–102, 107–11, 116–18, 127–35, 148; internalized, 13–14, 62, 66, 70–72, 74, 78, 100–101, 110, 132; justifications for, 23, 53, 56, 65, 82, 94–95, 115, 122, 128, 133; resistance to, 13–15, 67, 94–99; role of religion in, 62, 69–70
colorism, 14–15, 23–24, 53–54, 54n3, 105, 117
community, 16, 24–25, 28–30, 43, 76, 78, 125, 134–35. *See also* interconnectivity
Conan the Barbarian series (Howard), 4–7, 27, 44–48
Condé, E. G., 9n13, 10, 10n17, 10n19, 12, 12n23
Confucianism, 28–29, 88–89
conjurers, 64–78
Conrad, Joseph, 107, 108n23
consent, 88, 88n11, 95–96, 120
Cook, Glen, 84

Córdova, Zoraida, 17n26, 73, 76–78, 77n21, 78n22
Corrain, Cait, 145
counterstorytelling, 136–37
"Crash Course in the History of Black Science Fiction, A" (Shawl), 145
creatures, magical, 24, 30, 38–39, 41–43, 48–49, 59, 77, 100
Crenshaw, Kimberlé, 97n14, 114n28
crowdfunding, 142–43, 142n2, 146
Cruz, Angie, 76
Cruz, Vida, 9n13, 16–17
cultural erasure, 23, 32, 63, 95–96, 51, 56, 128–34; resistance to, 13, 51, 96, 129
curanderas. *See* healers
"Curanderas on the Ceiling" (Temblador), 73–74

Dandelion Dynasty series (Liu), 13, 31, 36–37
Daoism, 28–29, 71–72
Dark Fantastic, The (Thomas), 4n5, 4n8, 13–17, 56–57, 111–12, 136
Dark Lord trope / Dark Other figure, 7, 16, 20–21, 31, 52–78, 54n5, 111–36, 113n27, 119, 126
dark skin, prejudices against, 13–16, 23–24, 54–61, 54n3, 94–95, 114, 116–17. *See also* Blackness, depictions of; colorism
darkness as evil trope, 4, 7–8, 13–16, 22–25, 35–36, 52–78, 54n5, 107–13, 107n22, 108n23, 116, 119, 121–22, 124, 126, 130–31, 136. *See also* Blackness, depictions of; dark skin, prejudices against
Daughter of the Moon Goddess (Tan), 140
Davenport, N. E., 59–61
Davis, Milton J., 45–50, 142–43
"death of the sacred," 116, 116n1
Deism, 71–72
Delany, Samuel, 44, 87, 137
diasporic communities, 29, 49, 55–56, 63, 70–71, 73, 75, 77–78, 98
Diaz, Junot, 12, 19n28
Diene, Mame Bougouma, 4, 4n7
domestic violence, 85–86, 86n7, 97–98
Donaldson, Stephen R., 3, 83–84

Dong, Lan, 88–89
double estrangement, 19–21, 20n30. *See also* estrangement
Driggers, Taylor, 4n9, 8n11, 80–81, 122
Du Bois, W. E. B., 19
Due, Tananarive, 17, 17n26, 76, 137
Duncan, Scott Russell, 143

Ekman, Stefan, 36
Ekpeki, Oghenechovwe Donald, 9nn14–16, 10–11, 10n21, 20, 49–50, 63–64, 128–29, 137, 142, 145
El Porvenir ¡Ya! (Duncan et al.), 143
empathy, 24, 69, 92, 102, 111–12
Empress of Salt and Fortune, The (Vo), 41–42
Encyclopedia of Fantasy, The (Clute and Grant), 2, 7, 27, 55, 80
envy, 7, 52–78
epic fantasy, 6–7, 22, 26–51, 88–91, 93
equilibrium, 28–29, 37–38. *See also* interconnectivity
Erikson, Steven, 83
estrangement, 21, 54, 66, 78, 99, 113–14, 118, 120, 122, 127, 132–35; double, 19–21, 20n30
eucatastrophe, 30–32, 32n5, 35, 50
eugenics, 94–97, 109
Eurocentric Western fantasy, 1–17, 27–28; effects on readers of color, 20, 24–25, 25n32
evil woman trope, 82–93, 111–14

fairies, 77, 100
fairy tales, 31, 107–13, 108n24, 132n8; narrative structure, 125–26; retellings of, 54n5, 64–65, 68
Faithless, The (Clark), 119
family, importance of, 76–77, 89–90
fandom, fantasy, 2–8, 4nn5–6, 15, 22, 50, 64, 85, 85nn4–5, 141–46; backlash against diverse characters, 8n10, 9n13; fans of color, 12–14, 19–21, 25, 25n32; harassing authors of color, 138, 138nn3–4; influence over the fantasy genre, 2–4, 4nn5–6, 8–9
fantasy genre, definitions of, 1–21, 2n1, 9nn13–15
Fellowship, The (Zaleski and Zaleski), 5

female characters in fantasy, 80–114, 87n10
femininity, 34, 81–93, 113, 120
feminism, 80–114
Fernández Olmos, Lizabeth, 61
filial piety, 89–90
Filipino folklore, 107, 111–12
Fitzgerald, F. Scott, 16
Flo, Lysz, 12–13
Forged by Blood (Okosun), 140
Forna, Namina, 58–61
Fredrick, Candice, 82–83
Frodo (character), 27, 82–83
fuzzy set theory, 2–4, 2n1, 8

Game of Thrones (television series), 8, 84–85, 85n4
gender, 23–25, 30, 41–44, 55, 66, 80–114; binaries, 29–30, 58–60, 80–88, 108n24; Christian views of, 80–88; fluidity, 30, 82, 84, 87–91, 99–107; nonbinary, 30, 40–41, 44, 60, 102–7; nonconformity, 25, 82, 31–34, 43, 88–91, 102–7, 103n20, 113
"Gender in the Ancient Americas" (Joyce), 30
gender roles, 24, 29–30, 33, 80–114, 98n16; transgression of, 43, 88–114. *See also* women, subordination of
gendered violence, 24, 81–114, 85n4, 91, 91n12, 94–95, 97n14, 118
genocide, 13, 23, 31, 56, 96
genre bending, 102–7
genre hopping, 17–19, 17n26
ghosts, 25, 75–76. *See also* spirits
Gilded Ones series (Forna), 59–61
god-human relationships, 122–29
gold, symbolic importance of, 58–59, 58n10
Goldenberg, David M., 53
"Good Girls" (Yap), 107, 111–13
gothic genre, 107–11
Grace of Kings, The (Liu), 36–37
"Grandma's 'Bawena'" (Salmón), 95
Grant, John, 2, 7, 27, 55, 80
Great Gatsby, The (Fitzgerald), 16
Greek mythology, 58n10, 75–77, 76n19, 77n21, 113, 122

Green Bone Saga (Lee), 70
Griots anthologies (Davis and Saunders), 45
Guanzon, Thea, 116–17, 119–21, 131, 140–41
"Guardians of the Bright Isles" (Amberstone), 94, 100

habits of whiteness, 4, 4n6, 8, 57, 116, 116n2, 132
Hadithi & the State of Black Speculative Fiction (Bacon and Davis), 50
Halfblood Chronicles, The (Norton and Lackey), 58
Hansen, Christopher, 82–83
Harry Potter series (Rowling), 6, 13, 21, 27, 58, 107, 122n4
He Who Drowned the World (Parker-Chan), 93
healers, 72–74, 109–10
Heart of Darkness (Conrad), 107, 108n23
Herbert, Paul, 27
Here Be Dragons (Ekman), 36
Hernandez, Carlos, 11, 17n26
heroes, 2, 7, 14–16, 26–36, 40–51, 91–92, 116–21, 124, 132–34; female, 33–34, 87n10, 88–93, 119–23; virtuous white male savior prototype, 16, 21–27, 30–31, 30n4, 51, 81
hero's journey narrative, 2, 23; dismantling of, 51, 119
heteronormativity, 80–94, 84n3, 85n4; resistance to, 94–114, 120
Hey-Colón, Rebeca L., 55–56
hierarchies of power, 23, 35, 38–41, 122–27, 132; Christian, 3–7, 26–30, 70; gendered, 29–30, 80–118; racial, 50–78, 82, 122–29; reversal of, 94–99
high fantasy, 4, 22, 28, 31, 44
Hinduism, 33, 88, 90–91
History of Magic in North America series (Rowling), 10, 63
Hobb, Robin, 84
homophobia, 32–33, 33n6, 51, 84, 85n5, 100, 100n18, 102–7
Hopkinson, Nalo, 10n17, 17, 19n28, 137
horror genre, 76, 107–11
House of the Dragon (television series), 8
Howard, Robert E., 4–7, 27, 45–46, 48

Hua Mulan, legend of, 88
Hucks, Tracey E., 72
Hume, Kathryn, 1
humor, 86, 86n8, 102–7, 112–13
"Humor and Oppression" (Shrodes), 86n8, 102
Hundred Thousand Kingdoms, The (Jemisin), 121–23
Hundred Thousand Kingdoms series (Jemisin), 31
Hunger Games series (Collins), 13–14, 22, 106, 124
Hurricane Wars (Guanzon), 116, 119–21, 140–41
hysteria, 106, 106n21

Icarus myth, 113, 113n26
Ifa (religion), 69–70, 102n19
"Ifa" (Shawl), 69–70
Imaro series (Saunders), 45
imperialism. *See* colonialism
Indian culture and folklore, 32–36
Indigenous knowledges, peoples, and spiritualities, 10–11, 22–23, 27n2, 29–30, 52–78, 95–102, 109–10; colonial views of, 4, 23, 52–78, 81–82, 88n11, 109, 115–35; represented as magical, 9, 63–65
Inklings, the, 3n2, 5–7, 80, 82, 113, 116, 132
interconnectivity, 7, 23–24, 28–29, 37–38, 42, 88, 92–93, 100–102. *See also* community
intersectionality, 80–114, 114n28
Into the Riverlands (Vo), 41–43
Irizary, Jeremy, 143
Iron Widow (Zhao), 103, 105–6, 139n5
Irwin, W. R., 1
Islands of Blood and Storm series (Callender), 65, 68–70

Jackson, Rosemary, 1
Jade City (Lee), 70–71
Jainism, 33
Jamaican culture and folklore, 32–33, 33n6
James, Edward, 1–2
James, Marlon, 31–33, 32n5, 49–50, 137

Jemisin, N. K., 15, 17n26, 18–19, 31, 121–27, 138
Jennings, Willie James, 115
Jerry, Anthony Russell, 15
Jesus Christ, 26–27, 27n2, 52, 82; representations of, 31
Joyce, Rosemary A., 30
Judas, 52–53
juju, 11, 46, 61, 65, 67–68

Kaikeyi (Patel), 88, 90–93
Kane, Solomon (character), 6–7
Kang, Xiaofei, 24
Keene, Adrienne, 63–64
King Alfred, 6
Kingston, Maxine Hong, 89
kinship, 7, 24–25, 29–30, 29n3, 39, 46, 49, 88, 95–97, 123, 133–35. *See also* interconnectivity
Kuang, R. F., 8, 21, 31, 129–32, 132n8, 137–38, 140–41
Kundera, Milan, 16
Kurtz, Nicole Givens, 142

La Llorona figure, 111
La Pachamama, 81
Labyrinth Lost (Córdova), 76–78, 77n21, 78n22
Lackey, Mercedes, 58, 84
landscapes, 36–39, 43
language loss, 130–34
Languzzi, Ezzy G., 94, 97–98
Lara, Irene, 64
Larsen, Nella, 57
Latinx cultures and spiritualities, 11, 64, 73–78, 78n22, 81–82, 94
Lee, Fonda, 71–72, 137
Legacy of Orïsha series (Adeyemi), 14, 31
Leonard, Elizabeth, 8
"Let Us Go into the House of the Lord" (Saunders), 46
Lewis, C. S., 2n1, 3–4, 3n2, 27, 83, 116, 122n4
Lewis, L. D., 144
LGBTQIA+ community. *See* queer community

Lies of the Ajungo (Utomi), 130, 133–34
Light from Uncommon Stars (Aoki), 103–5
Littlejohn, Ronnie, 71–72
Liu, Ken, 13, 31, 36–38, 37n9, 137
Liutoldus, 53
Lord, Karen, 121, 124–25
Lord Foul's Bane (Donaldson), 83–84
Lord of the Rings, The (movie series), 6
Lord of the Rings: The Rings of Power, The (television series), 4n5, 6, 8
Lord of the Rings series, The (Tolkien), 2–3, 2n1, 12, 23, 27, 52, 54, 82–84, 83n2
love triangles, 106–7
Lovecraft, H. P., 6
Lucas, George, 27
Lyle, Graham, 134

machismo, 98, 98n16. *See also* masculinity
magic, 4, 4n7, 8–13, 18, 22, 24–25, 33, 46–49, 52–78, 54n3, 104–5, 118–20, 130–31; and agency, 86, 88, 93–99; definitions of, 10–13; and gender, 55, 64–78. *See also* black magic; blood magic
"Magic Is in the Roots, The" (Flo), 12–13
magical realism, 9, 11–13, 76
male dominance. *See* patriarchy
Malinche, 74, 74n18, 117n3
Mammoths at the Gates (Vo), 41–42
Manananggal figure, 107, 111–12
Manlove, Colin, 1
maps, 9, 30, 36–39
marriage, 82, 85–87, 92, 97–98
Martin, George R. R., 6, 82, 84–85, 85n4, 87, 120
masculinity, 32, 40, 85n4, 98n16, 120; toxic, 84, 85n4, 92, 113. *See also* machismo
Mason, Phillip L., 45–46
matriarchal societies, 44, 97–98; African, 67, 67n14, 73, 73n17
McBride, Sam, 82–83
McCaffrey, Anne, 83, 87n10
McLemore, Anne-Marie, 103, 105
Medical Apartheid (Washington), 94
medical experimentation, 94–96

medicine men/women, 10, 63
medieval Europe, 5, 36; people of color in, 3–4, 4n4; women in, 85, 85n6
medieval fixity, 3–8, 21, 36–38, 44, 80–85
Mendlesohn, Farah, 1–4, 20, 40, 76n20
messianic figures, 26–28
Mexican cultures. *See* Chicanx cultures
Mexican Gothic (Moreno-Garcia), 107–9
Meyer, Stephenie, 106
Milton, John, 53, 76, 76n19
monsters/monstrousness, 15–16, 32, 59, 100–101; empathy for, 23–24, 54n4, 102, 110–13; racialization of, 23–24, 54, 60
monstrous feminine, the, 82–83, 111–12
Moon Witch Spider King (James), 32n5
moral universe in fantasy storytelling, 4, 27, 31; non-Eurocentric, 7, 28–30, 40–43
"More than Pigs and Rosaries Can Give" (Hernandez), 11
Moreno-Garcia, Silvia, 17–18, 17n26, 107–10, 113, 137
Morris, Jan, 5
Morrison, Toni, 16, 76
Moses, 26–27
Motayne, Maya, 129–31
Mulan (character), 88–90
MV Media, 45, 50
mysticism, 28–29
Myth of the Flying African, 113, 113n26

Nachos, Anxious, 145
narrative structure, 125–26; closed, 40–41; multiple versions of, 41–43
natural resources, exploitation and theft of, 39, 71, 71n15, 128, 130–34. *See also* colonialism
nature, connection to, 34–36, 38–39, 77, 95, 100–101
New Testament, 52–53
Nielsen, Leon, 5–6
Nigerian cultural practices, 66–67, 66n13
Noah's curse of Canaan, 53–54
noble/god to commoner/human hierarchy, 59–61
Nocturna (Motayne), 129–31
non-English languages, 116, 118, 130–32

nonwhite characters, representations of, 21, 85–103; fan backlash against, 4n5, 8–9, 8n10, 9n13
Norton, Andre, 58

Obeah, 61–62, 72–73
Okorafor, Nnedi, 9nn14–15, 10–12, 10nn20–21, 17n26, 19, 19n27, 49, 65–68, 66n13, 137
Okosun, Ehigbor, 140
Older, Daniel José, 17n26, 73, 75
Oleander Sword, The (Suri), 33–36
Olokun, 128–29
Omenga, Joshua Uchenna, 9n14, 9n16, 10–11, 10n21, 49–50, 121, 127–29
"On Fairy Stories" (Tolkien), 2, 31
"one-drop" rule, 23, 57, 57n9, 94n13. *See also* blood
Onyebuchi, Tochi, 137
oral storytelling, 9–11, 41–43, 99–100, 121, 126, 131
orishas, 75, 77, 77n21, 128–29
Other, 4, 13–16, 23–24, 41, 48, 56–59, 122; acceptance of, 24–25, 54n5, 65, 99; gendered, 21; racialized, 13, 15–16, 21. *See also* Dark Lord trope / Dark Other figure
Oxford (Morris), 5
Oxford school of fantasy, 2–5, 3n2, 7, 80

pagan religions, 55–56
Pallapothu, Vaishnavi, 34n6, 90–91
Palmer-Patel, C., 2, 27
Palumbo, Suzan, 94, 99, 101–2, 144–45
Paradise Lost (Milton), 53, 76, 76n19
Paravisini-Gebert, Lizabeth, 61
Parker-Chan, Shelley, 24, 88–89, 91–93
Passing (Larsen), 57
Patel, Vaishnavi, 88, 90–93
Paton, Diana, 62
patriarchy, 4, 7, 23, 34, 66; challenges to, 80–114
Peake, Mervin, 2–3
"Peake and the Fuzzy Set of Fantasy" (Mendlesohn), 2
Percy Jackson series (Riordan), 58, 58n10, 76n19

"Phial of Olodumare, The" (Omenga), 121, 127–29
planes of existence, alternative, 29, 65, 75, 88
Polk, C. L., 137
polyamory, 106–7
polyphony, 24, 35
polytheism, 71, 73, 77, 116, 121–29
Poppy War series (Kuang), 31, 142
portal-quest fantasy, 7, 9, 12, 21, 40, 65, 76, 76n20
Potter, Harry (character), 27
Prater, Lenise, 84
Pratten, David, 67
precolonial cultures, 30, 73n17, 98, 100
Prida, Jonas, 44
publishing industry, 8n10, 16–18, 17n25; barriers to authors of color, 14–19, 86, 86n9, 137–48, 137n1, 139n5, 140n8, 147nn14–15; lack of diversity in, 8–9, 9n13. *See also* BIPOC publishers and publications
"Pull of the Herd, The" (Palumbo), 94, 101–2
purity, 34, 39, 54, 91, 93, 109; blood (or racial), 57–61; sexual, 82–88, 91, 94–95. *See also* chaste idealized woman trope

qì, 29, 106
Queen of the Conquered (Callender), 68–70
queer characters, representations of, 60, 82, 85, 85n5, 87n10, 93, 102–7, 118, 124
queer community, 86–87; empowerment of, 89–90, 102–7; violence against members of, 33, 84–85, 90–91, 93, 100, 100n18, 102
Queer Phenomenology (Ahmed), 87
Queering Faith in Fantasy Literature (Driggers), 80
quest fantasy, 31–32, 38, 76n20. *See also* portal-quest fantasy

Ra, Sun, 46
racial double consciousness, 19. *See also* estrangement
racial hierarchies, 55–57; creation of, 62; disruption of, 25, 94, 136

racial passing, 57, 60–61
racial self-consciousness, 54
racialized fantasy, 3–17, 4nn4–6, 22–23, 22n31, 52–78, 82
racialized violence, 112–13, 118; resistance to, 86–87, 94–99, 97n14
racism, 3–22, 9n13, 21, 50–78, 81–99, 107–9, 107n22, 115–21, 127; internalized, 14–16, 66, 118
Radiant Emperor series (Parker-Chan), 24, 88, 90, 92
radical joy, 86, 86n8, 102–7, 113–14
Ramayana, 88, 90–91
rape. *See* sexual assault
rationality, 4, 8, 10–12, 21, 50–78, 87, 97, 101, 104, 118, 123
reality, definitions of, 10–11, 20, 97
recovery/restoration, 8, 10, 13, 31, 35, 62, 65, 85, 94–99, 119, 131–35, 131n6
redemption, 121–29
Redemption in Indigo (Lord), 121, 124–26
Reformatory (Due), 76
"Reign of Diamonds" (McLemore), 103, 105
Remarried Empress, The (comic), 16
Rendón, Armando, 143
restoration of a bygone-era trope, 5–6, 20–21, 35, 37, 88–90
resurrection of Christ, 27, 27n2, 31
retellings of well-known stories, 87n10, 88–89
revenge, 31, 38, 47, 68, 111, 121–29, 133–34
Rhetorics of Fantasy (Mendlesohn), 2, 4, 20, 76n20
Rick Riordan Presents series, 17
Rings of Power, The. *See Lord of the Rings: The Rings of Power, The* (television series)
Riordan, Rick, 17, 58, 76n19, 122n4, 124
Roanhorse, Rebecca, 11
Rodriguez, Karlo Yeager, 94, 96–97
Rodriguez-Morales, Maria, 64
"Role of Patriarchy in Hinduism, The" (Pallapothu), 90–91
romance genre, 17–18, 17n25
Rowling, J. K., 6–7, 10, 13, 21, 27, 58, 63, 84, 84n3, 106, 122n4

Sachico Cecire, Maria, 3
sacrifice, 27, 92; critique of, 33–34, 51; ritual, 56–57, 56n7, 76, 122–23; self-sacrifice, 28–32, 43, 91. *See also* self-sacrificing God/Christ figure
Sad Puppy debacle, 138, 138n3
Sagara, Michelle, 138–39
Salmón, Enrique, 29n3, 95
Salvador, Brazil, 14–15
salvation, 4, 7, 23, 27, 27n2, 72, 101, 115–35
Samatar, Sofia, 137
Sanderson, Brandon, 142, 142n12
Sangster, Matthew, 12
Santería, 11, 46n10, 61–62, 69–70, 75–77, 77n21, 102n19
Satan, 52–53, 52n1
sati, 34, 34n7
Saunders, Charles R., 45–46
Saunders, Pharoah, 45
Sauron (character), 52, 54
Schuyler, George S., 57
science fiction, 1–4, 17–19, 45–46, 57, 103–4; postrace depictions in, 3, 3n3; respectability of, 19n28; visibility of, 144–46
secrecy/secrets, 61–62, 66–68, 76
secret leopard societies, 66–68
self-sacrificing God/Christ figure, 26–28, 31, 122, 122n4
selkies, 100–101
Senior, W. A., 31
sex, depictions of, 23, 44, 80–114, 120
sexism, 50–51, 66, 80–118, 85n5, 98n16, 127; internalized, 66, 93
sexual assault, 82–85, 93, 95–97, 104–5, 112, 120; victim blaming, 96–97, 97n14, 117
sexuality, 16, 30, 44, 60, 90–93, 114; Christian views of, 30, 81–88; deviant, 16, 95, 113; queer, 7, 32–33, 86–87, 92–93, 99–107
shapeshifters, 67, 94, 99–102, 99n17
Shawl, Nisi, 10n17, 47, 69–70, 137, 145
She Who Became the Sun (Parker-Chan), 88–89
Shen, Vincent, 28–29
Shrodes, Addie, 86n8, 102

Sims, James Marion, 95
Singing Hills Cycle (Vo), 24, 40–43
skinwalkers, 10, 63
Skywalker, Luke (character), 27
slavery, 3, 13, 44, 46–47, 46n10, 61–64, 68–69, 76, 94–95, 115–21, 130; justifications of, 22–23, 53, 56–57, 63, 115–17
Smart, Ciannon, 70, 72
social media marketing campaigns, 140–43. *See also* crowdfunding
Soledad (Cruz), 76
"Soledad" (Languzzi), 94, 97–98
Solomon, Rivers, 76
Song of Ice and Fire series, A (Martin), 82, 84–85, 85n4, 120
sorcery/sorcerers, 47–49, 55–56, 61, 67, 72
soul, 45–46, 48–49
spirits, 75–76; ancestral, 70–71. *See also* ghosts
Star Wars franchise (Lukas), 27
Strategies of Fantasy (Attebery), 2
Strickland, Galen, 36–37
Sunbearer Trials (Thomas), 24, 121, 123
Suri, Tasha, 31–36, 32n5, 50
Suvin, Darko, 19, 19n29
Swift, Taylor, 112, 112n25
sword and sorcery fantasy, 4, 55; African and African-diasporic revisions of, 22, 26–51
sword and soul fantasy, 44–50, 142
syncretic religious practices, 46, 46nn10–11, 61–62, 69–70, 102n19

"Tails That Make You, The" (Chan), 24
Tales of Nevèrÿon series (Delany), 44, 87
Tan, Sue Lynn, 140
Taoism. *See* Daoism
Temblador, Alex, 73–75, 78
Theseus and the Minotaur myth, 76–77
Thomas, Aiden, 24, 121–24
Thomas, Ebony Elizabeth, 4n5, 8, 10, 10n18, 13–16, 20, 54, 56–57, 111–13, 113n27, 124, 124n5, 136–37
Thomas, Sheree Renée, 137, 142, 144
time, perceptions of, 125

To Shape a Dragon's Breath (Blackgoose), 36, 38–39
Todorov, Tzvetan, 1
Toliver, S. R., 124, 124n5
Tolkien, J. R. R., 2–6, 2n1, 3n2, 8, 12, 23, 27, 31, 36, 52, 54, 82–85, 83n2, 87, 116
"Too Dystopian for Whom?" (Ekpeki), 20
trickster figures, 11, 73, 121–29
Turner, Tina, 134
Tschurenev, Jana, 30
Twilight saga (Meyer), 106

Ubuntu, 29
Unbearable Lightness of Being, The (Kundera), 16
Unbroken, The (Clark), 116–19
Unkindness of Ghosts, An (Solomon), 76
"Up in the Hills, She Dreams of Her Daughter Deep in the Ground" (Rodriguez), 94, 96–97
Utomi, Moses Ose, 129–30, 133–34

Van Beurden, Sarah, 128
Virgin Mary, 81–82
virtue, 7, 23, 26–51, 92–93
Vishnu, 91
Vo, Nghi, 17n26, 24, 40–43, 92
Vodun, 11, 61, 102n19

Walton, Jo, 44
war, 31, 42, 60, 84, 89, 91, 117–21, 129
Washington, Harriet E., 86n7, 94–95
water, 55–56
"Water's Memory, The" (Bacon), 49–50
"We Are the Mountain" (Cruz), 16
"We Don't Need Another Hero" (Turner), 134
West, Michelle, 138–39
Westfahl, Gary, 20, 20n30
When the Tiger Came Down the Mountain (Vo), 41–42

white male Christian fantasy authors, hegemony of, 1–17
white privilege, 1–17, 112–13
white supremacy, reinforced in fantasy narratives, 3–8, 20, 36, 57, 102, 80–81, 116, 133
whiteness, 13–15, 21, 23, 108–9, 112–13
Williams, Charles, 83
Wisdom of Solomon, The, 53
witchcraft, 63n11; accusations of, 54n3, 64–66, 74
witches, 23, 55, 64–78, 78n22
Witches Steeped in Gold (Smart), 70, 72
Woman Warrior (Kingston), 89
women, subordination of, 30, 34, 59, 80–115, 120
women as victim trope, resistance to, 84–85, 85n4, 87, 87n10, 92–113
Women among the Inklings (Fredrick and McBride), 82–83
worldbuilding, 9–10, 20–21, 30, 36–39
Wrongness to Healing narrative structure, 2, 51
Wuthering Heights (Brontë), 110

xenophobia, 8, 14–15, 32, 51. *See also* racism

YA fantasy, 17–18, 106, 139–40
yaksas, 33–35
Yap, Isabel, 107, 111–13
Year's Best African Speculative Fiction series, The, 50
Yoruba, 29, 128–29
Young, Clarence, 65
Young, Helen, 4n6, 8, 57n8, 85, 116n2

Zaleski, Carol, 5
Zaleski, Philip, 5
Zhao, Xiran Jay, 103, 105–6, 138, 139n5, 145
Zurara, 115

NEW SUNS: RACE, GENDER, AND SEXUALITY IN THE SPECULATIVE
Susana M. Morris and Kinitra D. Brooks, Series Editors

Scholarly examinations of speculative fiction have been a burgeoning academic field for more than twenty-five years, but there has been a distinct lack of attention to how attending to nonhegemonic positionalities transforms our understanding of the speculative. New Suns: Race, Gender, and Sexuality in the Speculative addresses this oversight and promotes scholarship at the intersections of race, gender, sexuality, and the speculative, engaging interdisciplinary fields of research across literary, film, and cultural studies that examine multiple pasts, presents, and futures. Of particular interest are studies that offer new avenues into thinking about popular genre fictions and fan communities, including but not limited to the study of Afrofuturism, comics, ethnogothicism, ethnosurrealism, fantasy, film, futurity studies, gaming, horror, literature, science fiction, and visual studies. New Suns particularly encourages submissions that are written in a clear, accessible style that will be read both by scholars in the field as well as by nonspecialists.

Dispelling Fantasies: Authors of Color Reimagine a Genre
　JOY SANCHEZ-TAYLOR

Reading in the Postgenomic Age: Race, Discipline, and Bionarrativity in Contemporary North American Literature
　LESLEY LARKIN

Black Speculative Feminisms: Memory and Liberated Futures in Black Women's Fiction
　CASSANDRA L. JONES

Anti-Blackness and Human Monstrosity in Black American Horror Fiction
　JERRY RAFIKI JENKINS

Gendered Defenders: Marvel's Heroines in Transmedia Spaces
　EDITED BY BRYAN J. CARR AND META G. CARSTARPHEN

The Dreamer and the Dream: Afrofuturism and Black Religious Thought
　ROGER A. SNEED

Diverse Futures: Science Fiction and Authors of Color
　JOY SANCHEZ-TAYLOR

Impossible Stories: On the Space and Time of Black Destructive Creation
　JOHN MURILLO III

Literary Afrofuturism in the Twenty-First Century
　EDITED BY ISIAH LAVENDER III AND LISA YASZEK

Jordan Peele's "Get Out": Political Horror
　EDITED BY DAWN KEETLEY

Unstable Masks: Whiteness and American Superhero Comics
　EDITED BY SEAN GUYNES AND MARTIN LUND

Afrofuturism Rising: The Literary Prehistory of a Movement
　ISIAH LAVENDER III

The Paradox of Blackness in African American Vampire Fiction
　JERRY RAFIKI JENKINS

www.ingramcontent.com/pod-product-compliance
Lightning Source LLC
Chambersburg PA
CBHW030139240426
43672CB00005B/187